A Guidebook for Teaching
STUDY SKILLS AND MOTIVATION

A Guidebook for Teaching Study Skills and Motivation

Second Edition

BERNICE JENSEN BRAGSTAD
National Consultant on Content Area Reading–Study Skills

SHARYN MUELLER STUMPF

Allyn and Bacon, Inc. **Boston ● London ● Sydney ● Toronto**

This book is part of A GUIDEBOOK FOR TEACHING Series

Library of Congress Cataloging in Publication Data

Bragstad, Bernice Jensen.
  A guidebook for teaching study skills and motivation.

  (A Guidebook for teaching series)
  Bibliography: p.
  1. Learning. 2. Study, Method of. I. Stumpf,
Sharyn Mueller, 1946– . II. Title. III. Series.
LB1060.B7 1987   370.15′4   86-14108
ISBN 0-205-08813-9

Printed in the United States of America

10 9 8 7 6 5 4 3 2   91 90 89 88 87

To my dear Glenn—
Susan, Paul, Richard,
Tricia and Mary,
whose love and active support enable me
to walk in new paths.
Bernice

In celebration of Carl
Christian
Aaron
and Angela Catherine
the sunshine of my life!
Sharyn

About the Authors

In 1983 the International Reading Association honored Bernice Jensen Bragstad with the Nila Banton Smith Award in recognition of her leadership in developing a unique, secondary reading study-skills program involving 150 staff members and 2,000 students at LaFollette High School, Madison, Wisconsin. She was the featured columnist on secondary reading in IRA's *Reading Today* during 1983–84.

Studying at the University of Chicago and the University of Wisconsin–Madison, Ms. Bragstad earned forty-eight graduate credits beyond her M.A. in Reading.

In *The Reading Teacher* Ms. Bragstad was cited with twenty others as sharing these characteristics: "sheer excellence in the teaching of reading, a seemingly vast store of energy, a pervasive faith in people and in education, and a marked openness to new ideas and fresh approaches."

Currently, Ms. Bragstad is a national consultant and has conducted in-service sessions and seminars on content area reading-study skills in twenty-five states and in major cities of Canada. She has been a speaker at numerous state, regional, and international reading conventions.

Sharyn Mueller Stumpf received her Master's degree in Reading from the University of Wisconsin–Madison. She has been a Reading/English teacher at LaFollette High School, Madison, Wisconsin. A former reading consultant, Ms. Stumpf has supervised practicum students and conducted in-service sessions for high school teachers.

Gene Stanford, Consulting Editor for the *Guidebook for Teaching Series,* received his Ph.D. and his M.A. from the University of Colorado. Dr. Stanford has served as Associate Professor of Education and Director of Teacher Education Programs at Utica College of Syracuse University and is a member of the National Council of Teachers of English and the International Council on Education for Teaching. Dr. Stanford is the author and coauthor of several books, among them, *A Guidebook for Teaching Composition, A Guidebook for Teaching Creative Writing, A Guidebook for Teaching about the English Language,* and *Human Interaction in Education,* all published by Allyn and Bacon, Inc.

Contents

Preface

We welcome those of you who are joining us for the first time and welcome back those of you who are with us once again. If you are interested in this book, you are a person with a special concern about students. You may care not only about the students' learning of particular content, but also about strengthening their desires to learn and teaching them *how* to learn. In our imaginations, you may be a classroom teacher in any field, a reading specialist, a school administrator, a professor of curriculum and instruction, or a college student preparing to teach at the middle-school or high-school level. In view of the continuing knowledge explosion, our common goal may be helping students become independent, lifelong learners.

In this guidebook we attempt to move theory into application by sharing ways in which teachers are fusing the teaching of learning process with the teaching of course content. Perhaps the most unique dimension of this effort is the active participation of and the great value placed on students themselves as developing persons who are capable of determining what is helpful for their own learning.

Although the authors often suggest a sequence of activities that might be useful in teaching a particular skill or concept, we assume that you will take the liberty of choosing those materials and strategies best suited to your students' needs and your own philosophy.

We have retained the practical format of the first edition:

- A brief *introduction* to the main concepts of each chapter.

- A list of *performance objectives* that the activities and materials in the chapter help students achieve.

- A wealth of *learning experiences* designed to stimulate students' interest and enhance their learning abilities in any course. Most important, each chapter includes *Reproduction Pages* of actual lessons and materials that can be duplicated for immediate student use.

- A list of *suggestions* or additional activities for *assessing* the student's *achievement of objectives*.

- An annotated list of *multimedia resources*.

In Chapter 12 you will find specific approaches for implementing a study-skills program across the curriculum and more materials geared to specific subject areas—science, social studies, and industrial arts, for example. In addition, Chapter 13 presents two schoolwide programs with dramatic results—the Reading Break and the Learning Center.

Most of the activities and approaches included in this book were developed for and used successfully in the classroom. We thank all LaFollette High School students and staff for being open to experimenting and discovering new directions for learning.

We also appreciate the professional spirit of Charles and Karen Carlson and Doug Vance, who willingly shared their ideas in the chapters on the research paper and strategic reading. The professional and personal interest of our editor, Hiram Howard, stimulated us to make this revision, and we have appreciated all his encouragement. Too, we thank Elydia P. Siegel for her care throughout production.

We are grateful to Dr. H. Alan Robinson for sharing his vision of a secondary content-area reading program in a course at the University of Chicago; to Dr. Richard J. Smith for his creative energy that moved an urban school district to initiate a content-area reading program with a reading consultant on each high school staff, and whose knowledge and enthusiasm continue to inspire us; and to Dr. Kenneth L. Dulin for his original ideas and fresh approaches to teaching study skills and his generosity in sharing his work with us.

Finally, we thank our parents and friends for simply being there for us. Above all, we are deeply grateful to our families for sharing their sense of humor at critical moments and loving us through it all.

Bernice Jensen Bragstad
Sharyn Mueller Stumpf

1

Motivating Students to Learn

What motivates high-school students today?

What arouses their excitement about learning?

How are a student's self-concept and academic achievement related?

What insights help students to assume responsibility for their learning?

How do we understand the adolescent as a developing person?

What teacher qualities create the personal atmosphere conducive to learning?

What teacher qualities do students value for effective learning?

As teachers we face these crucial questions every day. How we respond affects how students learn. Only through continuing research and interaction with the students in our classrooms are we able to affirm what is meaningful, what is effective.

In this initial chapter we will explore actual approaches used by teachers not only to deepen students' understanding of themselves and the dynamics of their motivation, but also to create a more effective learning atmosphere in the classroom, with students assuming more responsibility for their own learning.

PERFORMANCE OBJECTIVES

As a result of the learning experiences in this chapter, students will be able to:

1. Explain motivation.

2. Identify and apply Maslow's hierarchy of needs to their own motivation for learning, other students' motivation, and teachers' motivational experiences in education.

---

3. Demonstrate a knowledge of the difference between internal and external motivation.

4. Understand the complexity of motivation for learning.

5. Experience a personal classroom atmosphere that is conducive to learning.

CONTENT OVERVIEW

Topic 1: Source of Learning: The Brain

How can we capture their imaginations in a way that will excite students about their learning potential? How can we stimulate their desire to excel? Certainly there are scores of ways, but one approach that we find to be effective is sharing information about the instrument used for learning—the human brain:

Walking to the front of the room, the teacher asked: "What part of your anatomy is about a meter long and a half meter wide?" You could almost feel the students' brain cells working, but no one answered.

Further information: "You're using it now to solve this problem."

Instantaneous reaction—"The brain!"

"You're right. This large sheet of pinkish gray matter is crumpled into intricate folds beneath this hard shell (gently tapping a student on the head). In fact, you have your own individual arrangement of folds in your brain that are just as unique as your fingerprints.

"How many brain cells do you have? Jot down the number you would guess." (Responses were voiced from ten million to a billion.)

"Actually you have 13 billion brain cells![1] I can visualize 10 or 50, but 13 billion becomes incomprehensible. How can we make this number real? If you counted one brain cell every second of every minute of every hour, night and day, estimate how long it would take you to count your 13 billion brain cells. Counting continuously, you would need over 400 years. Think of that—over 400 years just to count your 13 billion brain cells.

"Will you put that into your long-term memory so you'll know it at the end of this year? Not only will I check you on the information but also on how you remembered it." (Later students may share their strategies for remembering.)

"This awesome instrument, the brain, is a sophisticated information processing center. Do you know that 'each neuron is connected to 100 others on the average and sometimes to as many as 10,000. . . . Learning, most research workers think, has something to do with changes in the strength and number of the connections.'[2] These interconnections encoding all your thoughts and feelings are so complex that the circuitry of the human brain may never be mapped. We really can't imagine such a complicated instrument. No computer even approaches the complexity of the brain.

"If you were to reproduce your brain as a computer, 'the total cost of duplicating all the brain's cells and connections, even at the ludicrously low cost of 5 cents per

---

1. Virginia L. Hoitsma et al., eds., *Understanding Psychology* (New York: CRM/Random House, 1977), p. 75.
2. Gilbert Burck and editors of *Fortune, The Computer Age* (New York: Harper & Row, © 1965 Time Inc.), pp. 126–127.

cell and 1 cent per connection, would come to more than $1 quintillion, or $1 billion billion.'[3] Think of the complexity, the potential, the value of this instrument that you possess and carry with you wherever you go! What a gift!

"Have you ever been taught how to use this complex instrument? In this class we'll experiment to find the most effective ways to use the brain in learning. For example, what helps the brain concentrate? How do you process information into long-term memory? After we experiment, we'll share our ideas. Your learning style may be quite different by the end of the semester."

Beginning a course this way is not just a gimmick. One of the biggest roadblocks to learning is a lack of self-esteem. Students think too little of themselves and of their potential. This in turn contributes to a lack of aspiration that damages motivation. Ultimately, less learning occurs.

On the other hand, helping students build strong, positive self-concepts results in improved achievement. After examining many studies, William Purkey concluded, "Over-all, the research evidence clearly shows a persistent and significant relationship between the self-concept and academic achievement. . . . A student carries with him certain attitudes about himself and his abilities which play a primary role in how he performs at school."[4]

What happens when students discover the wonder of the brain? They are amazed to know that they possess such a beautiful instrument for learning. They are impressed that they must have a great deal of unused potential. They become curious about how the brain should be used for learning. If they have not been achieving in school, they wonder if they have been using this instrument properly. Some even wonder why teachers spend so much time telling them what to learn and so little time teaching them how to learn, how to use such a complex instrument.

This thought-provoking introduction sends some students rushing to the library to check out books and articles about the brain. Later, they share their insights with the class. Others demonstrate their long-term memory as they pass the teacher in the hall by muttering (with a grin), "Thirteen billion brain cells. Four hundred years." Even in a shopping mall students remind the teacher, "One quintillion dollars." Another student adds, "I'll remember that all my life."

The interest is obvious. The students have discovered an amazing fact—that they possess a beautiful instrument with 13 billion parts worth $1 quintillion.

What is our continuing challenge as teachers? Through verbal and nonverbal communication, we have the opportunity to assure students that they have great potential for learning, that they have within them a need to fulfill their potential, and that we teachers are there because we care—we want to be a resource for growth. Our ultimate goal? To help students become self-motivated, independent learners. How can we communicate this perspective? The next approach reveals the relationship between motivation and using the brain effectively for learning:

"Today you will discover the power you have over the use of your brain. Because you are a person, you have feelings. How you feel has an effect on how well your brain operates. You've heard students speak about being 'turned on' or 'turned off' or about 'tuning in' or 'tuning out.'

---

3. Ibid. p. 127.
4. William W. Purkey, *Self Concept and School Achievement* (Englewood Cliffs, N.J.: Prentice-Hall, Inc., 1970), p. 70.

"For a moment let's imagine that we have an assembled computer right here with just one million parts and you are prepared to use it. What is the first thing you would have to do to make it function?"

From the back of the room: "Plug it in!"

"That's right. The computer does nothing without being plugged in. Now what do we call the current that stimulates the brain? What is it that gets us started?"

"Is it motivation?"

"That's what we call it. Motivation is that necessary current or spark that makes learning come alive. When we are curious, when we want to learn, our brain cells are activated. They become energized. We're with it! As a result, more learning occurs which then increases interest. Increased interest means more effective learning.

"Here's the big question! Who has the responsibility of 'plugging in' your brain, the responsibility of 'turning on the current'?"

One perceptive student responded, "Well, I suppose I have the responsibility and sometimes I do it. When I feel the need to know something, I'm motivated to learn it. That comes from within me. Then I work harder and longer. But sometimes I don't feel like that, so liking the teacher, wanting to get a good grade, impressing my friends, or just avoiding failure might be what gets me going. Sometimes my parents help me turn on the current!"

Another student responded, "Motivation is the difference between what I'm capable of doing and what I actually do. So much depends on what I'm willing to do. I really don't like to own all that responsibility. I'd rather blame the teacher if I don't feel like learning."

As the students explore the sources of their motivation, they discover the uniqueness and the complexity of motivation as a dynamic in learning. How can we further help students understand motivation and its relationship to learning? Knowledge of our human needs provides insight. When we experience a felt need, we are motivated.

Topic 2: Source of Motivation: Human Needs

In high school we are teaching adolescents who are in the process of making the transition to adult thinking. The brain is not fully developed until about eighteen years of age. As children, students could deal with what was concrete, what could be seen and touched. As adolescents, they now have more ability to think abstractly. They tend to become introspective, examining their own values, motives, and thoughts. Thus, they are curious about how they are motivated and how this process is related to who they are as individual persons. How can we make the complexity of motivation understandable?

Maslow's hierarchy of human needs makes sense to high-school students. It clarifies their understanding of themselves and others. Motivation becomes more real—more tangible. See Figure 1-1 and Reproduction Page 2.

The psychologist Abraham Maslow believed that all human beings have a need to grow, to develop abilities, to be recognized, to achieve. He viewed human needs in a hierarchical order. Some needs take precedence over others. As lower needs are satisfied, higher-order needs develop.

Maslow thus added to motivation theory the idea that teachers must be sensitive to those needs that precede the need to achieve. For example, a person's need for the real warmth of acceptance and closeness has priority over the need for competence

Figure 1-1. Maslow's hierarchy of human needs. According to Maslow, it is only after satisfying the lower levels of need that a person is free to progress to the ultimate need of self-actualization.

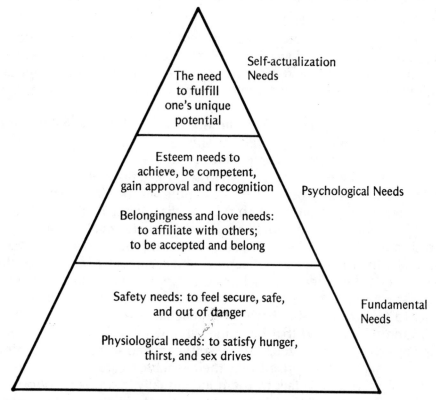

From Virginia L. Hoitsma et al., eds., *Understanding Psychology* (New York: CRM/ Random House, 1977), p. 132.

and achievement. As expressed by one inner-city teacher in Philadelphia, "Maslow clarifies why my caring about my students motivates them to learn." Thus, if we want our students to be motivated to achieve, we cannot ignore their need to be cared about as persons. Understanding Maslow's hierarchy of needs gives insight for motivating students to learn.

PHYSIOLOGICAL NEEDS
Maslow identifies the first level of basic need as the biological drives to satisfy hunger, thirst, and sexuality. A tiny baby needs to be held and loved in order to develop fully as a person. Eating is a basic need for living, so it has priority. Recognizing this reality, some schools furnish breakfast for children so that they are able to move beyond this fundamental need to a higher level of aspiration.

SAFETY AND SECURITY NEEDS
The next level of basic need is safety and security. If one is in physical danger, instantaneously adrenalin energizes the body in preparation for self-defense or flight. If a teacher is worried about tenure, or if a student's security at home is threatened by extreme conflict or parents' separation, resolving these fears will temporarily have priority over achieving, which is a higher-level need.

Often students do not see the relationship between personal experience in life and achievement at school. Yet the achievement of many students is adversely affected by personal problems that threaten security.

LOVE AND BELONGINGNESS NEEDS

Just as we need vitamins and proteins or protection from disaster, we need love and acceptance, according to Maslow. We fulfill the need for love and affection through relationship and interaction with other people. If a student does not feel cared about at home, a feeling of anxiety or tension may inhibit that student's ability to achieve at school.

Our surveys and interactions with hundreds of students reveal the adolescent's deep hunger for a caring, accepting relationship. As teachers today, we cannot ignore this deep need if we want to motivate students to learn.

What students want is not gushy words or emotional entanglements, but affirmation of themselves as persons. For example, in the first week of school three social-studies teachers of students with reading disabilities listened privately to each one of their students read materials at differing grade levels. Not only did these teachers learn about their students' reading capabilities but also about these students' special interests, their feelings about school, their learning problems of the past. In three class periods these teachers achieved a rapport with their students that had taken six weeks to establish in previous years. A level of trust developed that enabled the students to feel comfortable having the teachers know how miserably they had performed. One teacher said that he gained a new respect for his students: "Even though they murdered the language, they still managed to get the meaning."[5]

These students were surprised that their teachers cared enough to take three class periods to listen and to talk to them individually. Serious emotional problems were not being solved, but the teachers were helping to fill the real human need to be accepted and to be cared about. At the same time, they were gathering information that would be helpful in teaching these students. They were creating a warm, personal atmosphere that would help these adolescents take the necessary risks for learning.

The teachers' importance at the third level of Maslow's hierarchy (belonging, love, acceptance, friendship) is not underestimated by high-school students, who experience the strong correlation between being valued as persons and being motivated to achieve, the next higher level of the hierarchy. This is true to such a great degree that we have devoted the final segment of this chapter, "The Teacher-Student Relationship," to this correlation.

ESTEEM NEEDS

When we teachers hear the word *motivation,* we immediately think of motivation to achieve. We are ready to zero in on level four of Maslow's hierarchy: the need to be competent, to achieve, to gain recognition and approval.

Over a period of years the authors have discovered that students give almost equal value to effective instructional practices and to meaningful teacher-student relationships in motivating them to learn. They genuinely appreciate a teacher's effec-

---

5. J. Jefferson MacKinnon, former social-studies teacher at LaFollette High School, Madison, Wis. Remarks to Bragstad, September 1975.

tiveness because then they are enabled to do well. What helps students fulfill their need to achieve?

- "Teacher's ability to communicate clearly."
- "Teacher who cares enough to develop study guides and review sheets."
- "Teacher's intelligence and enthusiasm for the subject."
- "Giving good explanations with examples."
- "Teacher being able to involve students in good discussions."
- "Teacher with knowledge, effective communication, a caring attitude."

Students are so impressed with the important role of the teacher that they may overlook their responsibility in fulfilling this need to grow, to achieve. In a classroom survey identifying motivational factors affecting achievement, a few mature students revealed intrinsic motivation in the following responses:

- "Personal satisfaction in growing mentally helps me to achieve."
- "Proving that I can do what I set out to do."
- "Goals that I set motivate me to achieve."
- "I am my own source of motivation and I feel good about it."
- "My own desire to learn motivates me to achieve."

Even high-achieving students gain insight as they discuss the relationship of maturity (willingness to accept responsibility) to motivation. They soon determine that the more one is inner-motivated, the more likely one is to fulfill one's unique potential, the ultimate need of a human being. This insight gives students a perspective of life as a continuing process of growth beyond that time of formal education. Consequently, the top level of Maslow's hierarchy, self-actualization, begins to have meaning.

SELF-ACTUALIZATION NEEDS

The pinnacle of Maslow's hierarchy is self-actualization. This is an ongoing stage; it is a way of being, of continuously becoming what is intrinsically you. Self-actualized persons are moved by the need to grow, to discover, to develop all the various capacities that they might possess. They thrive on internal motivation. The needs for security, relationship, love, respect, and self-esteem are satisfied to such an extent that these individuals are free to become, free to be open to new experiences. They use their talents creatively. One person may develop latent artistic ability through photography or sculpture; another may find a whole new area for creative expression through serving others in new ways, in new places. Maslow has stated that many people do not arrive at this stage prior to sixty years of age, but within all of us the need for self-actualization lies dormant, waiting to be fulfilled. Since this level of realizing fully our intrinsic character and goodness calls for full maturity, it is more relevant to the life of the teacher than to the life of the student.

Self-actualized persons have not escaped pain, effort, and anxiety. However, in adapting to the frustrations and pressures of life, their being growth-motivated is analogous to the process through which an oyster, confronted with the irritation of a grain of sand, creates a pearl. "Adaptation to life means continued growth."[6] For self-actualized persons, problems become a means of growth.

Although achieving at one level of satisfaction releases new needs and motivations at the next higher level, we also realize that there may be exceptions. A student may expend inordinate amounts of energy in achieving to compensate for her lack of social maturity, her inability to relate, for instance.

Maslow's hierarchy does help both students and teachers to see their human needs in an understandable way. In fact, some students develop a whole new vision of life as a continuous learning process, a process of growing through an infinite variety of happy and unhappy experiences over an extended period of time. They can be reassured that their current introspection—examining their own personal meanings, motives, and thoughts—is a continuing life experience. For the growth-motivated person, to live is to change. This is exciting rather than threatening if one has a sense of unshakable self-worth. This sense of self-worth is the ultimate gift that a teacher may offer students in preparation for experiencing life.

Topic 3: Exploring the Teacher-Student Relationship

One of our primary concerns as teachers is reaching or getting in touch with our students. To teach effectively, we must know the learner. How do we understand the adolescent as a developing person? What is happening within these students who appear in our classrooms each day? Actually, we are teaching persons in transition—physically, mentally, and emotionally.

Puberty, or sexual maturation, is the biological event that marks the end of childhood and the onset of adolescence, the developmental stage between childhood and adulthood. Over a period of years adolescents experience physiological changes, awakening sexual drives, and a new kind of relationship with the opposite sex—all contributing to a feeling of uncertainty.[7]

Simultaneously, adolescents develop the ability to think more abstractly as they look inward to examine themselves, their meanings, their aspirations. A major developmental task for the adolescent is building an identity;[8] therefore, he or she is preoccupied with the question: "Who am I apart from my family and friends?"

All this questioning and corresponding change results in adolescents' becoming quite egocentric. They gaze into the mirror for periods of time with a new awareness of themselves. They control the family telephone for hours to interact with their friends, a necessary part of discovering who they are. Feelings of ambiguity are ever-present—appreciating their own uniqueness, but not wanting to be too different.

The struggle for identity is often complicated by peer pressure. As one student pondered, "How can I be myself, keep my personal values, and still belong to the group?" The dilemma is real. In reaction to this, one sensitive teacher observed, "If

6. George E. Vaillant, *Adaptation to Life* (Boston: Little, Brown, 1977), p. 105.
7. Hoitsma et al., eds., *Understanding Psychology*, p. 207.
8. Erik Erikson, *Identity, Youth and Crisis* (New York: W. W. Norton, 1968).

we can give students more emotional support and help them to become excited about developing their full potential, they will feel more comfortable being 'out of step' with others."[9] For any student, developing unique potential may mean being quite different from others. This we should affirm with a caring, supportive, and productive atmosphere for learning.

Erik Erikson asserts that "adolescents who are comfortable with their maturing bodies, who have a realistic sense of where they want to go in life, and who feel they are accepted by important people in their lives will experience less stress in building their identity."[10] Teachers are important people to students at this time of transition.

What can we teachers *be* as persons and what can we *do* to facilitate each student's growth and learning?

Students themselves provide leads. In an open-ended questionnaire, the *Teacher Qualities Survey,* we asked approximately 400 LaFollette high-school students (about 100 at each grade level, 9–12), "What teacher qualities are important for effective learning?" The results are revealing. Of these students, 69 percent cited instructional practices, while nearly the same number, 67 percent, cited personal attitudes and behaviors of teachers, as important contributors to an effective learning atmosphere.

What do students prize most highly? "Caring teachers"—those who are understanding, patient, and respectful toward students—was voluntarily mentioned by over 200 students. The need to be cared about—the longing for relationship—is real in our classrooms today. See Table 1-1.

Our findings are consistent with the research: that is, two factors—*instructional methods* and a *teacher's ability to relate personally to others*—are equally vital if students are to learn.[11] The way a teacher relates to others in the school setting is so powerful that one educator aptly refers to it as the "silent curriculum." Furthermore, he insists that acknowledging the dramatic impact of a teacher's personal qualities and working to improve this interpersonal dimension in schools is the key to resolving our basic skills problems.[12]

This assessment is validated by research. A study on an unprecedented scale, one involving more than 10,000 students and 550 elementary and secondary teachers of various ethnic backgrounds throughout the United States and several foreign countries, substantiates what many of us teachers have sensed.

The relationship between—

- a *teacher's ability to relate* to others and *student attendance* is positive and significant.

- a *teacher's ability to relate* to others and *enhanced student self-concept* is positive and significant.

- a *teacher's ability to relate* to others and *student gains on achievement test scores* is positive and significant.

---

9. Susan Erickson, English and humanities teacher at LaFollette High School, Madison, Wis. Remarks to Bragstad, May 1978.

10. Hoitsma et al., eds., *Understanding Psychology,* p. 208.

11. A. W. Combs et al., *Florida Studies in the Helping Professions* (University of Florida Social Science Monograph no. 37, 1969).

12. Philip L. Hosford, "The Silent Curriculum: Its Impact on Teaching the Basics," *Educational Leadership* 36 (December 1978): 211–215.

Table 1-1. Teacher Qualities Survey: What Teacher Qualities Are Important for Effective Learning?

Instructional Practices: cited by 69% of the sample, with comments categorized as follows:

Interesting—varies teaching style	29%
Understandable presentations, appropriately paced	24
Knowledgeable, extensive background	13
Organized course (lectures, assignments, etc.)	13
Provides special help	10
Enthusiastic about subject matter	6
Encourages student involvement	4
Student comments which could not be categorized	1

Personal Attitudes and Behaviors: cited by 67% of the sample, with comments categorized as follows:

Caring—understanding, patient, respectful	49%
Sense of humor—relaxed, but effective	24
Fair (no "pets"), but strict; controls class	17
Student comments which could not be categorized	10

Bernice Bragstad and Linda Shriberg, Teacher Qualities Survey. Unpublished study, Madison, Wis.: Madison Metropolitan School District, 1978.

The message is clear: in order to get students to school, to have them feel good about themselves, and to have them learn academic material, we must address the silent curriculum. Further, students' growth may actually be retarded by teachers who do not relate well to others![13] As teachers, then, our relating to students as persons facilitates their growth and their learning. Unequivocally, students achieve better when teachers care about them as persons.

Because students' needs for relationship must be met before they are free to focus on learning, we surveyed 800 high-school students to determine what, specifically, makes them feel valued. Students responded to a single open-ended question (henceforth referred to as the *Valued Survey*): "At any time in your educational career that you have felt cared about, what has contributed to that feeling?" An overwhelming majority—80 percent—pinpointed personal dimensions of the teacher-student relationship as being most significant. These students confirm what Carl Rogers, renowned psychologist and educator, asserts: that the three teacher attributes that facilitate students' becoming independent learners are (1) being real; (2) caring, accepting, and trusting; and (3) empathic understanding.[14] Since we wish to create prime conditions for our students' learning, we will now explore each of these three dimensions and their possible implications for our teaching.

---

13. David N. Aspy and Flora N. Roebuck, *Kids Don't Learn from People They Don't Like* (Amherst, Mass.: Human Resource Development Press, 1977), pp. 46, 56.
14. Carl R. Rogers, "The Interpersonal Relationship in the Facilitation of Learning," in *Humanizing Education: The Person in the Process,* ed. R. R. Leeper (Alexandria, Va.: Association for Supervision and Curriculum Development, 1967), pp. 1–18. Reprinted with permission of the Association for Supervision and Curriculum Development and Carl R. Rogers. Copyright © 1967 by the Association for Supervision and Curriculum Development. All rights reserved. A slightly revised edition appears in *Freedom to Learn* (Columbus, Ohio: Charles E. Merrill, 1969), pp. 103–127.

Being Real

About eight years ago a young teacher eagerly anticipated inspiring every student before her with the burning desire to learn for the sheer joy of learning! Volumes of her time and energy flowed into preparing for her first classes, anticipating every possible question students might ask so that she could fulfill her vision of the perfect teacher—knowing the answer to every question.

In fact, this teacher trekked to school each day truly fortified with knowledge. But any time that a student asked a question that the teacher could not answer— tension. The teacher's response? "I don't think we have time to deal with that issue now," or any other excuse to buy time to study the matter.

One day as students struggled to improve basic skill problems, a student the teacher was working with lamented, "You're so smart. I bet you got all *As* in school without even trying."

The others chimed in: "You know everything." "This work must seem like kids' stuff to you." "How'd you get so intelligent anyhow?"

Without thinking, the teacher retorted, "What do you mean! I got a *D* for a semester grade in college and I've made plenty of other mistakes in my life."

Silence.

Finally, hesitantly, one student said, "Aw c'mon. You did not." Another added, "You mean you got a *D* and you still made it?"

Then the students sat enthralled as the teacher talked of going off to college and getting so involved in plays, concerts, and other social events that virtually no time remained for study. And there were the inevitable consequences. . . .

As students left the classroom that day, their mood was unusually lighthearted.

Too often students come to us burdened with past failures. We teachers can guide students to understand that, for a person of any age, the freedom to make mistakes is integral to the freedom to achieve and the freedom to grow. And as teachers, we need to grant ourselves the freedom to be human, to make mistakes, before we can create that kind of space for others. In the classroom where no one has to expend energy saving face or worrying unduly about being wrong, everyone has greater energy and enthusiasm to learn.

How do students react to our acknowledged humanness, to our admission that we teachers have made and will continue to make mistakes since we, too, are learning and growing? They are heartened:

- "When a teacher lets us know him as a person and not just as a teacher."

- "When a teacher tells about a personal experience."

- "When teachers 'open up' and reveal themselves, students feel like 'opening up' too."

In these circumstances students say they feel cared about (Valued Survey).

Daring to be *real* rather than role takes courage. How are we teachers real? First and foremost, by accepting our own humanness. By daring to admit experiencing ambiguity—celebration and chaos, certainty and confusion, love and hatred. By meeting the student on a person-to-person basis. By being aware of our own feelings, accepting them, and sharing them with students, if this is appropriate. For example, the teacher who comments as follows dares to be real:

The materials and activities we'll be working with in class today are new to me, so I'm a little nervous. I'd appreciate hearing your honest evaluations of today's session when we meet here again tomorrow.

By communicating her feelings as she experiences them, this teacher authentically reveals herself, and, concurrently, the students discover that feeling nervous or upset is acceptable. In sharing her honest feelings this teacher not only allows herself to move beyond the nervousness but also encourages the class members to respond in more open, human ways as well. Realness elicits realness.

The initial step toward becoming real is to realize that feelings are neither good nor bad, but just are. This attitude implies accepting our humanness, which consequently frees us to deal more constructively with feelings like anger toward a student, without the complication of guilt because we experience that feeling. Only after identifying our feelings are we able to make conscious decisions about them. We then have a choice—to act or not to act on those feelings. Through this process—identifying and accepting our feelings, evaluating whether to act on them, then following through on our decisions—we continuously discover and acknowledge our own total humanity, involving the harmonious interplay of both intellect and emotions.

In the following exchange, too, the teacher is daring to be real, this time in response to a student's sharing:

Mark: Ms. Timm, that note-taking stuff we're doing in here really helps me a lot, especially in chemistry.

Ms. Timm: I'm happy to know the things we're learning are paying off for you, Mark. You've just brightened a bad day!

This kind of honest encounter certainly affirms each of the people involved. Such an utterly simple instance of sharing authentic, positive feelings can so easily be overlooked in the whirlwind of a typical school day. Yet these small interchanges are the foundation of a general sense of optimism and well-being in the students' and teachers' lives inside school as well as outside it.

Reflect for a moment: How do you feel when someone tells you how much your cheerfulness means or how special you are in his or her life? Now can we find the time to share such elemental, positive feelings within our schools?

Being real is not an easy thing. Invariably, it is risky, but without taking risks we cannot grow. Being authentic necessitates stripping away the facade of always being emotionally in control, always knowing the answers. Thus, we reveal ourselves as we are—caring but sometimes impatient, knowing but often groping for solutions. This is the beauty and complexity of being a person in process—not static, but dynamic.

Furthermore, being real challenges us because personal authenticity flows from the heart—identifying our feelings, accepting them, growing through them. Our Western culture, however, stresses logic, problem solving, analytical thinking—all "head" concerns; thus, we have little societal support for nurturing the emotional dimensions of ourselves. Not surprisingly, then, of seventy-five juniors and seniors polled, seventy-one students—fully 95 percent—strongly felt the need to understand their emotions and to learn how to cope with them. Moreover, a strikingly large majority agreed that the amount of attention given to this need by either their families or the school was not even worth mentioning.

Clearly then, we teachers facilitate our students' growth and our own growth as well by being not only knowledgeable in our respective subject areas but also courageous enough to risk being real.

Caring, Accepting, Trusting

In the Teacher Qualities Survey 49 percent of the students cited the caring teacher as paramount in creating an effective learning atmosphere. Students state in the Valued Survey that they feel cared about:

- "When teachers ask and value my opinion."
- "When a teacher trusts me and gives me the benefit of the doubt."
- "Being complimented by a teacher in class."
- "A teacher giving me special responsibility."
- "When a teacher makes me feel important regardless of grades."
- "When a teacher told me she was glad to see me back after I was absent. She was really concerned, not about my attendance record, but why I wasn't there. She cared."
- "Having a teacher who cares about every student, no matter if he is a brain or not very smart in that particular subject."
- "If teachers actually help me with my work or if I am upset, they ask why."
- "Talking outside class about interests, feelings."
- "When my teacher lets me know I have worth, regardless of anything."

In addition students state that they feel valued when a teacher laughs, smiles, calls on them by name, greets them in the hall, and writes comments on papers.

The value students place on simple personal touches is substantiated at every turn. When 1,115 students in a Gallup poll were requested to grade their schools, 25 percent of these students rated their teachers *A*. When students meted out any lower ratings, their justifications suggested that the teachers "were not attuned to students' emotional needs."[15]

Being in touch with students' emotional needs does have consequences. Our freely offering acceptance and love to students simply because they are persons—they do not need to earn it—creates a nurturing environment in which everyone, students and teachers alike, can risk learning, changing, growing. In this atmosphere each individual is apt to be enthusiastic about exploring his or her own potential.

Apparently, we all share the common human need to feel cared about as persons. When forty high-school teachers listed what influenced their motivation when they were students, they also recalled the significance of relationship as a source of

---

15. Pam Proctor, "Gallup Poll: What Your Kids Really Think about School," *Parade* magazine in the *St. Paul Dispatch* (April 1, 1979), pp. 4–5.

motivation. Specifically, when asked "At any time in your educational career that you have felt cared about, what has contributed to that feeling?" the teachers responded,

- "Having a professor believe in me and my capability."
- "Being given out-of-the-ordinary responsibilities."
- "Being praised even though my success wasn't that great."
- "Teacher taking sincere interest in correcting my disruptive behavior."
- "Knowing that a professor respected me as a person."
- "Being given personal help."
- "College professor talking to us as equals."

Upon hearing the results of this teacher survey, students were amazed and in-spirited by the fact that teachers' experiences and feelings are so similar to their own. Because their teachers seemed more human, students felt a new rapport.

Thus, as teachers we know that being experts in our academic fields is impera-tive, but we can do much more to foster our students' growth. We can—we must—care enough to expect a great deal of each and every student because usually a student fulfills whatever expectation he or she perceives that a teacher has of him or her. In fact, the potential that our positive expectations unleash in our students is inestimable. Our optimism can result in students' increasing their achievement scores and their IQ scores. In one classic study elementary-school teachers were told that 20 percent of their students could be expected to show significant gains in mental ability during the ensuing school year. This information was false; those students' names were merely chosen at random.

Nonetheless, these teachers later described the "spurters" as happier, more affectionate, more curious, and more likely to succeed in later life than the other students. Additionally, at the end of the school year, intelligence tests and other measures administered to the children revealed the potential spurters had, in fact, soared far beyond the other students—by as much as ten to twenty-seven IQ points! In other words, the teachers' high expectations were the keystone. This study sug-gests that through both verbal and nonverbal means, teachers convey their expecta-tions to the students, who, in turn, actualize these expectations in a self-fulfilling prophecy.[16]

There are certainly as many verbal ways to let students know that we care and expect a great deal from them as there are teachers. Commenting "This is a good start, Tom, but with a little more thought, I know you can do even better on this project" may be comfortable for some of us, whereas "Your thoughtful questions keep me on my toes, Marie," or a sincere "Hi Jim" or "Thank you, Brent" may be more natural for others. As students have mentioned, a common gesture, such as being called by name, matters. The specific words we use are not important. What is important is the fact that we do attempt to convey to students our feelings of appreciation for and our high expectations of each of them.

---

16. R. Rosenthal and L. Jacobson, *Pygmalion in the Classroom: Teacher Expectation and Pupil's Intellectual Develop-ment* (New York: Holt, Rinehart & Winston, 1968).

In addition to these verbal means, our nonverbal expressions speak loudly and clearly. Ask yourself,

- What is my typical facial expression and tone of voice in my classroom?
- When a student speaks to me, does he enjoy my full attention, or do I continue to shuffle papers or scan my files?
- What message do these actions convey to students?

Our smiling and laughing, for instance, carry more power to affirm than we often realize, as evidenced by the great number of students who cited these on the Teacher Qualities Survey. As teachers, we can become so accustomed to evaluating student performance and assigning grades that we unintentionally devote too little energy to creating the warm, personal atmosphere that stimulates deep involvement in learning.

On the Valued Survey and the Teacher Qualities Survey students repeatedly attested to their need for a teacher's unconditional caring if they are to truly thrive and grow toward their potential. Indeed, upon reading their own students' comments from these two surveys, teachers were so struck by students' expressed need for and appreciation of caring teachers that they were stirred to action. To assure that, henceforth, their students do actually experience their teachers' caring for them as persons, the teachers made commitments like the following:

- "Learning first names sooner the first quarter."
- "Try to get away from the subject matter and focus on student problems, thoughts, suggestions, once in a while."
- "Send positive progress reports instead of only negative reports."
- "Take more time going over difficult problems individually instead of assuming that the students have learned the process."
- "Expect more of each and every student!"
- "Give more praise for the amount accomplished."
- "Spend more time getting to know the students who are unappealing to me."
- "Refrain from 'losing my cool' with well-known problem students and try to treat them as I would treat a good student."
- "Show students I care by correcting and returning papers sooner."
- "Give more equal praise to good, medium, and poor students."
- "Give some personal attention to quiet students."
- "Be more sensitive to problems that students may be having that do not relate to the subject matter."

Once again, simple things are the secret to letting students know that we care.

Empathic Understanding

In addition to being real and caring persons, we teachers create a positive learning atmosphere by listening deeply to our students. The following remarks suggest the value that students place on empathy. Students feel appreciated (Valued Survey) in these situations:

- "When a teacher listens and really understands how I feel."
- "A teacher who just listens without giving a lot of advice."
- "When a teacher's nonverbal communication tells you she heard."
- "When a teacher understands your problem."

Empathic understanding is the third characteristic of a teacher who facilitates students' growing toward their potential. Specifically, students who perceive their teachers as understanding are more likely—

- to use their abilities
- to have a positive self-image
- to have a positive attitude toward school
- to relate personally with other class members.[17]

Empathic understanding is the walk-a-mile-in-my-shoes concept whereby we attempt to perceive life from another person's viewpoint rather than from our own. Judging and evaluating have no place in this kind of listening and understanding. The following exchange illustrates empathic listening:

> One day Glenn, typically jovial and gregarious, walked slowly and sullenly into class.
>
> Mr. Jones: You really seem down, Glenn. Wasn't today the day you took your driver's test?
>
> Glenn: Yeah.
>
> Mr. Jones: It didn't go so well, huh?
>
> Glenn: Nope.
>
> Mr. Jones: Do you want to talk about it?
>
> Glenn: No.
>
> Mr. Jones: (resting his hand on Glenn's shoulder)   I bet it's tough to start all over again when you were counting on getting your license now.

---

17. R. Schmuck, "Some Relationships of Peer Liking Patterns in the Classroom to Pupil Attitudes and Achievement," *School Review* 71 (1963): 337–359.

Whether we have the courage to enter into another person's pain may well make the difference in whether that person can be strengthened and grow beyond it through the healing power of being understood.

Empathic understanding is a great challenge, for it often calls us to hear beyond the words. For example, one day the students were given class time to begin an assignment. Suddenly, one student slammed down his pencil and slumped back in his chair, red-faced and muttering, "This is dumb!" This remark could have meant a host of things: "The assignment isn't clear to me. I need more help"; "I always get frustrated when I learn new things"; or "My girlfriend broke up with me last night. Who cares about school!"

The teacher simply stated, "You sound frustrated, Tom." After a brief discussion, Tom mentioned that the hour before this class, he learned that he had received a *D* on a social-studies exam for which he had really studied.

If this teacher had initially heard Tom's complaint and responded defensively with, "I've given you everything you need to know to do this work on your own. *Get busy!*" Tom's frustration probably would have escalated. Since the teacher was open to him, however, Tom ultimately felt more able to focus on the work. As Carl Rogers states, ". . . if any teacher set himself the task of endeavoring to make one nonevaluative, acceptant, empathic response per day to a pupil's demonstrated or verbalized feeling, I believe he would discover the potency of this currently almost non-existent kind of understanding."[18]

Empathic listening calls us to speak, not with solutions, but merely with our presence.

What we have learned through our experiences with high-school students is that students want and need teachers who are persons as well as professionals. This is also verified at the college level. In *Harvard Magazine* the most noteworthy attributes of four outstanding professors are cited: "enthusiastic, lives his material," "articulate, as skilled in teaching as he is knowledgeable in his field," "sympathetic, understanding of students' needs and problems," "accessible, good listener as well as good talker."[19] Apparently students at all levels need and appreciate teachers who are both knowledgeable and caring persons. Further, all of us are enabled to develop more fully, intellectually as well as emotionally, when we are first cared for as persons.

What can happen in our schools when we are committed wholeheartedly to teaching subject matter and to caring for one another?

> When a facilitator creates, even to a modest degree, a classroom climate characterized by all that he can achieve of realness, prizing, and empathy; when he trusts the constructive tendency of the individual and the group; then he discovers that he has inaugurated an educational revolution. Learning of a different quality, proceeding at a different pace, with a greater degree of pervasiveness, occurs. Feelings—positive and negative, confused—become a part of the classroom experience. Learning becomes life, and a very vital life at that. The student is on his way, sometimes excitedly, sometimes reluctantly, to becoming a learning, changing being.[20]

18. Rogers, "The Interpersonal Relationship," pp. 1–18.
19. Timothy Noah, "Four Good Teachers," *Harvard Magazine* (September–October 1978), pp. 96–97.
20. Carl R. Rogers, NEA source as revised in "The Interpersonal Relationship in the Facilitation of Learning," *Freedom to Learn* (Columbus, Ohio: Charles E. Merrill, 1969), p. 115.

LEARNING EXPERIENCES

Topic 1: Source of Learning: The Brain

1. Invite the school psychologist, a guidance counselor, a psychiatrist, or a science teacher to share insights about the brain. Questions that students generate may give some direction for the presentation, but the main focus may be how to use the brain effectively for learning.

2. Questionnaires are a relatively easy way to obtain information from students about themselves. As students respond, they often discover a need for change. Appropriate study habits contribute to the effectiveness of the brain in learning.

   Distribute copies of Reproduction Page 1, "How Am I Doing?" After students have responded to all the statements, they may use the answer key for evaluation of seven study habits. The answers are based on the recommendation of study-skills experts.

   On the answer key, ask students to circle the answers that are incorrect. On the study-skill chart, "What Are My Strengths and Weaknesses?," circle the question numbers that are incorrect for you. The student can quickly assess his or her strength or weakness in each study-skill area. Then the student may examine the questions in areas of weakness to see what study experts recommend.

   Finally, ask each student to focus on two areas for improvement. What changes need to be made? At a later date, the students may evaluate their progress with another assessment using this same instrument. (Chapter 12—Social Studies.)

3. Ask the school librarian to prepare a bibliography of available materials in your school on motivation and the brain (Resources for Teaching). Involve students in choosing interesting topics for research. Below is a brief list of possible student investigations:

   - Effect of positive or negative attitudes on the brain's ability to remember information

   - Difference between the right and left sides of the brain

   - Processing information into long-term memory

   - Intelligence, creativity, and the brain

   - Time line for brain development

   - Relationship of motivation to effective use of the brain

4. Recognizing that other students are not knowledgeable about the brain and its use for learning, ask your students to make small-group presentations on this topic in other teachers' classes. Although this may be a voluntary activity, frequently students enjoy becoming experts on the brain and sharing their insights for the benefit of others. Freshmen especially enjoy listening to upperclass students. The freshmen's positive attitudes help them remember what the older students say.

Topic 2: Source of Motivation: Human Needs

1. In this activity the students will discover the many sources of motivation to learn.

    Distribute Reproduction Page 3, "Students: What Motivates You to Learn?" This same sheet is used for Activity 2. Answer Key—Appendix B. Ask students to decide whether the source of each factor is internal or external. Place *I* or *E* in front of each item.

    In small groups the students may discuss questions like the following:

    • Is external or internal motivation more common?

    • What causes a person to develop internal motivation?

    • Would you choose to be internally or externally motivated? Why?

    • Why are not more people self-motivated to learn?

    In the authors' experience, at least 75 percent of students' motivational factors have an external source. Frequently students discover how much they are using the teacher as a "motivational crutch." They begin to examine teacher-student responsibility for motivation to learn.

2. Participating in this activity will make students aware of all the varying needs that motivate them in the classroom. As a result, students often gain a deeper appreciation of the challenging position of the teacher. How is it possible for a teacher to motivate so many different individuals in each class?

    a. Using an overhead projector and a transparency of Reproduction Page 2, "Maslow's Hierarchy of Needs," explain the hierarchy. Then give each student the triangular diagram depicting the five levels of human needs, Reproduction Page 2.

    b. Distribute copies of Reproduction Page 3, "Students: What Motivates You to Learn?" (These are responses from a junior class in high school.)

    c. Ask students to write the number of the level on Maslow's hierarchy that is the source of motivation for each particular response. Answer Key—Appendix B.

    After the students have finished scoring the identification activity, ask them to compare answers in groups of three. After sharing rationales for their answers, they may discuss the following questions:

    • Are some needs more important than others in motivating us?

    • Is motivation to learn at school a simple or complex process? Explain.

    • Is motivation the responsibility of the student or the teacher?

    • What is the role of each?

    • What motivates the teacher to keep trying to meet the needs of students?

    • Do students have any responsibility to encourage or stimulate the teacher's motivation to be effective?

    • Do experiences outside of school have an effect on motivation at school?

3. The purpose of this activity is to help students realize that teachers have experienced the same human dynamics of positive motivation that were meaningful to the students. First, distribute copies of Reproduction Page 4, "Teachers: What Motivates You to Learn?" Next, on the blank by each response, the students write the number of the level on Maslow's hierarchy that is the source of motivation for that particular response. Answer Key—Appendix B.

   After students complete this activity, they are aware that teachers are more than "brain cells." Teachers are real people with human needs and feelings. Based on positive motivational experiences, are the same human needs important to teachers and students? When teachers and students reflect on their own educational experience, the "silent curriculum"—trust, caring, belonging—is remembered as motivating them to learn.

   An alternative is to survey your faculty and use their responses for this activity.

4. This activity causes students to assess what "turns off" motivation to learn. Distribute copies of Reproduction Page 2, "Maslow's Hierarchy of Needs," and Reproduction Page 5, "Students: What Inhibits Your Motivation?" On the blank space next to each item, the students identify the level (Maslow's hierarchy) at which the damage to motivation is experienced (Reproduction Page 5). At which level is most of the damage experienced? Answer Key—Appendix B.

   Because teachers are important people in the lives of students, what they do (positive or negative) has real impact on the students.

   An alternative is to have your students answer the question, "What inhibits your motivation?"

5. As students experience this activity, they discover that to learn, one must overcome a variety of roadblocks. This is reality in the experience of both students and teachers. How can problems be handled in a positive way?

   Distribute copies of Reproduction Page 6, "Teachers: What Inhibits Your Motivation?" On the blank space next to each item, the students identify the level (Maslow's hierarchy) at which the damage to teachers' motivation is experienced. Answer Key—Appendix B.

   Now the students can compare the negative experiences of the two groups. The teachers' roadblocks to learning are quite different from those of the students. One teacher's explanation: Perhaps the teachers were thinking of their most recent educational experience in college, when they were very motivated to learn and had less opportunity to interact personally with their professors. As a result, their disappointments were experienced at the achievement level since they expected little personal attention.

   The student survey results suggest that secondary-school teachers must be sensitive to the feelings of high-school students if they want to motivate them to learn. In their search for identity, adolescents are very vulnerable, especially in the presence of their peers.

   Small-group discussion may center on coping skills needed in negative situations. How can problems such as "disorganized lectures" and "lack of trust in students" be handled in a positive way? (Most students have never discussed positive and negative dimensions of motivation in any class.)

Figure 1-2. Circle of Responsibility.

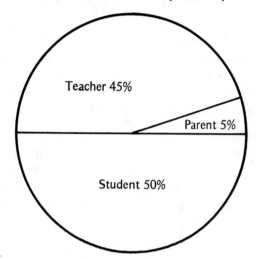

6. For teachers, a continuing challenge is to stimulate each student to want to develop his or her own potential. Now that students understand something about motivation, how much responsibility do they assume for their own learning?

Ask each student to draw a large circle on a clean sheet of paper, labeling it "The Circle of Responsibility for My Learning" and recording the date beneath that. See Figure 1-2 for an illustration.

This circle represents 100 percent of the responsibility for learning. Ask each student to decide how this circle is currently divided, considering the following components: (1) student, (2) teacher, (3) other influences (parents, peers, society, etc.). Have students divide the figure, recording percentages in each category.

Next, small-group discussion might focus on the following questions:

• Until now, have you given much thought to the issue of responsibility for your own learning? Explain.

• How does this diagram compare with one you might have drawn three years ago?

• How is your learning affected if you perceive the teacher's responsibility as high, yours as low? Vice versa?

• How do you feel about what you have put down (pleased? upset? etc.)?

Finally, base total class discussion on the question, "What is the ideal division of responsibility for learning?" Emphasize the point that human growth and change are continuous and, one hopes, in the direction of one's assuming greater personal responsibility, both in school and outside it. Repeating this activity, for instance at the end of each quarter or semester, allows both you and the student to observe progress.

7. Ask students to break into small groups to respond to the following questions:

What teacher qualities are important for effective teaching in the classroom? What qualities should a student develop to be an effective learner?

As the teacher shares in the discussion by going from group to group, students see more clearly that effective learning is the result of a joint venture of students and the teacher working together.

8. Invite students to work with you in developing an instrument that helps students clarify their motivation to achieve. The process stimulates self-evaluation.

Distribute copies of Reproduction Page 7, "Assessing Motivation to Achieve." Answer Key—Appendix B. Ask students to follow directions given for the activity.

Topic 3: Exploring the Teacher-Student Relationship

1. Explain the fact that, like your students, you, too, need a little time to get acquainted with the new people in your class. This activity affords students the chance to express themselves—their interests, their meanings—in a collage entitled "Who Am I?" and gives everyone the opportunity to know each other better. (The teacher can become less "mystery," more "person" by creating one, too!)

Supplies: magazines to cut, scissors, glue, poster paper. Pass out large sheets of construction paper or tell the students to use some sort of firm paper (tag board); approximately 18″ × 30″ is a reasonable size. Tell students to feel free to do whatever they wish in terms of the backing, pictures, words, as long as they clarify the question, "Who Am I?" (One avid musician created his collage in the form of a musical note, for instance.)

Spending some class time on this, especially for students with special learning needs, encourages much person-to-person interaction in a pleasantly busy atmosphere. Allow a minimum of several days if this project is to be completed outside class.

Tell students to write their names on the backs of the collages. Once you receive these projects, a number of options are open:

- Student-teacher conference: the collage is a springboard to know each other better.

- Small groups: students and teacher (as another class member) share in groups of five to seven, rotating until everyone has shared with the entire class.

- Total class: a guessing game—number all collages and post them on the front wall. Each student tries to guess who did what. A free paperback book rewards the best guesser. Then invite students to volunteer to explain their respective collages.

An appreciation for uniqueness and a heightened group feeling should be two of the outcomes of this activity. Emphasize how enriching the classroom experience can be with such diverse interests and viewpoints represented.

2. Initiate a "Reading Break" in your class! That is, at a regularly scheduled time each day, earmark ten to fifteen minutes for you and every student to sit back and pull out a book or magazine for leisure reading. The goal of this activity? Solely enjoyment—no tests, no comprehension questions, no projects.

   As a consequence of this break, expect students to gradually become reading enthusiasts. Expect, too, that students will be more ready and able to handle study assignments as a result of their growing proficiency in reading. And, delightfully, expect changes in your relationships with many students. For instance, a business teacher and several students discovered a common bond when they all noticed each other reading about their great love, horses.[21] And after hearing their physics teacher's chuckles over Mark Twain's writing, the students insisted that they get to share in the fun by having their teacher read the short story to them during the Reading Break the very next day[22] (Details in Chapter 13).

3. Have every person in class (the teacher included) write answers to the questions on Reproduction Page 8, "Getting to Know You." Then, in small groups or through individual conferences, share the results.

4. On each of four separate sheets of paper, print the words *Strongly Agree, Agree, Disagree, Strongly Disagree.* In that same order, post these signs along one wall of your classroom. Then ask students to listen to the statements you will read and respond by walking to the sign that most accurately reflects their opinions.

   • I'd rather have a banana split than a hot fudge sundae.

   • I prefer steak to pizza.

   • If I had to get more exercise, I'd rather jog than swim.

   • I wish I were older than I am.

   • I wish I were younger than I am.

   • I am more of a spender than a saver.

   • I have decided upon a career after high school.

   • I think that calling teachers by their first names is a good idea.

   • I'd rather have one very good friend than several friends I don't know so well.

   • I wish I had more brothers and sisters.

---

21. Jean Sholts, business education teacher at LaFollette High School, Madison, Wis. Remarks to Bragstad, November 1979.
22. Paul McIntosh, science teacher at LaFollette High School, Madison, Wis. Remarks to Bragstad, December 1979.

- I wish I had fewer brothers and sisters.

- I prefer being alone to being with others.

An alternative is to explain this activity to the class, then, in small groups, have students draw up their own questions.

5. Create a "class quilt" early in the school year! As an original and effective means to build a more personal relationship between students and teacher, view together pictures of quilts or quilts themselves to underscore the paradox of unity through diversity: each quilt block remains unique while contributing to a unifying pattern. This is a perfect metaphor for the students that form each class.

   To illustrate physically this principle, invite each student to design a personal quilt block. Each student's block, 8½" × 11" in size, can depict important experiences and accomplishments, family heritage, significant relationships, key personality traits, future goals, or even a motto that reflects a philosophy of life.

   To represent this material, students might choose to be detailed and concrete or symbolic and abstract. Encourage the use of color, which may also be symbolic. Reluctant artists might use magazine pictures for their portrayal. The range of student designs is often astonishing and always delightful! (One "photographer" threaded film around her block, each frame illustrating a new aspect of "her." An "artist" drew a palette, each dab of paint being a significant item, while a third student transformed the pepperoni on her pizza into important pieces in her life.) Also, have students write an explanation of the block for you so that you can then comment on individual interests.

   Assemble the blocks on a colored paper background and, finally, have students design a "class logo" block. Then display the quilt to highlight each student's uniqueness while fostering *esprit de corps!*[23]

6. Invite students to see the real you! Bring to the classroom things like:

   - Photos of your family, pets, special interests, and casually talk about them.

   - Eye-catching posters of personal interests (favorite ski slopes or vacation spots).

   - Posters with philosophical comments.

   Then invite the people in class to help create a more personal atmosphere by bringing:

   - A plant or two from home. (Hanging plants are loaned.)

   - Giant floor pillows for leisurely reading. (You buy the stuffing; students choose the fabric and do the sewing.)

   - Art they may have created (pottery, drawings, paintings, macramé, if you have a safe place to display them).

   - One of their favorite posters.

23. Susan Dean, English teacher at LaFollette High School, Madison, Wis. Remarks to Stumpf, May 1985.

- Quotations that have especially inspired them. (We recommend designating a special bulletin board or blackboard area for these.)

7. Ask your students to respond to the following question: "What teacher qualities contribute to an effective learning atmosphere?" Students are often pleasantly surprised when a teacher is genuinely interested in their opinions and insights. After tallying the responses, you might compare the data with those of Table 1-1. Students will also be interested in your evaluation of an effective atmosphere for learning.

   Further, you might pose the following question for discussion: "What *student* qualities contribute to an effective learning environment?" Frequently, students are unaware of their contributions to learning atmosphere. This activity helps them see that effective education is a cooperative venture, while revealing to us what steps we teachers can take to enhance the learning environment. Then act on the students' suggestions.

8. Students with a positive self-concept have more confidence in their ability to learn. What kind of experiences cause students to have a sense of self-worth? Administering this simple questionnaire to students could provide insights: "At any time in your educational career that you have felt cared about, what has contributed to that feeling?" "When you have felt like a number, a nonentity, what has contributed to that feeling?" Students are very willing to tally the responses to this questionnaire. In class, the results may be discussed with this focus: "How does a feeling of self-worth affect motivation to grow, to become, to achieve?"

ASSESSING ACHIEVEMENT OF OBJECTIVES

In assessing this unit on motivation, not only do we want to know what students have learned but also what they perceive to be helpful to others. We want them to know that we value their insights.

For an overall evaluation of students' understanding of motivation, ask them to:

1. Explain motivation in relation to human needs.

2. Respond to the following questions:
   What insights have you gained from the study of motivation? What changes have you made as a result of these insights?

3. Prepare a handout for the student-council members who want to help freshmen become aware of internal as well as external motivation.

4. Teachers have asked for your insights on learning atmosphere and motivation. Write suggestions on the following topic: Teachers—Tips for Motivating Your Students. (The range of recommendations will reveal the student's understanding of the complexity of motivation.)

5. Write a letter to the principal with your suggestions for creating a more personal atmosphere in school. The principal appreciates student input on this subject.

RESOURCES FOR TEACHING

Below is a list of selected resources for teaching the concepts and topics of this chapter. It is divided into two categories: "Books, Pamphlets, and Articles" and "Other Resources." Addresses of publishers can be found in the alphabetical list in Appendix A.

Books, Pamphlets, and Articles

Aspy, David N., and Roebuck, Flora N. *Kids Don't Learn from People They Don't Like.* Amherst, Mass.: Human Resource Development Press, 1977. Focuses on the effect of personal qualities of the teacher (particularly warmth, personal regard, and empathy) and the tremendous impact these have on students' learning. Includes specific communication approaches that facilitate becoming one's best self.

Bourne, Lyle E., and Ekstrand, Bruce R. *Psychology,* 3rd ed. New York: Holt, Rinehart & Winston, 1976, "Motivation and Emotion," pp. 235–291. Presents basic concepts and various dimensions of motivation, including intrinsic and extrinsic motivation.

Cofer, Charles N. *Motivation and Emotion.* Glenview, Ill.: Scott, Foresman, 1972. A short, comprehensive paperback textbook covering drive and incentive theories, biological aspects of motivation, the need for stimulation, and cognitive consistency theories.

Combs, Arthur W. "Humanism, Education, and the Future," *Educational Leadership* (January 1978): 300–303. Cites and elaborates on five reasons why humanistic education is essential in contemporary schools.

Ginott, Haim G. *Teacher and Child.* New York: Avon Books, 1972. Presents a myriad of concrete, practical suggestions related to such issues as homework, praise, motivation. Congruent communication—language that fits feelings and situations—is illustrated. Affirms that the teacher basically sets the classroom tone.

Laurent, Jama. "On Motivation," *Senior Scholastic* 112 (October 18, 1979): 13. Focuses on an adolescent's motivational problems related to parental pressure. Maslow's recognition of our basic need to succeed is discussed. This provocative article stimulates discussion of motivation and related problems when it is presented to students. Write to Scholastic Magazines, Inc. for further information.

Levine, Ann. "Motivation and Emotion," in *Understanding Psychology,* ed. Virginia L. Hoitsma et al. New York: CRM/Random House, 1977, pp. 125–155. Explains various theories of motivation and the relationship between motives and emotions. McClelland's research on the achievement motive is presented as well as Maslow's hierarchy of needs.

Rogers, Carl R. "Beyond the Watershed: And Where Now?" *Educational Leadership* 34 (May 1977): 623–629. Presents a definition of person-centered education, explores the current state of humanistic education and its ramifications, the research that supports it, and the means of sustaining it. Suggests that the inner (intuitive) person is the next great frontier of education.

Rogers, Carl R. *Freedom to Learn.* Columbus, Ohio: Charles E. Merrill, 1969. "A view of what education might become" if a climate of freedom within limits existed in our educational settings. Includes both the practical and philosophical—always acknowledging the wisdom and uniqueness of individual persons. To facilitate each person's becoming fully functioning is the goal.

Smith, C.; Smith, S.; and Mikulecky, L. *Teaching Reading in Secondary School Content Subjects: A Bookthinking Process.* New York: Holt, Rinehart & Winston, 1978, "Motivating Positive Reading Habits," pp. 75–107. Presents a host of impediments to positive reading habits and attitudes at the secondary level. Emphasizes the students' needs for adult models. Presents a number of approaches, techniques, and methods to motivate reading and improve reading habits.

Other Resources

Motives and Learning (tape). New York: McGraw-Hill, College Division. Points out that students differ in motivations. Shows how teaching stimulates differing motives and how improper teaching methods often overwhelm rather than promote motivation.

"The Persistence of Memory," program 11 in the *Cosmos* series. Los Angeles: Carl Sagan and KCET. Dr. Sagan covers the study of genetic information, functions of the human brain, and discusses brain size and behavior, relationship of brain and environment, the chemical-electrical process that enables us to think. Write the Television Licensing Center for further information.

2

Concentration:
Learning to Focus

Frequently, students complain about their inability to concentrate: "I can't keep my mind on what I'm supposed to be doing. I just can't concentrate." This is true not only for low-achieving students but also for gifted students; not only for high-school students but also for college students.

What students mean by lack of concentration may vary. Some students mean that anxiety takes over as a result of procrastination; others mean that their minds wander—thinking first of one thing, then another; still others mean that they are unable to study consistently for two to three hours. Sometimes the students' expectations may be unrealistic.

Very often lack of concentration represents some form of conflict between studying and other interests or desires. All students experience such conflicts: wanting to socialize versus thinking through a theorem in geometry; wanting to daydream about dates or a Florida vacation versus doing a social-studies assignment; wanting to watch a favorite TV program versus learning new vocabulary terms. Mentally resolving the conflict is crucial to concentrated thinking. Deciding to telephone a friend after each hour of work, taking a five-minute break for daydreaming, making a schedule of the week with planned time for watching TV—all are ways of resolving conflicts in order to strengthen concentration. Acknowledging that such conflicts are a reality for everyone helps students feel more comfortable as they seek their own solutions.

What happens when we really concentrate? Our thinking becomes so focused that we are not even aware of happenings around us or of the passage of time. Joan experienced this in science class. Two minutes before class was to start, Jeff hurried into the room with a note for her. Immediately, Joan was in another world as she avidly read the note. She was assessing what Jeff said, what he had not said, why he said what he did. Thinking creatively, she was sensitive to problems and possibilities in whatever she read! Concentration? Joan was too absorbed to hear the bell ring for class to begin. Students identify with this example of deep concentration. They see it every day. Joan's total involvement exemplifies a real concentration experience.

If concentration is purposeful, directed thinking, what does this definition suggest about assignments? To concentrate effectively, students value knowing why they are to do an assignment, what to do, and how to do it. Not only does this result in better concentration but also in students' making the best possible use of their study time. Students appreciate knowing that we are trying to save their time by clear, purposeful assignments so that they can concentrate and learn more effectively.

Having a study-skills section in their notebooks is an invaluable aid for stimulating students to make positive changes. Therefore, ask each student to reserve a twelve-page section in his or her notebook for recording both basic information on various study skills and personal commitments to alter poor study habits as the year progresses. This study-skills section will be referred to throughout this guidebook. For additional details on notebook organization, consult Reproduction Page 36 and Chapter 12.

This chapter initiates our work on study processes, then, by centering on concentration. Creating awareness and stimulating positive change will be the purpose of all activities.

PERFORMANCE OBJECTIVES

As a result of the learning experiences in this chapter, students will be able to:

1. Assess their own concentration.

2. State what contributes to concentration.

3. State what interferes with concentration.

4. Take steps to improve their concentration.

LEARNING EXPERIENCES

Topic 1: Creating Awareness

1. Realizing that effective concentration is not an inherited trait but a developed behavior can be encouraging to students. Most students would like to improve the quality of their concentration, but without stimulation and help few of them make a concerted effort to change their habits.

   First, in a nonthreatening way, help students to think about their own study experiences through a guided fantasy. Although the questions asked in the activity may vary, the intent is to cause students to examine their usual experiences in studying. Next, ask students to share insights in small groups. Finally, each student is to assess briefly in writing what currently interferes with attentive studying and what changes might be helpful. Inform students of the three stages.

This guided fantasy may be used for stimulating students to imagine their usual study experiences:

> Close your eyes, relax all your muscles, and take deep breaths as I count from ten to one. (Countdown) You are now deciding to study. Where do you usually go? Do you have all your materials organized? Are people talking? Is the TV on? Is your stereo playing? Is anything interfering with thinking about your homework? Can you tune out interferences? Are you daydreaming? Are you feeling frustrated about the distractions or aren't you that intent on studying? Are you accomplishing what you set out to do? Now your time to study is over.

The following questions may be a guideline for small-group discussion:

- How do you feel about studying? Is it difficult to decide to study? Do you look forward to studying, or do you dread it?

- What kind of study environment do you usually have? Does this affect what you accomplish?

- What interferes with your studying? What do you do about these distractions? Can you find ways to quickly bring your attention back to studying when your thoughts wander?

- Do you have a feeling of satisfaction or of frustration when you finish studying? What causes these feelings?

- Do you see any need for change? Are you satisfied with your concentration? Your achievement? If not, is concentration part of the problem?

- What changes can you make to improve your concentration?

2. The purpose of this activity is to enable students to experience intensive concentration and to analyze what causes them to concentrate. Distribute the first page of Reproduction Page 9, "How Well Do I Concentrate?" or any other printed sheet. Give the students two minutes to cross out the letter e whenever it occurs. Only one strike mark is necessary to delete a letter.

   As students work, make a few observations. Do students quickly make a single mark or do they waste time by marking x or by blacking out the e entirely? (Because of the lack of instruction, some students are not efficient test takers.) Are there any signs of anxiety? Are some students working harder than others? Later, report your observations to the class. Usually this activity causes a class to become a model of concentration.

   When the two minutes have passed, provide another two minutes for students to respond in writing or in discussion to the following question: What helped you concentrate so intently?

   Usually the students mention the following five factors: wanting to do the work, having a limited time to work, knowing exactly what to do, knowing how to do it, and having absolute quiet in the room with everyone working.

   Next, ask the students if they concentrate with the same intensity when they study as they did during this exercise. How could this quality of concentration be duplicated in their study experiences? How could they apply these five factors in doing homework? Who must assume ultimate responsibility?

Aiding students in becoming conscious of their concentration patterns frequently stimulates students to desire change. Through this activity students discover that concentration contributes to efficiency in accomplishing a goal.

Topic 2: Stimulating Positive Change

1. The purpose of Activities 1–6 is to help the students to:

   • Discover that they already possess insight about concentration.

   • Realize the complexity of concentration.

   • Realize that they are largely responsible for their own concentration habits.

   • Determine what action they can take to improve their concentration.

   First, ask the students to respond to an open-ended questionnaire:

   a. What is concentration? (Final decision of our students: To concentrate is to focus one's attention, thought, and effort on a particular content or activity. Concentration is purposeful, directed thinking.)

   b. What contributes to concentration?

   c. What interferes with concentration?

   Second, in our experience, students are very willing to help tally these responses (outside of class) because they are interested in each other's comments.

   The following is a sample tally of interference responses from fifty-two freshmen in two advanced social-studies classes: What interferes with concentration?

• People talking	38
• Daydreaming	37
• Noise, music, TV	36
• Lack of interest in subject	13
• Lack of understanding	8
• Family interruptions	6

   Third, after typing the tallied items in the order of frequency as in the above example, invite the students to discuss how concentration can be improved. How can teachers help? What is the role of parents? What positive steps can students take to improve their concentration?

   Remind students that they should congratulate themselves on any positive strides forward since habits developed over a period of years are not easily changed. Any struggle experienced by one student may give insight to other students, so we encourage students to share their experiences.

2. The purpose of this activity is to involve students in assessing their concentration. Then they are to experiment with making changes in their procedures in

order to improve concentration. Make and distribute copies of Reproduction Page 9, "How Well Do I Concentrate?" To evaluate progress, the students may respond to this questionnaire before and after the work on concentration. Answer Key—Appendix B.

Remind students that a variety of study habits contribute to concentration. Budgeting time and making a study schedule (Chapter 3), listening carefully to assignment instructions in order to know what to do and how to do it, asking questions to clarify purpose and procedure—all contribute to concentration in studying. By experimenting with such changes in study habits, students soon discover what is effective in their varying situations.

3. Students in various classes have contributed to the formulation of the assessment instrument, "How Well Do I Concentrate?" Reproduction Page 9. After your students have responded to the questionnaire, solicit their reactions to this instrument. Are some items unnecessary? Should other items be added? Have students consult various study-skills books (Resources for Teaching). With this increased involvement in diagnosis and evaluation, students are more likely to make positive changes.

4. Ask students to make a chart with the following format:

Winning the Struggle to Concentrate

Obstacles to concentration   *Solutions*

After students have listed their concentration problems and possible solutions, invite them to share ideas in small groups. As a result, students discover new approaches for meeting the challenge of concentration.

5. Conduct a survey of teachers to determine their opinions on what contributes to their concentration and what detracts from it. Students enjoy compiling teacher comments, particularly if the teachers are asked to respond from their own experiences in high school and college. In class, compare teacher and student insights. Our faculty agreed with the students that "wanting to learn" is the top contributor to concentration.

6. The purpose of this activity is to stimulate students to synthesize what they have learned about concentration by producing material that will be helpful for them and for other students in the future. Distribute copies of Reproduction Page 10, "Concentrate? Of Course You Can!," which a junior class produced cooperatively with the teacher. This may be a model as well as a resource for ideas in having students devise their own tip sheet.

Inform the entire staff, including the administrators, that your classes wish to prepare a concentration guideline to help students become effective learners. Because staff members have had many years of experience in going to school and apparently have been successful, the students enjoy incorporating the staff members' suggestions within the guideline. Simply ask staff members to respond to two questions: Based on your experience, (1) What interferes with concentration? (2) What contributes to effective concentration? Combine staff and student insights. Use study-skills books as additional resources.

The final guideline your students prepare may be used the next fall as a handout to help orient freshmen to high school. Freshmen will listen carefully in homeroom to upperclassmen who use the handout for explaining how to improve concentration. All this participation communicates the message "We care" to the freshmen, and the upperclass students feel that they are truly valued as an important resource for helping others know how to become effective learners.

Students at our high school decided to publish Reproduction Page 10 "Concentrate? Of Course You Can!" in the school paper so that all students could benefit from the suggestions of the juniors.[1] This made it easier for teachers to reinforce in their classes what was presented in the guideline for effective concentration. The following fall the social studies teachers used this material with 500 freshmen.

ASSESSING ACHIEVEMENT OF OBJECTIVES

The extent to which students have achieved the objectives of the Learning Experiences can be measured by having students submit activity sheets for evaluation.

For further evaluation, on any test the teacher may ask:

• What is concentration?

• What contributes to concentration?

• What interferes with concentration?

• Analyze how your concentration habits have changed since you have become more aware of your concentration.

RESOURCES FOR TEACHING

Below is a selected list of resources for teaching the concepts and topics of this chapter. Addresses of publishers can be found in the alphabetical list in Appendix A.

Books, Pamphlets, and Articles

Farquhar, William W.; Krumboltz, John D.; and Wrenn, Gilbert C. "Controlling Your Concentration," in *SR/SE Resource Book*, ed. Frank L. Christ. Chicago: Science Re-search Associates, 1969, pp. 119–126. How to improve one's concentration is the subject of this article. Identification of distractors is a central theme.

Moore, J. William, and Schaut, Judith A. "Increasing Instructional Effectiveness Through the Use of a Problem-Solving Approach to the Design of Instructional Systems," *Journal of Experimental Education* 47 (Winter 1978–1979): 156–161. This article discusses student nonlearning and teacher inefficiency of instruction. How to increase teacher's effectiveness in respect to atten-

---

1. Published in *The Lance,* LaFollette High School, Madison, Wis.

tion, concentration, and learning is its subject. Write to the Helen Dwight Reid Education Foundation for further information.

Norman, Maxwell H., and Norman, Enid S. Kass. "The Fine Arts of Concentration and Remembering" in *How to Read and Study for Success in College*. 2nd ed. New York: Holt, Rinehart & Winston, 1976, pp. 230–236. This article discusses identification of distractors to concentration and how to improve one's ability to concentrate.

Pauk, Walter. *How to Study in College*. 3rd ed. Boston: Houghton Mifflin, 1984, "Concentrating to Learn," pp. 59–80. Gives information on external and internal distractions, physical and mental fatigue, and a secret technique: the pencil. Suggests a variety of solutions.

Spargo, Edward. *The Now Student*. Rev. ed. Providence, R.I.: Jamestown, 1977, "How to Concentrate," pp. 173–180. Presents ten suggestions for improving concentration followed by a comprehension test.

3

Time Management: Overcoming Procrastination

At the end of a day, teachers often wonder, "Where did all the time go?" Students face the same dilemma. They may have had good intentions to study but they became distracted. Most of us have experienced the feeling of frustration when we have not accomplished what had been planned for a specified period of time. Roughly 75 percent of entering Harvard students identify procrastination as a problem of concern to them.[1] Frequently, high school students are not aware that overcoming procrastination is a continuing challenge even for adults.

Why is procrastination such a common problem? In relation to doing their assignments, students have shared these distractions and disabilities:

- Telephone conversations with friends

- Television

- Daydreaming

- Personal problems

- Not knowing exactly *what* to do

- Not knowing *how* to do an assignment

- Lack of interest in a course

- Not planning a *specific* time to do the work

At first, some students may be quite skeptical about scheduling their time; to them, time management suggests a rigid, restricting efficiency with no flexibility or

---

1. Kiyo Morimoto, Bureau of Study Counsel, Harvard University, "Some Hints on Studying and Concentrating," (© Copyright 1984 President and Fellows of Harvard College).

freedom to do spontaneous things. After being involved in some of the activities in this chapter, they discover that organizing time is a way of gaining perspective on what needs to be done and setting priorities so they do not have to face all responsibilities at once. Many students claim that being organized releases more free time to do what they most enjoy without the stress of unfinished assignments. They learn that schedules tend to be idealistic about what is possible. As a result, they don't waste energy regretting what was not possible but learn where they need to allow more "breathing space." A daily list of schedule changes becomes a resource for developing a more realistic schedule.

When teachers give guidance in time management, students do become more purposeful and more efficient in their use of time. In addition, according to a mathematics teacher, "My students became real persons to me as I learned through their schedules what was important to them. The students learned to know themselves and each other in a different way."

An approach for teaching time management across the curriculum is presented under "Focus of the Month," in Chapter 12.

We have organized this chapter on time management around three topics: rationale for time management, evaluating current use of time, and exploring changes to provide a flexible schedule for meeting study and recreational needs. The materials were developed cooperatively by teachers and students who enjoy making suggestions based on their experiences in overcoming procrastination.

PERFORMANCE OBJECTIVES

As a result of the learning experiences in this chapter, students will be able to:

1. Assess how well they are currently using time.

2. Realize the amount of free time over which they have control.

3. Prioritize their activities that need to be completed.

4. Organize their time in an effort to meet their study and recreational needs.

5. Share insights on effective management of time.

LEARNING EXPERIENCES

Topic 1: Rationale for Time Management

1. How can we overcome the students' initial reluctance to scheduling time? Give your class other students' opinions based on their experience. After sophomores had experienced planning their use of time, they were asked to list the values of having a schedule. Distribute copies of Reproduction Page 11, "Why Bother with a Time Schedule?" to the class. In small groups, invite the students to discuss the sophomores' reactions. During this short discus-

sion students are to anticipate what may change in their lives as a result of experimenting with the use of time. If you ask them to record their anticipated results, these expectations can be compared with the actual results after completing activities in this chapter.

2. Many graduates of our high school claim that efficient management of time is crucial to success in college. During vacations they are very willing to share their experiences with our high-school students. As they show all their textbooks and discuss the professors' expectations, the time problem becomes apparent. Then the college students reveal how they schedule their study and social activities in order to maintain a good balance. These former high-school students give strong testimonials about the necessity of organizing their time to accomplish all the musts and still have extra time to do things that are fun and stimulating. Even if a college student shares the time problem without knowing how to solve it, he or she motivates high-school students to become concerned about organizing time.

   Inviting the principal or other adults in the community to share their time problems and solutions from their respective viewpoints results in students' gaining additional insights. (You may wish to videotape or film one presentation for use in other classes.) As a result of these experiences, the students begin to realize that time-management skills are needed in a variety of situations throughout life. This realization provides impetus for their time-management experiments.

Topic 2: Evaluating Use of Time

1. In this activity students are to record their daily time use for one week. Procedures for analyzing their use of time will be presented in subsequent activities.

   Duplicate copies of Reproduction Page 12, "Coping with Stress—Scheduling," and distribute them to the class. First, ask the students to write their class schedules in the appropriate time slots, which they need to label. Next, record fixed activities such as meals, employment, church, team practices. The rest of the schedule is to be completed at the end of each day. Daily, the schedule is brought to class for self-evaluation, thereby increasing each student's sensitivity to time usage. For example, if students make a star by interruptions, they may discover problem areas like hour-long telephone calls; this may lead them to rethink their priorities and revise their schedules.

2. Distribute copies of Reproduction Page 13, "Where Has the Week Gone?" Using the results from the previous activity, ask the students to record the total number of hours that they spent on a particular activity during the week. Then have students determine how much free time they had during the week. This is unscheduled time over which they had control. (In the same class, the amount of free time per week has varied from four hours to fifty-three hours. One conscientious, overcommitted, senior girl had only thirty minutes of free time per week. Later she became aware of her time treadmill as she discussed

"Where Has the Week Gone?" with other students and made plans for change.)

3. Using the information from Activity 2, list the hours of free time on the board so that students can assess the diversity within the class. Discuss the following questions: What are the reasons for varying amounts of free time? Can a person have too little free time? Are there areas of overcommitment like employment or TV viewing? Do you plan your use of free time or does this time just slip away? What is your responsibility in the use of your time? What percentage of your time was used for activities at school or in the community? Did you have time for yourself—to do what you enjoy?

A brief discussion of these questions creates further awareness of current use of time. You may wish to collect the students' schedules and analysis sheets. Their usage of time may indicate special interests or responsibilities that help you know each student as a unique person.

4. Some students like to work with a simplified plan for scheduling their time. Ask students to make the following three columns on a lined sheet of paper:

Date	Assignment	Planned Time for Study

Ask them to make a check mark in the margin for those assignments that were completed. At the end of each week they may make a list of recommendations for themselves.

5. This activity is designed to help students gain perspective on their current use of time. Make copies of Reproduction Page 14, "How Do You Organize Your Time?" and distribute them to the class. As students respond to this questionnaire, developed by juniors in high school, they are often motivated to change after discovering procedures that save time.

Toward the end of the quarter, ask students to respond to the same questionnaire in order to evaluate how their habits have changed. Based on their experience, the students may have ideas for improving the questionnaire to make the experience more meaningful for other students in the future.

Topic 3: Exploring Changes in Use of Time

1. Explain to the students that we sometimes feel overwhelmed by all we must do because we have not set any priorities. Make copies of Reproduction Page 15, "To Do List," and distribute it to the class. An expert on time management who advises corporation executives recommends "working smarter rather than harder." Ask the students to follow his plan.[2] Using the back of Reproduction Page 15, ask students to list all the activities or tasks that they must complete in the near future. Next, they are to assign to each task an *A*, a *B*, or a *C* priority. *A* means "I have no choice. I must do this immediately"; *B* means

---

2. From *How to Get Control of Your Time and Your Life* by Alan Lakein, copyright by Alan Lakein, © 1973, published by Peter Wyden, Inc. and reprinted by permission of David McKay Co., Inc., pp. 46–48.

"This is quite important but I could wait a little while"; C means "I could postpone this. I may not even do it." After the tasks have been prioritized, ask students to list them under the appropriate letter on Reproduction Page 15, "To Do List." Remind students that A activities are to be finished before moving to the B list. By categorizing their activities according to importance, the students use their time for what is most valuable.

During the week, as the students enter class, ask them to ABC their day. Soon they get into the habit of deciding what is most important for each day.

This is a very helpful step prior to setting up the next time schedule. The students learn to focus on what absolutely must be done. In the process a few students always discover that they have been spending their time on their Cs while their As just have not been completed.

2. Give each student three schedules (Reproduction Page 12) for an ongoing three-week experiment: Each day after finishing ABCing their activities for that day, ask the students to set a tentative time limit for each A activity before planning their daily schedules. If your students are ready, they may prioritize their weekly activities, estimate time needed, and make a schedule for the week. At the end of each day, ask students to list the changes daily that they made in their schedule. This list will be helpful for making next week's schedule more realistic.

   Here are a few suggestions for making a schedule based on other students' experiences:

   • Put first things first by listing what absolutely must be done (ABCing).

   • Make your schedule realistic—not so severe that you know you cannot possibly follow it. Include some built-in space for the unexpected.

   • Balance work and organizational activities with other things that are fun for you.

   • Do not be heroic in your belief that you can easily follow a schedule. You may become discouraged—particularly in the beginning. It is, however, very important to keep making a schedule so that you can find out what is possible.

   • Revise the schedule if necessary. Occasionally you may need to "toss the plan," but it can still be a guide to efficient effort.

   • Reward your daily successes by marking through your schedule with a colored pen or pencil each time you meet the hourly commitment you set for yourself. All the color will tell you that you are gaining control over your time.

   • Spaced review—a weekly review period for what you have had in each course—should be planned into your schedule. As a result, you will need less time for study before a big test.

3. Distribute copies of Reproduction Page 16, "Twelve Tips for Studying and Managing Your Time." These tips may be discussed prior to experimenting with organizing time; also, they may be revised at the end of the three-week experiment when your students have additional insights to share. In small

groups, have students determine what tips to recommend to students at your school.

Developed by a chemistry class, "Twelve Tips for Studying and Managing Your Time" was published in the school paper.[3] After reading the article, students were aware that the chemistry students' insights were relevant to effective work in other courses. Learning how to manage time gains prestige as students share their insights.

4. Give students the opportunity to read about scheduling time in various study-skills books such as those recommended at the end of this chapter. The school librarian may be willing to compile a time-management bibliography of available material in your library. These resources may be used by students in planning their schedules for the next week.

ASSESSING ACHIEVEMENT OF OBJECTIVES

The extent to which students have achieved the objectives of the Learning Experiences can be measured by having students submit activity sheets for evaluation.

To further evaluate the experiences with managing time, ask students to:

1. Make two columns on a page and respond to the following captions:

   I am pleased with my time   *I need to improve my time*
   use concerning   *use concerning*

2. Evaluate any change in use or amount of free time that are the result of the time-management experiment.

3. Hand in the current week's *ABC* list and schedule or an alternative plan developed for organizing time. (The students should be aware that to learn is to change. Has purposeful use of time become a habit so the weekly schedule is always planned?)

4. Make a chart, "Evaluate Your Experience," with the following format:

   Time problem   *Solution*

   (Analysis and response may be based on each student's own experience and observations of other people. Later the responses can be combined to make a class chart to be discussed in class and shared with others.)

5. Prepare suggestions, entitled "Tips for the Wise Investment of Time," for other students wanting help in using time effectively.

---

3. Published in *The Lance*, LaFollette High School, Madison, Wis.

RESOURCES FOR TEACHING

Below is a selected list of resources for teaching the concepts and topics of this chapter. Addresses of publishers can be found in the alphabetical list in Appendix A.

Books, Pamphlets, and Articles

Brieve, F. "Time is Money," *Phi Delta Kappan* 59 (December 1977): 282. This article outlines a 17-point suggestion list for the most efficient use of time. Although the list was designed primarily for school administrators, the suggestions are generally applicable.

Chapman, Elwood N. "The Time Message," in *SR/SE Resource Book,* ed. Frank L. Christ. Chicago: Science Research Associates, Inc., 1969, pp. 3–8. Ten "messages" serve as the basis for Chapman's discussion on the importance of being well organized. Discussion questions follow.

Cross, Ray. "How To Beat the Clock: Tips on Time Management," *National Elementary Principal* 59 (March 1980): 27–30. An elementary-school principal discusses his discoveries about how to control one's time. Write to NAESP for further information.

Holmes, M. "What Are You Doing with Your Time?" *Orbit* 10 (December 1979): 10–11. The relationship between instructional time and high achievement is discussed.

Research on the topic is cited. Write to Ontario Institute for Studies in Education for further information.

Norman, Maxwell H., and Norman, Enid S. Kass. "Organizing Your Time" in *How to Read and Study for Success in College.* 2nd ed. New York: Holt, Rinehart & Winston, 1976, pp. 26–31. Time organization and its value in college life are the topics of this article. The basic principles of how to budget one's time are discussed. The ideas can be applied at the secondary level.

Pauk, Walter. *How to Study in College,* 3rd ed. Boston: Houghton Mifflin, 1984, "Controlling Your Time," pp. 34–55. An in-depth view of how to develop a schedule of one's time and how to program for most efficient use of one's time.

Robinson, J., and Godbey, G. "Work and Leisure in America: How We Spend Our Time," *Journal of Physical Education and Recreation* 49 (October 1978): 38–39. The emphasis of this article is on how we develop leisure-time activities. Its value in education rests with the idea that leisure and recreational time must be budgeted and planned; in addition, recreation can contribute to whole-being achievements.

Spargo, Edward. *The Now Student.* Rev. ed. Providence, R.I.: Jamestown, 1977, "How to Manage Your Time," pp. 219–225. An outline of important considerations for becoming efficient at organizing one's time is provided. Questions for discussion follow.

4

Remembering:
Storing and Retrieving

One of our most distinctive gifts is memory. Memory—that rich, mysterious territory unique to each of us. Our storehouse of memories and learning, the brain, is a magnificently complex instrument. It allows us to be present in all dimensions of time—looking lovingly or painfully at what childhood was for us, being present now at the moment of "recording" our experiences and knowledge in memory, anticipating what the turn of the century will bring.

Yet many of the workings of this matchless instrument remain enigmatic to us. Though they have not yet discovered precisely how, for instance, many psychologists speculate that the brain may file multiple copies of learnings instead of just one, much as materials in a library are cross-referenced. Another mystery related to learning:

> Precisely how the brain puts things together has never been adequately charted. We still don't understand how the human brain constantly delves into the subconscious to retrieve buried fragments of knowledge and experience which it then instantaneously fuses with all the new information.[1]

Undoubtedly, all of us experience exhilarating moments of insight and creativity when our previous knowledge and new learnings meld to form "new life," new designs. This fusion of what is known with what is new not only enhances memory, but also gives greater meaning to what is learned.

Without a "meaning or relationship connection," details are rapidly forgotten. Hence, students learn more effectively when teachers relate new ideas and new terms to what students already know, and when teachers challenge students to do that for themselves as well. For example, students can better understand and remember new ideas about the functioning of cells when that information is linked to students'

---

1. Roy Bowman, "Those Business Hunches Are More than Blind Faith," *Fortune* (April 23, 1979), p. 113.

existing knowlege about the makeup or structure of cells. This building of relationships between previous and present learning, then, not only strengthens retention of the new information, but also enriches one's background of knowledge. When students understand the importance of this linking process, they become more actively involved in seeking connections. This kind of involvement further enhances remembering.

In order to give students the opportunity to learn about and experiment with memory principles, this chapter is organized as follows: the first topic is intended to pique students' curiosity about memory. Topics that underscore general memory strategies, then the necessity of organizing study content for learning follow. Next, we explore the value of reciting and spacing reviews. Finally, the chapter focuses on mnemonics (specialized memory systems) as a memory aid.

When is the best time to teach the principles for remembering? Hand in hand with any of these study skills: SQ3R (Chapter 6), mapping (Chapter 7), or note-taking (Chapter 8). Hence, after students hear about the importance of organization, that is, of searching for relationships of ideas in order to understand and remember, they will experience a specific method like mapping that incorporates this principle.

When teaching students about memory, an overriding emphasis should be that memorizing data is not an end in itself. Rather, learning and remembering new information is a steppingstone in building a vast storehouse of knowledge which, in turn, facilitates the learning and remembering of more new information. This "knowledge bank," then, is a valuable resource upon which a person draws for thinking and problem solving more creatively. Thus, enhancing memory ultimately enriches not only one's knowledge but also one's experience of life itself.

PERFORMANCE OBJECTIVES

As a result of the learning experiences in this chapter, students should be able to:

1. Experience greater awareness and appreciation of that remarkable gift, memory.

2. Realize that memory can be improved.

3. Analyze the effect of attitude on remembering.

4. Experience memory improvements through learning—

   a. to organize ideas in study material

   b. to self-recite

   c. to space reviews

   d. to employ mnemonics.

5. List seven tips for improving memory and analyze the actual applications of these to academic work.

LEARNING EXPERIENCES

Topic 1: Heightening Awareness

1. Ask students to write either the heading "How to Sharpen Memory" or another one of their own choosing in the study-skills sections of their notebooks (Reproduction Page 36). Then invite them to reflect and to write their thoughts on the following questions:

   • What would your life be like if you had no memory?

   • If you could not remember, do you believe that life would be more or less satisfying than it is now? Explain.

   Discuss together the results of students' reflections. (In response to the first question, students might state that they would have no friends, experience no recall of past painful experiences, have no prejudices.)

   Sometimes we best appreciate our gifts in life when we imagine life without them.

2. This activity helps students discern factors that affect their remembering; consequently, they may harness these for better learning results. Request that students draw three columns on a sheet of paper in their notebooks and write answers to the following:

   • In column one list five things from both in school and outside school that are easy for you to remember. (If students have trouble, suggest these: things they learn about friends, plots from novels, song lyrics.)

   • In column two list five things from both in school and outside school that are difficult for you to remember.

   • In column three compare the first two lists. Then write at least three reasons for the differences between these two lists. (Students may arrive at insights such as the positive effects of motivation, of interest, and so on.)

   • Based upon what you have just learned about yourself, decide and write specifically how you can improve your remembering in school.

   Encourage the entire class to share their personal observations. You may wish to have a volunteer at the blackboard recording a list of the students' comments on the last two questions.

3. Ask students to imagine that people who sit near them in class are having trouble remembering information in the course. What suggestions could each student offer, based on memory strategies he or she currently uses? Have each student record these.

   These suggestions may then be consolidated on a master list, to be handed out to all students and used as a record of students' preinstruction practices. This can then be compared to a postinstruction list (Topic 2, Activity 4).

4. Request that students guess the answers to the following two questions:

   • After reading an assignment, within what time span do you forget *most* of what you have read? (Answer: 24 hours)

   • If you do not use any special methods to remember, how much of a reading assignment do you forget within two weeks? (Answer: 80 percent)[2]

   These facts often shock students into action!

Topic 2: General Memory Strategies

1. To diagnose students' current memory techniques, use Reproduction Page 17, "A Memory Habits Checklist." You may wish to use this now, and again at the end of the quarter, to nudge students into continuously "stretching" their applications of memory strategies.

2. Distribute "Memory Tips," Reproduction Page 18, a concise summary sheet of memory suggestions. After experimenting with the activities in this chapter, have students evaluate and, if necessary, revise this material.

3. Provide class time for students to skim study-skills books (Resources for Teaching) to glean any additional tips on memory that may help them. Have them record any good suggestions in the "How to Sharpen Memory" sections of their notebooks. You may want to have students shout out loud the best tips so everyone can learn them.

   Note: One resource, *Superlearning,* by Sheila Ostrander and Lynn Schroeder with Nancy Ostrander (Resources for Teaching) fuses knowledge about relaxation, the logical capabilities of the human mind, and the mind's creative capacity into memory strategies that have shown amazing results.

4. Assign students, in groups of five to seven, to pool all the methods they can think of that improve their remembering. One person in each group may be responsible for recording a master list. After receiving instruction in and experimenting with memory procedures, students may volunteer to consolidate and refine all class suggestions. Pass on this final list to incoming freshmen or perhaps to the school newspaper, as well as to each student in the class. To evaluate change, compare the original preinstruction list (Topic 1, Activity 3) with this final list.

Topic 3: Organizing—A Key Factor

1. The following activities captivate students' attention and sensitize students to the value of organizing ideas as they read and study. This is accomplished by

---

2. H. F. Spitzer, "Studies in Retention," *Journal of Educational Psychology* 30 (December 1939): 641–656.

allowing students to experience the frustration of not being able to remember because they did *not* perceive any structural pattern.

Using the overhead projector, allow thirty seconds for students to view a transparency of the figures on Reproduction Page 19, "Try to Remember." After students reproduce as many figures as they can, ask how they tried to remember (i.e., in the order the figures appeared, according to how many sides an object has).

2. Inform students that you will give them forty-five seconds to study the transparency of Reproduction Page 20, "Organizing Confusion," which contains twenty words they should attempt to memorize. After having students write as many of these as they can remember, ask how many words people recalled, as indicated by hand vote. In addition, ask how students tried to remember these words (i.e., by writing them down, by grouping them so they make sense like "painting-artist-brush," by position on the page, by same first letters). Have students who were most successful at this activity explain their methods; then reinforce the importance of students' searching for organization as they read and study.

3. First, distribute to students a sheet of paper containing the following words:

way	on	the
this	my	school
to	?	Did
friends	a	morning
tire	have	flat

Tell students that they will have fifteen seconds to memorize this list; after that time, they will be asked to write on a fresh sheet of paper all the words they can recall.

Next, pass out to students a sheet of paper containing this sentence:

"Did my friends have a flat tire on the way to school this morning?"

Again, after fifteen seconds, ask students to record what they recall.

Finally, pose these questions:

• After comparing your word list to the original one, what do you notice about the words you recalled? the words you forgot (i.e., position in the list or degree of meaning associated with the word)?

• Which was easier to recall—the list or the sentence? Why?

Students may arrive at these valid conclusions concerning memory:

• One remembers more from the beginning and the end of a study session, less from the middle.

• One remembers best what has meaning or some kind of powerful association (the sentence versus the seemingly unrelated word list).

• One remembers most easily what is original, unique (*?*, *Did*).

4. Prepare a tray with the following twenty items on it:

thread	keys	wallet	tea bag
pocket knife	pen	facial tissue	salt shaker
spoon	cigarettes	hand lotion	cup
thimble	apple	sugar cube	comb
matches	banana	credit card	pin

Keep these objects covered with a cloth or newspaper until you explain the activity (same as Activity 2: forty-five seconds viewing time; then students record all the items they remember). Be certain that this tray is located centrally so that all students can surround it to scrutinize the variety of items.

This time students may organize according to categories such as what is found in a kitchen, a purse, and so on. Praise any student attempts to search for structure!

5. Divide the class into small groups of four or five, and have each group categorize all the objects on the tray in the previous exercise. This activity allows you to lead students inductively to these facts:

- Categories are based on such things as *experience*, the *setting*, and *observation* using the senses. Keen powers of observation are indispensable.

- Categories result from searching for *common characteristics*.

- Categories also result from noting what is *unique* about objects, words, and ideas.

- An object, word, or idea may be classified in a *variety* of ways (i.e., the key: with pocket knife, facial tissue, pen, wallet, credit card, comb, cigarettes, and matches, labeled "items commonly found in pockets"; with pin, spoon, thimble, etc., labeled "metal objects"; with spoon, pin, pen, etc., labeled "facilitating tools," and so on). Create categories that are *personally meaningful!*

- Categorizing greatly *enhances memory*.

Then have students return to their small groups to quiz each other by calling out a category "title" and challenging each other to recall the specific items included under that heading. Finally, ask students which was easier— remembering twenty isolated objects or recalling them according to category titles. Inquire how this information relates to students' study of a textbook chapter wherein they may need to learn a great many facts. Is it easier to learn these facts individually or as they relate to major headings?

6. Carl Sagan posits, "The brain is like a library of looseleaf books, constantly adding new pages—new volumes." Further, he claims that the brain can hold as much information as twenty million books and that long-term memory has virtually unlimited capacity: a large computer can hold ten million bits of information per cubic centimeter while the human brain can accommodate

ten *billion* bits per cubic centimeter![3] However, the great problem in remembering is not storage, but retrieval. Professor Jerome S. Bruner of Harvard University asserts, "The most basic thing that can be said about human memory, after a century of intensive research, is that unless detail is placed into a structured pattern, it is rapidly forgotten. . . . The key to retrieval is organization."[4]

The primary truth about memory, then, is that perceiving the structure or organization of material that students read, hear, or view is absolutely essential if they want to remember it. Tell students, when you give them a reading assignment, that they can "just read it" sentence by sentence and hope that its contents will "stick" when that next test is announced, or they can actively search for the major concepts and supporting information related to them. Why? Because remembering major concepts will trigger the memory of supporting details. When ideas are seen in relationship to each other, the whole meaning of the study materials "jells," or crystallizes, thereby facilitating memory.

In reading an article, for example, students may need to learn only the title or thesis statement and perhaps four or five major concepts to grasp the essence of that article. Of course they would need to study the important details, too, but learning those in relationship to the major concepts they illustrate or clarify is much easier than attempting to memorize each fact in isolation. Inform students that they will be learning about a number of study techniques to help them discover relationships among ideas and categorize them as they study so that remembering is facilitated: SQ3R, a method for studying a textbook and/or article (Chapter 6); mapping (Chapter 7—a note-taking substitute that is original and particularly useful to students); and note-taking (Chapter 8). All these methods focus on getting the essence of the content.

7. Inform students: Seven is a magic number. It is the approximate limit of unrelated items we can remember.[5] If you need to go to the store for bananas, broccoli, milk, oranges, ice cream, apples, cheese, peas, lettuce, and beans (write these items on the blackboard), you might have difficulty remembering these foods, unless you group them. If you do that, instead of ten individual items you would need to keep in mind only three general categories (have students formulate these): fruits, vegetables, and dairy products. These "category words" would then trigger the details, i.e., the word *vegetables* would trigger *lettuce, peas,* and *beans.* What you have done then is called "chunking." Each chunk, like *fruit* (*apples, oranges,* and *bananas*), is considered only one unit. You have just diminished the amount to remember from a frustrating ten to a more manageable three. Consequently, you have also just increased the amount of additional information that you will be able to remember.

3. Carl Sagan, "The Persistence of Memory," *Cosmos,* KCET TV, Program 11, 1982.
4. Jerome S. Bruner, *Process of Education* (New York: Alfred A. Knopf and Random House, 1960), p. 24.
5. George A. Miller, "The Magical Number Seven, Plus or Minus Two: Some Limits on Our Capacity for Processing Information," *Psychological Review* 63 (1956): 81–97.

Since applying this concept eases even the task of remembering simple items on a grocery list, ask students to think how much more helpful it can be for studying effectively a chapter, an article, and class notes.

8. To prepare for this activity, use a chapter from your textbook as the basis and devise fifteen to twenty questions that are answered throughout that content material. (Questions at the beginning or end of the chapter are a ready source.) Type these questions, double spacing between them, and duplicate enough for your largest class plus ten extras. Then cut apart the questions on each sheet and insert these into an envelope.

   When introducing this activity, jot the major headings of the chapter, numbered consecutively, on the blackboard. Next, distribute one envelope to each student and have him or her sort the questions into columns according to the major heading that probably contains the answer (i.e., students form one column for each major heading). This activity not only exemplifies that study requires thinking and organizing but also highlights the fact that headings are great aids to comprehension and remembering.

9. Select a portion of the index of your class text. Then assign small groups and ask students to categorize the topics into as few categories as possible. Discuss.

Topic 4: Reciting and Spacing Reviews

1. Once students have decided how ideas are related to each other in their study materials and have somehow recorded this, they are ready to apply another powerful weapon to fight forgetting: frequent reciting and reviewing. The fact that most forgetting occurs within twenty-four hours of initial learning is a compelling reason to review and, thereby, check such an "evaporation" of knowledge.[6] In fact, even one minute of review after learning can double retention.[7]

2. Psychologists report that self-recitation is the most powerful defense against forgetting. Inquire why this is true and let students, in pairs, come up with three speculations. Reasons such as the following are valid:

   • Students are more purposeful and more intent on understanding the content when they hold themselves accountable immediately after reading.

   • In addition to *seeing* the material to be learned, the student also *hears* it while reciting aloud. The more senses involved in learning, the greater the chance of remembering. That is why *writing* what one recites is also judicious.

   • Checking one's recitation against the material to be learned reveals any gaps or inaccuracies in knowledge at this early stage when they can easily be remedied, before "wrong learning" becomes a habit. Accurate initial learning is paramount.

6. Spitzer, *Journal of Educational Psychology*, pp. 641–656.
7. Walter Pauk, *How to Study in College*, 1st ed. (Boston: Houghton Mifflin, 1962), p. 76.

- As one's mind actively "works over" the new material, the original neural trace (the brain's record of an experience) becomes more deeply etched in the brain. Thinking about and involving oneself with the learning results in ideas moving from short- to long-term memory.

  Specifically, when we perceive auditory and visual stimuli, they enter a sensory storage system for twenty to thirty seconds. To retain this information, it must be transferred to short-term memory (STM). Then, through *self-recitation* the new information will finally enter long-term memory (LTM), where it seems to remain forever.[8]

- Since self-recitation is so effective, students will have a richer "knowledge bank" to which new knowledge can relate.

3. Inquire, "How would you like to take a year-long course with your grade determined by a single test in June? What study methods would you use for long-term memory?"

   This is the challenge encountered by first-year law students at the University of Minnesota School of Law. Relate that Professor David Bryden, a graduate of Harvard Law School, therefore suggests to his students: "After the first three weeks in my course, whenever you study, spend *half* your time in *review*. Then in May you can focus on current learning since you will have already mastered what you had in the fall and winter."[9] Professor Bryden's recommendation is based on his own successful study experience at Harvard.

4. The next time that you will be doing two consecutive days of lecturing, try this experiment to prove the importance of reviewing for long-term remembering.

   Without explaining why to the students, in one class (experimental group) save five to ten minutes at the end of each of these two class sessions for the students to review what they have just heard. In another class (control group) simply lecture to the end of the class hours, never mentioning the importance of review for long-term remembering. On the third day and again one week later, give the experimental group another five-minute "refresher shot" of review time; perhaps review with them.

   Compare the performances of these two groups on the chapter test. Then, two weeks later, administer to both groups a surprise quiz on the two-day lecture contents. The results? Our experimental group of students has scored at least 40 percent higher than the control group! Do not forget to tell the students in each class about the outcome. The facts speak! Then have students themselves write an article or report the results of this study to the school newspaper so that the entire student body has the opportunity to benefit from these striking findings.

   Inform students that research indicates that with no review at all of what one reads, within two weeks one forgets approximately 80 percent of the content. On the other hand, with review, one *remembers* 80 percent and forgets only 20 percent.[10]

---

8. Robert A. Baron, Donn Byrne, and Barry H. Kantowitz, *Psychology: Understanding Behavior* (Philadelphia: W. B. Saunders Company, 1977).

9. David P. Bryden, Professor of Law, University of Minnesota. Taken from Tricia Bragstad's class notes, September 1978.

10. Spitzer, *Journal of Educational Psychology*, pp. 641–656.

5. Tell students: Angela has just read a chemistry chapter. She then spends one entire hour studying and reviewing the chapter contents to be certain that she thoroughly understands it. Meanwhile, Catherine has just read the same chemistry chapter. She also studies and reviews the material for one entire hour, spacing out her reviews over six weeks. Ask students:

   • Six weeks after the initial reading of the chemistry chapter, who will remember the most—Angela or Catherine? Justify your speculation.

   • Are you more like Angela or Catherine in your study habits?

   The two graphs that follow illustrate the difference between one extended review and several brief, spaced reviews when long-term retention is the goal.[11] The results are remarkable!

   The student in Figure 4-1 (a) studied one hour on September 30, then steadily lost much of that knowledge over the next six weeks. The student in Figure 4-1 (b) studied the same amount of time—one hour—but spaced his reviews. Six weeks later? The first student lost much of his original knowledge, whereas the second student maintained his same high-level mastery of the material. Clearly, spaced reviews are a smart investment!

Topic 5: Mnemonics—Memory Systems

1. Inquire, "When you need to learn and remember a list of ten or so items—for instance, the causes of the Civil War (or cite an example from your course)—how do you do it?"

   Students are so frequently required to learn lists of dates; items; causes and effects of political, social, and economic events; laws of science; etc., that teachers often assume that students effectively cope with this learning task. Yet your asking students their procedures for remembering lists of elements integral to your course may reveal rote learning (repetition) as virtually their only method. If this is the case, time-tested, special memory systems known as *mnemonics* can increase students' options, and concurrently, their chances of "memory success."

2. At the outset of this section, the authors reaffirm that the very best way to learn and remember material is to organize it, thoroughly understand it, frequently recite and review it, and actually use it. We discourage mnemonics as a substitute for understanding; however, these special memory systems can be useful in memorizing lists of unrelated items or laws of science, causes and effects of historical events, and so on. According to current research on the brain's functioning, mnemonics is closely correlated to how the mind appears to work.

   Present and discuss with the class: The term *mnemonics* is derived from Mnemosyne, the goddess of memory in Greek mythology. It refers to the science or art of improving memory by using formulae or other aids.

   Mnemonics has been with us since the ancient Greeks used it to perform

---

11. Thomas F. Staton, *How to Study*, 6th ed. (Nashville: HOW TO STUDY, 1977), p. 47.

Figure 4-1. (a) "Massed" study. (b) Spaced reviews.

(a)

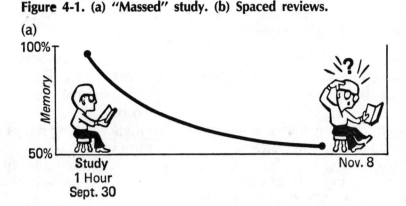

(b)

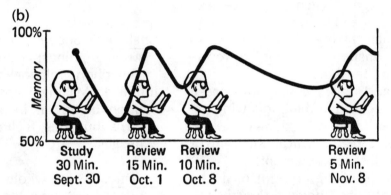

Thomas F. Staton, *How to Study*. 6th ed. (Nashville, Tenn.: HOW TO STUDY, P.O. Box 40273, 1977), p. 47.

outstanding feats of memory—delivering hours-long orations without notes, memorizing hundreds of items in any order. How did they accomplish this? Each orator imagined himself in a very familiar spot, such as his own home or hometown. As he mentally walked about this location, he associated points from the oratory with a chair here, a table there. When speaking, then, he simply mentally walked that same territory and recalled the lines he "found" along the way. Students might experiment with this method using their bedtime or rising routines.

3. Using mnemonic aids to remember is more than mere trickery or gimmickry; it is a sound educational approach to learning long lists of items for classroom use or everyday living. Specific memory systems such as *peg-words* or *narrative-chaining* (explained in activities that follow) draw on facets of the brain that have recently been gaining attention—namely, the sensory, imaging, and visualizing potential that we each possess.

   As the burgeoning current literature on the brain reveals, we are penetrating more deeply the mystery of how the human mind operates. What seems clear is that we have been neglecting a critical facet of our mind's potential—not its ability to analyze, to think logically, or to be rational, but rather its genius for creating images.

Some researchers talk of the two hemispheres of the brain: the left and the right brain. Purportedly, each segment encompasses diverse characteristics, some of which follow:

Left Brain	*Right Brain*
Verbal: Using words to name, describe, define.	Nonverbal: Awareness of things, but minimal connection with words.
Analytic: Figuring things out step-by-step and part-by-part.	Synthetic: Putting things together to form wholes.
Symbolic: Using a symbol to *stand for* something. For example, the drawn form ◐ stands for *eye*, the sign + stands for the process of addition.	Concrete: Relating to things as they are, at the present moment.
Abstract: Taking out a small bit of information and using it to represent the whole thing.	Analogic: Seeing likenesses between things; understanding metaphoric relationships.
Logical: Drawing conclusions based on logic: one thing following another in logical order—for example, a mathematical theorem or a well-stated argument.	Intuitive: Making leaps of insight, often based on incomplete patterns, hunches, feelings, or visual images.
Linear: Thinking in terms of linked ideas, one thought directly following another, often leading to a convergent conclusion.	Holistic: Seeing whole things all at once; perceiving the overall patterns and structures, often leading to divergent conclusions.[12]

Whether the brain is so neatly divided is highly controversial: what seems certain, nevertheless, is that our culture and our schools laud "left-brain" functionings (schema above). For example, one previous topic in this chapter—organizing and categorizing ideas—is the kind of analytic task this society values highly. At the same time, "right-brain" potential is virtually dormant and ignored: the artist, the poet rarely enjoy great status in our country. Many giants in their fields, however, do capitalize on the "whole-brain" approach: thinking and reasoning *as well as* imagining and dreaming, following hunches and gut feelings. For example, Buckminster Fuller; Chester Carlson, the lawyer and inventor of Xerox; and Conrad Hilton, the hotel magnate, are just a few of many prominent persons who rely on getting the facts *and* following their hunches. In fact, Buckminster Fuller has reported that, in a study of famous scientists' diaries, every scientist revealed that the most significant factor in each of his discoveries was, not knowledge, but intuition.[13]

Thus, although we do not yet perceive precisely how, we do know that our minds are capable of bringing far more to bear on our learning and living

12. Betty Edwards, *Drawing on the Right Side of the Brain* (Los Angeles: J. P. Tarcher, Inc., 1979), p. 40.
13. Sheila Ostrander, and Lynn Schroeder with Nancy Ostrander, *SuperLearning* (New York: Dell Publishing Co., Inc., 1979), pp. 201–204.

than solely the thinking skills our society so highly esteems. Like the outstanding persons mentioned above, each of us and our students also possesses a wellspring of intuitions and imaginings that could greatly enrich our capacity to learn and to problem-solve. Let's focus now on mnemonics, which can unleash this expansive potential for visualizing and creating to aid remembering in fresh, new ways.

4. Ask students to cite individual mnemonic devices that aid them in recapturing basic information: "*I before e except after c*"; "*Every Good Boy Does Fine*" for the lines of a music staff, *FACE* to recall the spaces; "Thirty days hath September . . ." are a few illustrations.

   Likewise, "*Kings play cards on fine green sofas*" aids memory of the biological classification system:

Kingdom	*Family*
Phylum	*Genus*
Class	*Species*
Order	

5. Ask students how they would go about remembering 120 individual items. Then relate this information: One group of college students (experimental) was given twelve successive lists of ten items to learn using one specified memory technique. A second group (control) was given the same task and told to memorize in any way its members could. Later, a test administered to each of the subjects indicated these findings: the experimental subjects remembered almost 93 percent of the 120 items, while the control subjects, who typically used rote learning, recalled just 14 percent![14]

   What technique led to such astonishing recall by the experimental group? *Narrative-chaining,* whereby items to be remembered are woven into a story. Using the biological classification system as a basis, an illustration of narrative-chaining follows:

   > The *kingdom* was in chaos, so the knights sharpened their weapons. *"File 'em!"* they were directed. The peasant *class* had revolted and the knights were to impose *order.* Every *family,* even those containing *geniuses,* was to be investigated to eradicate traitors from the *species.*

   Have students, in pairs or trios, apply the narrative-chaining method to at least one or two lists of data they must master in your course. Then have the class share "tales"! Repeatedly hearing the data in itself will reinforce remembering while giving students the opportunity to experiment with a new memory technique to see whether it is helpful for learning and remembering.

   The narrative-chaining method is highly effective, particularly when a great many lists must be learned. On assignments you may wish occasionally to ask students to apply this technique and record their "stories," to be shared with the class. Since this technique is often new to them, students need experience in applying it before evaluating its usefulness.

---

14. Gordon H. Bower, "Improving Memory," *Human Nature* 1 (February 1978): 69.

6. Inform students: Another method for learning a listing of items is the *number-rhyme,* or *peg-word,* system. In this system, each number from 1 to 20 is linked with a rhyming word. The first ten numbers are linked to the following, for instance:

1	bun	*6*	sticks
2	shoe	*7*	heaven
3	tree	*8*	gate
4	door	*9*	vine
5	hive	*10*	hen

When attempting to learn a list of items, then, the student creates a vivid image which associates the number *1,* the word *bun,* and the first word on the list of items to be learned. One study-skills expert recommends making this association exaggerated, absurd, sensual, dynamic (rather than static), colorful, imaginative, sexual, and vulgar! In addition, he suggests keeping the association as "pure" as possible by avoiding intricate, confusing images that may be difficult to recall accurately.[15] Then focus on this image for several seconds to be sure that it is imprinted in the brain.

To illustrate, if one were to try to memorize the biological classification system using the number-rhyme approach, it would entail the following:

1	*bun*	kingdom	Imagine an immense bun with a medieval kingdom oozing out the edges—a "kingdom sandwich."
2	*shoe*	phylum	Imagine a card catalog shaped like a chartreuse shoe with a librarian who continues to "file 'em" (the reference cards).
3	*tree*	class	Imagine a majestic tree bedecked with a crown and flowing mantle—"a classy tree."

Have students work in pairs several times to apply this peg-word system to your class content before assessing the value of the method.

7. Over a two-week period have students experiment with mnemonics in three different situations. You may wish to specify that two of these situations be academic. The assignment might be organized as follows:

Situation?	*Mnemonic Device Used?*	*Effectiveness?*
1. _____		
2. _____		
3. _____		

Then have students share their "research" results.

---

15. Tony Buzan, *Use Both Sides of Your Brain,* rev. ed. (New York: E. P. Dutton, 1983), pp. 64–66.

8. Ask students to interview three of their teachers to determine helpful mnemonics in each of their subject areas. The student might also inquire what mnemonics from grade school, high school, and college the teacher still remembers and whether the teacher uses mnemonics in any other situations in life, i.e., meeting new people, remembering a social-security number. If the teachers do use specific strategies, have students get a detailed description of what types so that the students themselves can report on and experiment with these techniques.

ASSESSING ACHIEVEMENT OF OBJECTIVES

Several activities in this chapter can be used for evaluating student achievement. In addition, the following suggestions may be used for evaluation or as additional learning activities:

1. Either create a drawing or write a brief summary, including specific details, of how your view of memory has changed as a result of your learning in this unit. (You might employ a "before" and "after" column format to elicit this information.)

2. Specifically, what is the relationship between memory and each of the following:

   a. organization of ideas

   b. self-recitation

   c. spaced reviews

   d. mnemonics

3. Without using any particular means for remembering, one forgets ____ percent of what one has read within two weeks. However, applying specific memory strategies, one remembers ____ percent after two weeks.

4. What is mnemonics? When is its use most appropriate and effective?

5. (Refer to some listing of causes, effects, laws, etc., related to your course, and ask students the following.) List three ways that can facilitate your learning and remembering this material. Then elaborate on one method you would actually use to cement this information in long-term memory.

6. List seven suggestions to improve memory. Then analyze your current application of these to academic work.

7. The Student Council is compiling a study-skills booklet, and the editor of the project invites you to write the article entitled "A Treasure Chest of Memory Tips." What will you say?

RESOURCES FOR TEACHING

Below is a selected list of resources for teaching the concepts and topics of this chapter. It is divided into two categories: "Books, Pamphlets, and Articles" and "Other Resources." Addresses of publishers can be found in the alphabetical list in Appendix A.

Books, Pamphlets, and Articles

Bower, Gordon H. "Improving Memory," *Human Nature* 1 (February 1978): 64–72. A clear, readable exposition of how remembering occurs, mnemonics, the role of meaning, interference. Filled with concrete illustrations. Excellent for teachers and students.

Buzan, Tony. *Use Both Sides of Your Brain.* Rev. ed. New York: E. P. Dutton, 1983, "Memory," pp. 43–70. Involves the reader in specific activities to discover some of the most important memory principles.

Devine, Thomas G. *Teaching Study Skills: A Guide for Teachers.* Boston: Allyn and Bacon, Inc., 1981, "Remembering, Relating, and Test-taking," pp. 279–301. This excellent sourcebook explores kinds of memory and provides a wide array of specific activities involving students.

Gerhard, Christian. *Making Sense: Reading Comprehension Improved through Categorizing.* Newark, Del.: International Reading Association, 1975. An activity-filled source to teach students how to organize ideas in general, then how to organize ideas when reading and writing. Intended for middle grades, but easily adaptable to high-school students. Excellent material.

Lorayne, Harry, and Lucas, Jerry. *The Memory Book.* New York: Ballantine Books, 1974. An exposition of memory techniques to aid in remembering foreign and English vocabulary, information in the arts and in readings, long-digit numbers, names, and faces.

"Memory and Thought," in *Understanding Psychology,* ed. Virginia L. Hoitsma et al. 2nd ed. New York: CRM/Random House, 1977, pp. 51–61. Contains information on taking in, storing, and retrieving information, and on the central processing of information through thinking, problem-solving, creativity. Well-written and informative.

Ostrander, Sheila, and Schroeder, Lynn, with Ostrander, Nancy. *Superlearning.* New York: Dell, 1979. This exciting book will have special appeal to the innovative teacher. Backed by research, the authors present inventive approaches that combine relaxation techniques and baroque music with knowledge of logical and creative capabilities of the person to "free" untapped potential. Their thesis: that "supermemory" is within the reach of each of us. Originally developed to help people learn foreign languages, this system is also applied to other situations both inside and outside of school.

Pauk, Walter. *How to Study in College.* 3rd ed. Boston: Houghton Mifflin, 1984, "Forgetting and Remembering," pp. 82–113. This excellent study-skills book focuses first on studies of and causes of forgetting, then on the basic principles of remembering.

Spargo, Edward. *The Now Student,* Rev. ed. Providence, R.I.: Jamestown, 1977, "Training Your Memory," pp. 135–142. A concise summary of memory principles, followed by two comprehension tests and six related activities for students.

Weinland, James D. "Memory Improvement: General Principles," in *SR/SE Resource Book,* ed. Frank L. Christ. Chicago: Science Research Associates, 1969, pp. 127–142. A discussion of the factors affecting memory.

Other Resources

"The Brain," New York: WNET-TV, 1984. This 8-part documentary telecourse has a study guide and text, if you wish. The functioning of the brain, learning and memory, and the two sides of the brain are explored. Write or call the Annenberg Project.

Computers and Human Behavior. Bloomington, Indiana: Indiana University. In this film theories and findings on human mental processes such as memory and problem-solving capabilities are explored through computer studies at Carnegie Technological Institute.

How Do We Know What We Know? Bloomington, Indiana: Indiana University. This film traces the thinking process from the original stimulus to sophisticated verbal abstractions.

"The Persistence of Memory," program 11 in the *Cosmos* series. Los Angeles: Carl Sagan and KCET. Dr. Sagan covers the study of genetic information and functions of the human brain, and discusses brain size and behavior, relationship of brain and environment, the chemical-electrical process that enables us to think. Write the Television Licensing Center for further information.

5

Technical Vocabulary:
Absorbing Specialized Meaning

"A good mind means a good vocabulary and a good vocabulary means a good mind. Which comes first? Which causes the other? It is more accurate to say that they are interactive—each is an inseparable part of the background and abilities of the learner."[1]

In a social studies classroom this quotation on the blackboard sparked a discussion on the importance of having an extensive vocabulary. Students were surprised to learn that vocabulary test scores correlate highly with school grades, scores on IQ tests, and scores on reading tests. The teacher also informed them about the research showing that having formal instruction in vocabulary is much more effective than simply relying on informal, unplanned acquisition of words. Then, relating the etymologies and roots of words in the next assignment, the teacher stimulated and challenged the students to extend their vocabularies in listening, reading, speaking, and writing.

Students not only must acquire new understandings and insights in each course, but also must remember and apply what is learned. The initial step in remembering is to fully grasp the meaning of new terminology. We cannot remember what we do not understand. Long-term memory of technical terminology is semantically encoded; we are not likely to forget what is meaningful. Knowing the meaning plus frequent review or usage is crucial for rapid retrieval of informational terminology stored in the brain. Assimilating the specialized vocabulary is basic to accumulating fundamental knowledge in any field.

For all of us an extensive vocabulary is a very important tool for gaining knowledge. Are students sharpening this tool? Here are the responses of 467 freshmen in

---

1. Edgar Dale and Joseph O'Rourke, *Techniques of Teaching Vocabulary*. (Palo Alto, Calif.: Field Educational Publications, Inc., 1971).

our high school to the following question: Do you attempt to get the meaning of new terms in your courses?

More than half the time	44%
Half the time	30
Less than half the time	26

Since the specific knowledge of a field is transmitted through words, this lack of effort to understand new terms cannot be ignored.

How can the teachers who are the vocabulary experts in their fields motivate students to learn technical vocabulary? If motivation is response to a felt need, we must find ways for students to experience the need for knowing technical terms. Based on positive student reactions, the following four-step approach is effective:

- Create the felt need to know specialized vocabulary.

- Cooperatively discover effective strategies for understanding and learning vocabulary.

- Involve students in experimenting with learning strategies of their choice.

- Share results of this cooperative project and determine what learning strategies are effective.

This sequence is delineated in the activities of this chapter. Each student develops his or her own effective learning style for assimilating the technical language used to communicate the knowledge of each field.

PERFORMANCE OBJECTIVES

As a result of the learning experiences in this chapter, students will be able to:

1. Understand the relationship between technical vocabulary and comprehension.

2. Realize what approaches are effective through experimenting with methods for learning technical vocabulary.

3. Formulate a plan for vocabulary learning in their classes.

LEARNING EXPERIENCES

Topic 1: Technical Vocabulary: Roadblock to Comprehension

1. Since technical vocabulary is used to transmit the specific knowledge of a field, knowing that subject-matter vocabulary is crucial for understanding. In

planning direct instruction in vocabulary, teachers have found the following suggestions helpful as a guideline for developing activities:

Do's and Don'ts in Teaching Vocabulary[2]

Do . . .

a. Teach new subject-matter vocabulary in context and before students' initial reading of the new material; all teachers have this responsibility.

b. Explain new words in terms of structural analysis—prefixes, roots, suffixes—whenever possible. This way, students will learn families of words, not just a few new "big words for the day."

Don't . . .

a. Don't rely solely upon "incidental" approaches to vocabulary growth; actively, consciously pursue a program of vocabulary development, but avoid deadening drill.

b. Don't gamble with mere verbalisms; make definite provisions for extending new words into speaking, writing, and thinking vocabularies. That way you are building concepts, not simply encouraging the acquisition of many isolated "labels" that fit equally isolated "package" definitions.

Do . . .

c. Constantly direct pupils' attention to words—their appropriateness, power, and specific nuances of meaning. Offer two choices when a word is needed; give the students practice in choosing exactly the right word for exactly the right meaning.

d. Occasionally bring the class into this decision; try to foster a respect for the well-chosen word and the well-turned phrase.

Don't . . .

c. Don't forget the connotative implications of certain words; these are as much a part of the definition as are denotative ones.

d. Don't teach roots, affixes, etc. completely isolated from actual words; try to approach these word elements inductively, and then apply them.

Do . . .

e. Teach your students definite forms or patterns for succinctly stating definitions; the following work well for the major parts of speech:

Nouns	State the word, the class it is in, and how it differs from other words in that class.
	A desk is a piece of furniture that is used for writing and storage.
	Then, to sharpen the definition, narrow the class.
	A desk is a piece of office or school fur-

---

2. Courtesy of Professor Ken Dulin, University of Wisconsin-Madison.

	niture that is used for writing and storage.
Verbs	Use the infinitive form followed by a synonym or phrase. To ratify is to approve.
Adjectives and most adverbs	Use *to be* in the same way. To be fatigued is to be tired out.

Don't . . .

e. Don't make your definitions more difficult than the words to be defined. Carefully select the definitive words and examples of a lower (more concrete) level of abstraction.

Do . . .

f. Teach students how to consciously make use of the major context clues used by authors; occasionally take time to practice this important skill with the whole class. Remember, students will not always have you and/or Webster along when they are reading!

Don't . . .

f. Don't neglect the "different" ways of approaching definitions. The analogy is a good way of getting at meaning; so is asking for antonyms occasionally, rather than always for synonyms. For many words, the posing of an absolute opposite is the best way to give a definition.

Do . . .

g. Teach your students a "system" or "strategy" for unlocking unfamiliar words. The following CSSD is a good one, since it so strongly emphasizes *meaning.*

Context	First approach the word through its setting or use. Does it make sense here? What should it probably mean? What does its surrounding context suggest? Make an intelligent guess.
Structure	Take the word apart; are there familiar "pieces" you recognize? Any root word? Does this give you its pronunciation or meaning?
Sound	Analyze the word phonetically. Break it into sound units. Can you get it now? If not, go to the last step.
Dictionary	If all else fails, go to "the big book" and straighten it all out. But remember—language is alive! New word meanings develop and may not be recorded except in new or specialized dictionaries.

Don't . . .

g. And, finally, don't stop here! Go on to develop your own unique ways of presenting new words. Just remember these few suggestions:

- Encourage use on all levels—reading, writing, speaking, and thinking.

- Aim for concepts, not mere verbalisms. Work from the concrete to the abstract.

- Utilize the novel and the different. A new approach always has an appeal.

- Always define a word in context, and always from a structural approach.

2. In this activity the students will experience technical language as a roadblock to understanding what is being communicated. First, the teacher asks if any of the students have had a course in spyloctogy. Since no one has had this experience, everyone is at the same level of understanding. Spyloctogy is a mathematics course that is offered on the planet Mars. (This same approach with different technical material has been effective in other subject areas.)

    Next, as the teacher seriously reads the spyloctogy material from an overhead transparency, the students are to analyze: (a) what prevents their understanding of the material, (b) what kind of thinking is required, and (c) what study skills are important for achieving in spyloctogy.

An Example from Martian Mathematics
Taken from a Text in Spyloctogy[3]

In this chapter, we will be concerned with a study of the Pexlomb. A Pexlomb is defined as any Zox with pictanamerals which flotate the Zox into five berta Zubs where each Zub is supramatilate to the Rosrey of the Ord. For example, consider the Zox defined by 3 berta Ooz. It is obvious that any pictanameral which is Blat must necessarily be Cort to the Ord. This follows from our knowledge of the relationship of a dentrex to its voom. However, if the Ord is partivasimous then the Zox must be Zubious. Thus, if we kizate the dox pictanameral, our Zox will be flotated into 5 berta zubs. But remember, each zub must be supramatilated to the Rosrey of the Ord. If any one of the zubs is not supramatilated, we then have a pixilated Pexlomb which requires a completely different procedure.

We can represent the necessary conditions by the following:

1. Q??----¢ (note: Q is nubbed according to the principle of Plasimony)

2. By Axdrellation we arrive at: X Q/?---!!* Thus, it is evident that the solution must be:

3. M---/?? (Really quite simple if you remember to obscone in step 4 of the Axdrellation process.)

After the reading is completed, the teacher quietly asks if anyone had any difficulty understanding the material. The students' reactions are immediate: "We don't know the vocabulary so how can we understand?" Some students have already counted the number of unknown technical terms—over twenty in the first paragraph. They are impressed by the relationship of vocabulary to comprehension.

Beyond the problem of the technical vocabulary and symbols, what other insights do students have? First, they notice the thinking that is required. A thorough, working knowledge of the concepts is needed since they must also be understood in relationship to other concepts, that is, ". . . any pictanameral which is Blat must necessarily be Cort to the Ord." What is meant by "Cort to

---

3. From Donald E. P. Smith et al., *Learning to Learn* © 1961 by Harcourt Brace Jovanovich, Inc. Reprinted by permission of the publisher.

the Ord"? Being able to define conceptual terms in isolation is not enough. How are they interrelated?

Second, a very heavy concept load combined with the cumulative nature of mathematics places a premium on understanding and remembering—"This follows from our knowledge of the relationship of a dentrex to its voom." Understanding new material is dependent on the understanding and remembering of previous concepts studied.

Third, words like *thus* and *therefore* reveal that a logical reasoning process is basic to understanding, thereby making careful reading-thinking essential. The teacher adds: "Speed readers have difficulty in spyloctogy. In fact Martian teachers often recommend reading the material twice." The students recognize that the logical reasoning process is impossible without first knowing the terminology used for transmitting knowledge.

Fourth, abstract thinking is a very important component of mathematics since the processes involved are frequently not visible to the naked eye. Equations heavily laden with symbols are a reality only as mental concepts; thoughtful study is required.

Since this kind of abstract, conceptual thinking is built progressively upon mental interaction with previous learning, daily study and review is crucial. Missing class for two days, a student might be lost! Frequently, students do not understand why they should make up their homework after being absent. Through this activity, they perceive the "building of learning." Any knowledge gap from the past may obstruct the reasoning and learning process in the future.

The students' abilities to do abstract thinking improve as the brain develops more fully during adolescent years. When students know also that they will gradually become more capable in abstract thinking through experience and continuing review, they are encouraged to persevere.

In mathematics classes teachers may further advise: (a) learning "what symbols are used, what they mean, and how they are interrelated"; (b) studying intensively the explanatory or illustrative material that precedes the problems, since problems are "miniature tests" of a student's ability to apply knowledge or to consolidate past learnings; (c) working through steps of problem examples to see "what is being done, how it's being done, and why."[4]

What is meant by *learning process* becomes more real as the students examine the material from Martian mathematics. Using this material is effective for creating awareness of the need for knowing technical vocabulary in any course. This same approach may be used with your textbook as a follow-up activity so that students learn to analyze material in your course and to determine the best procedures to use for learning. By reading paragraphs from technical journals you may also create awareness of the need for knowing technical vocabulary. Since so much knowledge is communicated through the use of technical terms and symbols, specialized terminology must be understood and remembered.

---

4. Ibid., p. 81.

3. Before students will purposefully study technical vocabulary, they must be convinced of its important role in learning now and in the future. Invite adults from the community to share their insights. You may invite adults whose work is relevant to your course.

    In an auto-mechanics class, the teacher invited the manager of a garage who shared difficult, technical materials that must be read and understood by his mechanics. The manager stressed that he has no time to read the material to them. These mechanics must have the expertise to understand what they read and to visualize the processes. Then he showed students the instruction manuals for repairing new cars. The students were impressed. They suggested that, in the future, the garage manager should come at the beginning of the semester because of the positive influence on their motivation to learn.

    During college vacation time teachers invite former students to bring their college textbooks for the high-school students to examine. One student brought seven social-studies books. By reading certain sections, the college students demonstrate the need for an extensive background of general and specialized vocabulary. They emphasize what study skills are needed in addition to the habit of studying regularly and reading extensively. This sharing is so meaningful that each year high-school seniors volunteer to return from college the following year to share their own struggles and their success experiences.

    Attorneys, engineers, and business representatives have been willing to talk to students about the importance of vocabulary in their fields. Videotapes of these sessions were made for use with other classes.

Topic 2: Experimentation: Source of Strategies for Learning

1. When students experience the real need for knowing the specialized language in any field, they are open to discovering a variety of strategies for learning, to experimenting with those strategies, and to evaluating their effectiveness for gaining knowledge in the course. Inform the students that for the next three weeks one blackboard in the classroom will be reserved for listing strategies for learning technical vocabulary. During the three weeks they may continue to choose strategies for their own experimentation, but at the end of three weeks they are to determine what has been the most helpful for learning the specialized language of the field. The activities that follow help students discover a variety of strategies.

2. Because class time is limited, students must assume responsibility for study and review of the technical terminology in each course. How can we convince them that short "refresher shots" or review results in instantaneous recognition and long-term memory? This activity serves that purpose. Students are to read "Ledgusllaiteive Yshooz," Reproduction Page 21.

    First, ask students to be aware of how they are helped by context clues (the meaning of the passage) and language clues (structure and spelling).

    Second, explain that one student will read the first paragraph aloud, but other students are to help whenever necessary with words that are difficult to decode. Then the first reader or the teacher chooses another student to read the second paragraph. (Usually so much help is offered that everyone is participating.)

Third, immediately after the material has been read aloud, ask students to write their answers to the comprehension questions without looking at the material again. (After an English teacher struggled to read this material during an in-service training session, he said he could not answer any of the questions. Emotionally, he had experienced the trauma of the student who has so much difficulty with vocabulary that the meaning is lost.)

Fourth, after discussing students' answers, the teacher reads the second paragraph rapidly and with expression. Then you quietly ask the students, "Why don't I have any difficulty reading this material?" Students immediately respond that you've read it many times so you are familiar with the vocabulary and the ideas. This gives you the opening to discuss the importance of frequent review in learning terminology. The students also may see how your knowledge of the ideas helped you become fluent in reading the material.

Fifth, discuss application of this experience to reading and studying technical material. What is the message? Keep reviewing daily that technical vocabulary, or a month from now reading the textbook will be an exercise in frustration. Week by week, in any course, the vocabulary demands increase. Since many courses are cumulative, with one concept building on another, gaps in knowledge of the conceptual terminology prevent comprehension. Think! Reflect! Review! With a solid base of knowledge, the students will be able to read and assimilate ideas faster as they continue in a course. Frequent review results in greater speed, better understanding, and improved memory.

3. In the previous activity the students discovered that frequent review and practice is important. The next step is to make students aware of strategies that facilitate this self-recitation and review. Year after year the "divided-page approach" has received the top rating for effectiveness by our students. List new terms on the blackboard in this format so that students see it in operation.

Here is information you may wish to share. With the "divided page" the students have a special section in their notebooks for technical vocabulary. The students record difficult terms and meanings within the following structure drawn on pages in the vocabulary section of their notebooks:

New Term or Concept	Context	Meaning, Stated Briefly

Ask your students to speculate on the advantages of this system. According to students who have tried it:

- If the information is recorded chapter by chapter, the list of terms becomes a concise, progressive study and review tool.

- Covering the column of definitions, the student can state the new term, recite the definition, then quickly check to see if the right meaning was given.

- Covering the column of new terms, the student reads the definition, then states the term that is defined, or writes it in the far-right column.

- To avoid knowing the terms in listed order only, a friend or relative can easily quiz a student on the terms in a different order. Since all the material is written out, the friend does not need to be familiar with the subject and may check which ones are right in the final column. Shared review of this type increases motivation.

- Using multiple senses—seeing, speaking, hearing, writing, or drawing—improves retention.

- In three minutes many terms can be reviewed.

4. Record another vocabulary learning approach on the board (Activity 1)—the "1 × 3 card approach." Using 3 × 5 unlined cards and a paper cutter, make a larger number of 1 × 3 cards so that students will be inspired to experiment with this approach. (A university student taking Hebrew and Greek simultaneously used this method to help him earn an *A* in both courses.) The cards are used in the following way:

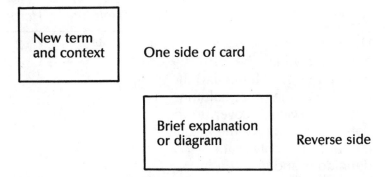

Synonyms and original sentences are also helpful. Students like flipping these little cards for frequent review. Often they test each other. When a term is in long-term memory, the card is removed from the pack (held together with a rubber band) and reviewed infrequently. (One student taped cards of known terms to her bedroom wall which was covered by the end of the year!)

5. Using all the study-skills textbooks in the library, ask the students to research the best ways to study vocabulary according to the experts. (Resources for Teaching) As students discover new methods, they list them on the blackboard.

   Another resource for students is the specialized materials that have been prepared for helping students know how to study at state universities. Frequently guidance and counseling centers are willing to make these materials available for classroom or library use in the high school. Students are impressed when materials come from a university.

   Some students have discovered new approaches by asking other teachers on the staff for ideas. Continuing to add strategies to the list on the blackboard keeps the experiment alive.

6. Through this activity the students discover what study approaches have been effective for each other. Individual style is encouraged, so that no one hesitates to list a strategy for learning that is helpful. For example, in one of our classes, three students used small blackboards in their bedrooms for recording new vocabulary terms. Self-recitation became automatic upon entering the room. Through the following activity, the sharing of approaches is made possible.

After three weeks of experimentation, ask each student to list or describe any study approaches that have been effective. Then outside of class all the strategies are tallied jointly by the teacher and a few students. The next day a Ditto copy of the total list is given to each student. Then give the students one more week to try any of their classmates' suggestions. Following this final experimentation, take a vote to determine the methods effective for the most students. (Students do not evaluate any method they have not used.)

The final vote on the strategies for learning technical vocabulary in two geometry classes at our school follows:

What is the best way for you to learn vocabulary?

	Helpful	Not Helpful	Have Not Tried It
a. Using the "divided page" method in which the term is written in one column and the meaning in the other column. Then for review, I cover up the definitions and give the meaning, or I look only at the definitions and give the term.	44	2	2
b. Taking notes on new concepts in class.	43	2	3
c. Reviewing every day by reciting to myself. Much repetition results in long-term memory of vocabulary.	28	7	13
d. Finding some trick to the word—some association for remembering the meaning.	31	3	14
e. Drawing diagrams that help understand some definitions. Understanding is necessary for remembering.	31	7	10
f. Taking practice tests.	14	3	31
g. Reading definitions over and over.	35	7	6
h. Quizzing by friends.	31	5	12

		Helpful	Not Helpful	Have Not Tried It
i.	Saying new terms out loud and thinking about the meaning.	35	5	8
j.	Reviewing whenever I come upon a technical term again after having studied it; I make sure that either I know it or I look it up in my list.	35	4	9
k.	Expressing the meaning of terms in my own words to see if I can give the exact meaning.	38	0	10
l.	Using 1 × 3 flash cards with the term on one side and the definition on the other.	18	2	28
m.	First, examining the word for familiar parts—prefixes or roots. Second, writing the word and focusing on the meaning.	38	0	10
n.	Sitting in a quiet room and thinking out the meaning of the concepts, then drawing diagrams to check my understanding.	9	9	30

Over a period of time teachers may develop a list of effective strategies that gradually may be shared with students during the three-week experiment.

When students experienced this "experimental approach" to learning in the third quarter, they strongly urged that the teacher implement the project in the fall. Even during the third quarter, over 50 percent of the students improved their grades as a result of the increased emphasis on learning process. Request students' suggestions for improving the project.

7. How can we stimulate students to search for meaning? How can we be certain that a student knows how to use context clues? How can we reinforce these skills in classroom exercises or in tests?

The following learning format can be used effectively in various content areas. In responding to the questions, the students must underline the word clues for their answers. Then the number of the question is written above those words. With this required accountability, students discover the importance of context clues. When students discuss their answers, the focus is on meaning and proof of each answer. Gradually, they become more conscious of technical vocabulary, language structure, and style of writing in various fields. Eventually students are willing to prepare exercises to prove their expertise. Sentences may be developed that contain important information. Later, paragraphs may be used.

Prove Your Answer[5]

Underline the words that answer the question; then write the number of the question above those words:

The portion of the cell substance outside[1] the nucleus and within[1] the cell membranes[2] has been named the cytoplasm.[3] It is a region[3] and not a[3] single substance[3] any more than the nucleus[4] is a single substance.

1. Where is the cytoplasm found?

2. What does the "it" in the second sentence refer to?

3. What is cytoplasm?

4. Name another structure that is not a single substance.

You have learned that life, whatever it is, is part of a genetic process; living organisms of today are descendants of other living organisms.

1. What is a part of a genetic process?

2. What words tell you that scientists are not sure what life is?

3. Where do living organisms come from?

4. The phrase "living organisms of today are descendants of other living organisms" describes what process?

An alternative is to make a transparency of paragraphs from your textbook. Divide the class into two groups to compete in answering the questions that you ask orally. They must know the words that supply the information. Exercises of this type also may be one part of a unit test. Then the students know that the teacher really values knowledge of learning process as well as of content.

8. Vocabulary in context is a major contributor to comprehension of textbook material. Frequently, context clues are the source of meaning for technical vocabulary. Students are forced to use the context for this purpose when they must find the meaning of nonsense words. Distribute copies of Reproduction Page 22, "Context Clues to Nonsense Words." Ask students not only to respond to the multiple-choice questions but also to underline those words that are clues to the meaning of the nonsense words. In small-group discussion students may compare rationales for their answers.

On any test or on the blackboard nonsense words may be substituted for technical vocabulary in sentences from the textbook. Ask the students to define the nonsense words and list the technical terms if they are known. Request your students to bring this type of exercise to class for others to do.

9. Words have families and ancestors. For example, the word *turbulent,* meaning disorderly or tumultuous, has the Latin ancestor *turba* meaning tumult or crowd. Included in this family are the words *perturb* and *disturb;* both imply agitation or disorder.

---

5. Moira Marshall, former biology teacher, LaFollette High School, Madison, Wis. Shared with Bragstad, May 1976.

Figure 5-1. Root word—meter.

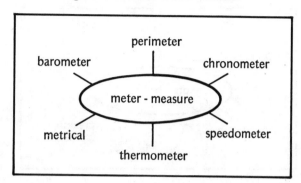

In the vocabulary section of the notebook, ask each student to make diagrams of word families relevant to the course. An alternative is to give students 1 × 3 cards for this purpose. Figure 5-1 makes the family relationship real so that the meaning is not forgotten. Recommend frequent review for long-term memory.

10. The meaning of a word may be complicated and modified by a prefix. The following prefixes affect the meaning of so many words that students appreciate having this information:

Word	Prefix	Common Meaning
premonition	pre-	(before)
descend	de-	(away, down)
interstate	inter-	(between, among)
inject	in-	(into)
monopoly	mono-	(alone, one)
unimportant	un-	(not)
community	com-	(together, with)
nonviolent	non-	(not)
extend	ex-	(out, beyond)
reassure	re-	(back, again)
propaganda	pro-	(forward, for)
inaccurate	in-	(not)
disagree	dis-	(apart, not)
submarine	sub-	(under)
misbehave	mis-	(wrong)

As the prefixes appear in technical vocabulary, the student may make a diagram like the following:

Figure 5-2. Prefix—pre.

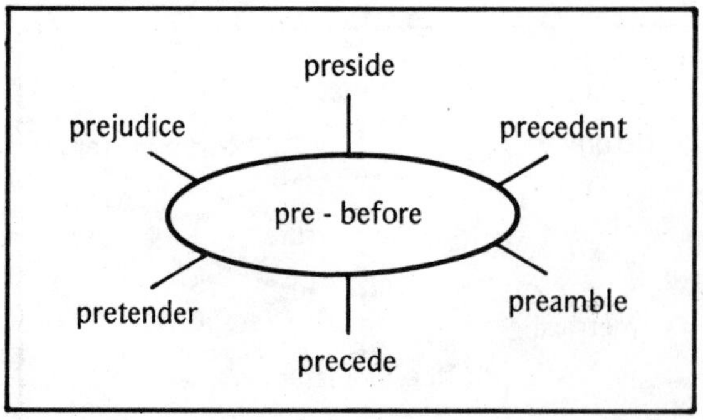

As an alternative, students may make a family tree with the root on the trunk and all the "relatives" on the branches. Some students like to post their creative diagrams on the bulletin board.

Frequently this approach to learning vocabulary helps students see that words are alive. We have a living language: words grow and change; new members of the family appear. For example, *astrology* and many *nautical* terms have a long history in comparison to the modern *astronaut*—a sailor in a space ship among the stars. The study of vocabulary enriches the meaning of what is read. Meaning enhances memory. As a result, the student brings more knowledge to the printed page when he or she studies in each course. An extensive vocabulary contributes to achievement in any content area course.

ASSESSING ACHIEVEMENT OF OBJECTIVES

The extent to which students have achieved the objectives of the Learning Experiences can be measured by having students submit some of the activity sheets for evaluation.

For further evaluation you may ask students to respond to the following questions:

1. What is the relationship between technical vocabulary and comprehension of course material?

2. What changes have you made in vocabulary study?

3. How have these changes affected your learning and understanding of the subject?

4. Imagine that you are a science or English teacher. How would you stimulate interest in vocabulary development? What study procedures would you recommend? Why?

RESOURCES FOR TEACHING

Below is a selected list of resources for teaching the concepts and topics of this chapter. It is divided into two categories: "Books, Pamphlets, and Articles" and "Other Resources." Addresses of publishers can be found in the alphabetical list in Appendix A.

Books, Pamphlets, and Articles

Bergman, J. R. "Reducing Reading Frustration by an Innovative Technique for Vocabulary Growth: Vocabulary Margin in Textbooks," *Reading Improvement* 14 (Fall 1977): 168–171. This article examines the various problems inherent in present techniques in technical vocabulary teaching and learning. A technique using the vocabulary margins is presented. Write to Project Innovation for further information.

Duffelmeyer, Frederick A., and Duffelmeyer, Barbara Blakely. "Developing Vocabulary Through Dramatization," *Journal of Reading* 23 (November 1979): 141–143. Using foreign language as a model, Duffelmeyer and Duffelmeyer suggest that dramatization may be the key to vocabulary learning in that it provides for meaningful, albeit vicarious, experiences essential to language development. Write to the International Reading Association for further information.

Einbecker, P. G. "Use of Multi-media Programs to Increase Adult Vocabulary," *Phi Delta Kappan* 61 (January 1980): 360–361. The author discusses her multi-media-program approach to vocabulary learning and describes research on the approach. The study focused on college-student vocabulary learning.

Ignoffo, Matthew F. "The Thread of Thought: Analogies as a Vocabulary Building Method," *Journal of Reading* 23 (December 1979): 519–521. The author suggests that the most effective method of vocabulary building is through use of analogy and sentence-completion exercises. Research is

discussed and examples are given. Write to the International Reading Association for further information.

Pauk, Walter. *How to Study in College.* 3rd ed. Boston: Houghton Mifflin, 1984, "Your Vocabulary," pp. 269–301. Presents information and techniques for building vocabulary including prefixes, roots, and the frontier vocabulary system.

Rowell, C. G. "Vocabulary Development in the Social Studies," *Social Education* 42 (January 1978): 10–14. Citing research in the area, Professor Rowell discusses strategies such as using cloze procedures, games, and classification problems for developing content area vocabulary. The author also stresses the importance of maintaining the relationship between vocabulary and concept development. Write to the National Council for the Social Studies for further information.

Thomas, Ellen Lamar. *Reading Aids for Every Class: 400 Activities for Instruction and Enrichment.* Boston: Allyn and Bacon, 1980, "Helping Students Learn the Meanings of Words," pp. 58–91. Includes activities and materials for study of vocabulary including context clues, structural analysis, word origins, and dictionary competence.

Witty, Paul. "How You Can Build Your Vocabulary," in *SR/RE Resource Book,* ed. Frank L. Christ. Chicago: Science Research Associates, 1969, pp. 85–91. The author discusses techniques for learning the meanings of new words.

Other Resources

Working with Vocabulary. New York: Guidance Associates. This program (2 filmstrips, 2 cassettes, 2 LPs, Library Kit, Teacher's Guide, Ditto Masters) employs the locale of a movie set to teach vocabulary. Using cinematic vocabulary as examples, students are shown how to use context and clues to reason out the meanings of new words.

6

SQ3R:
Streamlining Your Study

One of the most common assignments made in high school is to study a chapter in a textbook. Yet it is appalling to discover that even the best students do not utilize an efficient method for accomplishing this task. Here is an actual experience.

After sharing some basic information on the brain (Chapter 1), the teacher gave three separate classes of unusually bright freshmen in social studies the following directions: "I would like to see how you use this complex instrument, your brain, in reading a chapter. Please open your book to page 49. Just begin reading the chapter. I'll stop you when I have finished my observation."

In each class, the students looked very curious, wondering how this teacher thought he could observe the use of the brain. The teacher had no difficulty. After a whole minute had passed, the entire class was still on the first page. Very obviously the students were reading sentence by sentence without any idea of where they were going. Not one student had looked ahead to detect the author's clues to the organization of the information. No one examined the main divisions, the headings, of the chapter. No one checked the summary for a mental map giving direction for study. The students did not seek any mental structure of the major concepts into which they could fit all the information. Without this structure, detailed information is rapidly forgotten!

At the end of three minutes the teacher said, "Please stop. Close your books. I would like you to write down the title of this chapter. Then write three major concepts presented in the chapter."

Even the students were amazed that not one person had read the title of the chapter. When citing "three main concepts," the students pinpointed various details within the first few paragraphs. This was the reading procedure for the brightest students in a freshman class of more than 500 students! They did not have an organized method of attack for studying a chapter in a textbook. Without instruction and supervised practice, students usually do not use the brain efficiently in reading to learn. Organizational clues to the relationship of ideas within the chapter are ignored until students experience how organization can facilitate learning and long-term remembering of the content.

Is the situation different for highly intelligent college freshmen? One LaFollette graduate had this experience as a freshman at Harvard College: all freshmen were directed to study a chapter in social studies as if they had two hours to complete it. After approximately twenty minutes, they were asked to stop reading in order to take an objective and essay examination.

This former LaFollette student reported that when he heard the word "Stop!" he flipped the pages to the end of the chapter, where he found a beautiful one-page summary entitled "Recapitulation." Immediately he knew that page should have been read first. Too late to be of help, he remembered SQ3R (Survey, Question, Read, Recite, Review), that intelligent approach to study.[1] Under the pressure of the situation, this Harvard freshman resorted to the plodding method that was deeply ingrained prior to learning about SQ3R during his senior year in high school. A study by Perry at Harvard revealed that only 10 percent of the Harvard freshmen explored beyond the page that they were reading.[2] Only 10 percent may have read the summary first. In response to the essay question only those who took time to survey the chapter knew the major concepts presented by the author.

In these two situations highly intelligent freshmen in high school and in college did not have an organized, purposeful approach to study. As teachers we need to revise our emphasis in education. Traditionally we have focused on all the information in each course that students must learn, understand, and remember. With the knowledge and publication explosions, we emphasize more information each year while we neglect improving the ability of students to absorb all this information. Instead of this solitary emphasis on content, we must first focus on the students—helping them to discover new, more effective ways of studying their textbooks, new ways of using their natural abilities to think, question, analyze, reflect, and create. With this student-centered approach both teaching and learning become more exciting and more productive. As experienced by a social-studies teacher, "Since I have taken some class time to help my students know how to learn, how to study a chapter, they are learning more content than they did previously. Spending time on study process is a good investment because of the students' increased learning."[3]

Instead of "reading blind" without direction, what is an effective method for study reading? In his book, *Effective Study,* Francis P. Robinson presents a study system often referred to as SQ3R, which makes study reading more efficient and long-term remembering more probable. Robinson, an expert on the psychology of learning, developed the procedures after thirty years of investigation. Within the Reproduction Pages for this chapter (26–28) Robinson's procedures for effective study and the purpose for each step will be explained. However, prior to a sequential introduction of each step of the SQ3R approach to students, other activities are necessary to

---

1. Francis P. Robinson, "Steps in the 'SQ3R' Method," in *Effective Study,* 4th ed. (New York: Harper & Row, Inc., Copyright 1941, 1946; Copyright 1961, 1970 by Francis P. Robinson).

2. William G. Perry, Jr., "Students' Use and Misuse of Reading Skills: A Report to a Faculty," *Harvard Educational Review* XXIX (Copyright © 1959 by President and Fellows of Harvard College), 193–200.

3. Charles Carlson, social-studies teacher at LaFollette High School, Madison, Wis. Remarks to Bragstad, September 1978.

stimulate students' awareness of the need for changing their approaches to study-reading.

As secondary teachers, we have three challenges: first, to convince students that having an organized study approach does make sense and does result in more learning; second, to help students become skilled in using the study method, SQ3R; third, to seek the cooperation of teachers in all areas in reinforcing SQ3R whenever a chapter or informative article is assigned to be read. Only through continuing practice will students automatically use an efficient approach to study-reading. Only then will they learn *more* in *less* time with *greater* retention.

PERFORMANCE OBJECTIVES

As a result of the learning experience in this chapter, students will be able to:

1. Evaluate their current approach to study-reading.

2. Develop skill in using SQ3R.

3. Experiment with SQ3R in all content area courses where it is relevant.

4. Evaluate the effectiveness of SQ3R.

LEARNING EXPERIENCES

Topic 1: Stimulating a Commitment to Change

1. Frequently students are not really aware that studying is quite different from casual reading. Because they do not understand the difference in motive and goal, they do not differentiate in reading method; they may read a chapter in a textbook in the same way that they read a newspaper. To create awareness, ask the students to list their motives for reading a newspaper or a favorite magazine in contrast to their motives for reading a class assignment. Next, ask them to list their goals in each of the above situations. In small groups, they may compare their perceptions to the differences identified by a university professor:

   • Study-reading is required. The student has no choice in the matter.

   • Since the student is held accountable, he or she must achieve intellectual mastery over the material.

   • Instead of being pulled into the reading act by interest, the student may be pushed into it by need.

   • In study-reading the goal is learning and the ability to recall information at will.[4]

---

4. Courtesy of Professor Ken Dulin, University of Wisconsin-Madison.

2. After students have determined the difference in motive and goal between studying and recreational reading in the previous activity, ask them to respond in writing to the following question: How does your method for reading a newspaper differ from your method for reading a chapter in a textbook? (The major operational difference frequently expressed by students is that they read the textbook material more carefully. Too often, reading carefully means only reading more slowly without any other change in the process.) List differences on the blackboard for discussion before distributing Reproduction Page 23, "Improving Grades with SQ3R: A Study Approach That Works." As you explain this approach to study, the students may determine if they are currently using any of the steps in this study method.

   Warning: Students' first reactions to this study method frequently are that SQ3R is too complicated, that it will take too long, and that they doubt whether they will be able to change their habits. Assure the students that you do not expect them to implement the whole method at once. The only purpose for distributing Reproduction Page 23 now is to make the students aware of the total method. The first two steps, surveying and questioning, take only a few minutes and will be practiced in class. The first step alone—surveying—has resulted in students' reading material 24 percent *faster*.[5] Although using Reproduction Page 23 makes students aware of the entire method, in class the focus is on mastering one step at a time. The gradual assimilation of the method through the activities in this chapter will keep the process alive and meaningful. Habits are changed as short refresher shots are given when assignments are made, that is, *five minutes* to survey and question before reading.

Topic 2: Surveying

1. To the students: Pretend that you are the author of a textbook. How would you let students know what you have included in your book?

   Using your own course textbook, ask the students to turn to the table of contents. Give them three minutes to study this map of the book. At the end of that time, with books closed, first have students write down how the author organized the material for the book. What are the major sections? Second, discuss why an author includes a table of contents. How does it help a student in learning? Third, ask students whether they voluntarily consult the table of contents when they get a textbook for a new course.

   Now give students one minute to look again to see what they can learn from this content map of the textbook. As students analyze the organization of the content in the textbook, they experience the value of knowing where they are going. Frequently, students are surprised to discover how much they have learned about a book in a few minutes.

---

5. H. Y. McClusky, "An Experiment on the Influence of Preliminary Skimming on Reading," *Journal of Educational Psychology* XXV (October 1934): 521–529. Copyright (1934) by the American Psychological Association. (Reprinted by permission)

2. Through this activity the students will experience the need to survey material before they begin to read.

  Before you do any teaching of SQ3R, ask students to read an article or a chapter with headings. (In a reading class, use a study-skills book.) Before they begin reading, tell the students that in twenty minutes you will give them a quiz on the material. At the end of three to four minutes, ask them to write down the title and major concepts presented in the material. The only students who will be able to do it are those who have surveyed for that mental map of major concepts by reading the title, the introduction, the headings, and the summary.

  As described earlier in this chapter, this experience has a real impact on the students, whether they succeed or whether they fail. Our experience has been the same as that at Harvard: seldom do more than 10 percent of the students check out where they are going before they start. They do *not* survey prior to reading the material.

  In any course, the students need occasional three- to five-minute practices in class when assignments are made in order to experience the value of getting that mental map. (Remedial classes have done well in seven minutes.) Teachers at our school claim that using five minutes for surveying and questioning in class before the students begin reading the assignment results in improved discussion of the material next day.

3. When we ask students to use SQ3R, we are asking them to make a behavioral change. This is not easily accomplished. A student's knowledge of the process is not the same as implementing the process. We want knowledge plus action!

  After the "brain observation" experience presented in the introduction to this chapter, what other approach causes students to see the need for changing their study habits? The following presentation (substituting towns in your area) helps students realize the value of surveying before they begin reading:

  "I have a problem for you to solve. Here's the situation. I've seen you cruising around the area in a new sports car of which you are very proud. I've decided to accept your offer to give me a ride, so I ask you to take me to Pumpkin Center. What would you do?"

  The usual answer—"I'd ask you where it is."

  "All I know is that it is near Beaver Dam, northeast of our city. Now can we leave?"

  "I'd have to get a map to check out the best way to get there."

  "That takes too much time. I want to start immediately. Why don't we just leave now? We know it's northeast of Madison. We can go east for a while, then go north about ten miles. If we don't find it, we can change directions or ask someone. We can get started right now if we don't take time to study that map! Let's go! Why waste any more time? Forget about the map!"

  After a moment of shock, the usual student responses: "First, we'll save time by looking at a map because we'll know where we're going. It's better to take five minutes to study a map than to spend hours wandering around and being lost. Second, we'll get where we want to go. We may never find Pumpkin Center without using a map. Third, we could be wasting precious gas while we were driving around without any direction. Fourth, we would prevent a lot of frustration. When we know where we're going, we feel more secure. We can enjoy the trip more." (List student responses on the board.)

The teacher continues: "You've just sold me on using a map whenever I'm going to some unknown place. This is what seems puzzling to me. Whenever we are physically going to some new place, we make careful preparations before we start out. Yet whenever any teacher assigns a chapter for you to read, he or she is asking you to travel mentally in new territory where you may never have been before. Do you start that mental trip without any preparation? If you don't read the title, you don't even know you're going to Pumpkin Center. At least I knew my destination. The map you should check for a mental trip is found in the title, the first paragraph, chapter headings, and the chapter summary. Only three to five minutes are needed to give you all that valuable information."

In small groups ask students to figure out reasons for taking three minutes to survey before reading a chapter. Later, group insights may be listed on the blackboard. Here are some reasons given by students:

- "Read faster when you know the territory."

- "Remember better when you have the information organized in your mind."

- "Less likely to drift away mentally when you know where you are going."

- "Less likely to become bored when you search for information about the headings."

- "Feel more secure."

- "Understand better when you survey the summary before reading the chapter."

When 467 freshmen were surveyed at LaFollette High School, only 65 students claimed that they regularly look at the chapter map before they start reading the chapter. Only 65 preview the title, the headings, the first and last paragraphs! The other 402 students regularly start reading sentence by sentence—not knowing where they are going. Then they wonder why they do not remember what they read. Also, when they haven't surveyed before reading, they naturally must read more slowly.

4. Students are compelled to survey a chapter before reading if the teacher gives them a map (Chapter 7) with blank lines for chapter headings that students must fill in prior to reading the chapter. Then students add more information as they read. The example that follows shows what students would write initially for the headings on the structure skeleton supplied by the teacher. See Figure 6-1.

The question marks are a reminder to turn headings into questions: How do the atoms combine? What is the anatomy of an atom?

Since the map is limited to one page, students must determine what information is most important as they complete the map. Mathematics teachers claim that mapping forces students to read the explanatory material

Figure 6-1. Living chemistry.

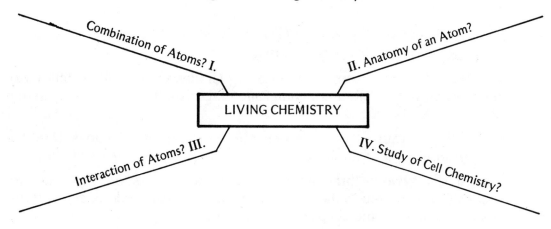

prior to working the problems. If only part of a chapter is assigned, the students map only that portion. During class the next day the maps are shared, with student innovation and originality noted. See Chapter 7 for more information.

This activity improves achievement because students must group the ideas in a meaningful order. This technique also strengthens memory because students identify supporting information for the logical divisions of thought. They perceive the relationship of ideas, the structure, which further enhances their understanding. Later the one-page map may be used for short periods of frequent review. Students using this approach do not need to cram for hours the night before a major test.

5. In this activity the students are not given any clues to the placement of headings. They must choose appropriate places for the headings and determine what each heading should be. Being skilled in detecting the organization of ideas without the help of headings is highly valued by students—after they have developed expertise!

- Make a transparency of a short article or a few pages from your textbook without any headings indicated.

- Distribute copies of Reproduction Page 24, "Help! This Article Has No Headings!" and discuss the clues to location and content of headings.

- Have students choose appropriate places for headings on transparency material, and determine what each heading should be.

- Ask students to identify the clues used for the above determinations.

- Have students compare their headings and their placement with the author's organization.

Students do not ignore headings after a few exercises of this type. They understand the thought process behind the choice of a heading, appreciate the author's headings as clues to organization, and experience improved comprehension through detecting the relationship of ideas.

Topic 3: Questioning

1. The purpose of this activity is to have the students experience the value of predicting questions that may be answered in the material.

   - Give each student a copy of "Improving Grades with SQ3R: A Study Approach That Works," Reproduction Page 23. Explain the survey and question steps.

   - Ask students to survey a textbook chapter or article with headings. Limit the time to three or four minutes.

   - Give students two or three minutes to write down questions that they predict will be answered in the material. (Students must not look at any questions at the end of the chapter.)

   - Take a few moments to hear predicted questions. Then place on the overhead projector a transparency listing the questions that you would ask if you were giving a quiz on this material.

   The students will undoubtedly discover that some of the teacher's questions are the same as their questions. They may also discover the difference between their "surface" questions and some of the teacher's "depth" questions about the interpretation or application of the information. Do not underestimate the importance of these discoveries! This experience reinforces the value of this questioning step in study-reading. The students gain confidence in their ability to predict questions that could improve their test grades.

   In a study of 467 freshmen only 17 percent regularly tried to predict questions that might appear on an examination. Our faculty was shocked that 83 percent of the freshmen did not anticipate what questions might logically be asked on a chapter test.

   Using a questioning approach in studying makes learning more interesting and more productive. Predicting questions causes students to think more deeply about what they are learning. Some students say that questioning (curiosity) makes their brain cells "sticky" so that they hold the information better when they get the answers to the questions. Questioning also improves concentration and remembering because the students are involved—searching for answers as they read.

   An alternative is to gather all the questions, read a question, and have the students decide under which heading the question is relevant. In a short time many questions can be read. This familiarizes the students with the material prior to reading. When they read the chapter, ask students to notice if they feel more secure or if they can read the material faster when they know what to expect. SQ increases speed.

2. This activity tests whether surveying and questioning prior to reading have become a habit for your students.

   If a colleague teaches some of your students in a course with a regular textbook, ask him or her to take three minutes to see if any students have developed the habit of surveying and questioning. When this teacher is assigning pages in a textbook, he or she may give the students ten minutes to start reading the assignment. At the end of a few minutes the teacher interrupts: "Close your books. Write down the title of the chapter, list the main concepts, and three questions you predict will be answered by the author." At this point your students will experience a moment of glory or of despair! In either case, they can explain the survey and question steps of SQ3R and the rationale for the approach to their classmates.

Warn your students to be "on their toes" because they may be checked on SQ3R and asked to explain the procedure in any of their classes. These surprising refresher shots help students change habits and also stimulate the interest of other teachers. By the time this is experienced in several content areas, all your students will be on the alert whenever a reading assignment is made in any class. Thus, through cooperation across departmental lines, students develop the habit of learning more efficiently through surveying and questioning.

Topic 4: Reading and Reciting

1. The purpose of this activity is to make students aware of the section-by-section thinking approach to reading instead of the sentence-by-sentence approach. Using a chapter in a textbook, give the students five to six minutes to survey the chapter and write possible questions. What are the major concepts presented? What questions are likely to be answered?

Now introduce the read-and-recite steps of SQ3R. Each heading represents one section of material. All the ideas within that section are related to the heading. To read effectively is to search for the relationship of ideas within that section. Relating concepts to the supporting information contributes to understanding and remembering. Details in isolation are rapidly forgotten. Ask the students to read with a questioning, searching attitude, knowing that they must recite the information as soon as they finish reading each section. Holding themselves accountable improves concentration.

After they have read the first section, ask students to look away from the book and quickly recite what they have learned. Then give them twenty seconds to review the first section to see what they have remembered and what they have forgotten. Did they understand and remember the main concepts and supporting information? Students also may write what they recite.

Without taking a minute for immediately recalling or paraphrasing what they have learned in each section, students will find that SQ3R loses much of its impact. Immediate recall helps establish interconnections within the material and the brain. Through timing the procedures, we prove to the students that the survey, question, recite steps take very little time, but make a great difference in helping the brain to operate efficiently. Our students have experienced that immediate recall of each section is a definite aid to understanding and retention. The evidence is improved grades in the courses they are taking.

Topic 5: Reviewing

1. Through this activity, students will learn the value of the final step of SQ3R—review. In a survey of 476 freshmen only 4 percent regularly reviewed. These students did not know that reviewing is crucial for long-term memory.

Ask the students to experiment with methods for reviewing. You may want them to check the amount of time they use to review. Encourage them to make use of odd moments that ordinarily would be wasted.

The following true story has been the experience of many students who have dared to take SQ3R seriously. Dave was a *B–C* student in physics. He was not happy with that grade. When he learned about SQ3R, he decided that he would test it out. On Monday he surveyed, questioned, read, and recited at the end of each section of the chapter, but became frustrated when he attempted to review mentally the whole chapter. To assimilate all the information, he decided he would review by mapping the physics chapter (see Chapter 7). Making the map, which covered one page, took thirty minutes.

During the days that followed, Dave reviewed the map for a short time *daily* to be sure that he understood the concepts and the relationships. When Dave had a test on the unit in physics the following Friday, he received an *A*. Dave reported that the review-writing step caused him to see clearly the logical interrelationship of ideas. His success motivated him to use the same method in studying the next chapter. Again, he received an *A* on the unit test. When the time came for the semester test, Dave found reviewing the maps to be a time-saver.

Another student made a flowchart for her review; others tried reciting aloud or outlining. Being encouraged to find the review method that works for them is appealing to students, who feel challenged and motivated because their uniqueness is recognized even in learning style.

Posting maps, flowcharts, and outlines on a bulletin board helps to maintain the momentum. On a unit test, you may want to ask students to report briefly on their study procedure for the unit. Later, procedures may be shared with students. Success experiences in learning more and improving grades encourage students to continue using SQ3R.

2. The purpose of this activity is to improve grades through short periods of frequent review in a one-month experiment. Students like to test the value of this final step in SQ3R.

Designate that for one month the first ten minutes of the class period every Wednesday and Friday will be used for review of what students have learned during the week or during the quarter. Sometimes the review will be teacher-directed so that students learn how to integrate new information with what is already known. Ask students to set aside another fifteen minutes at some other time during the week for further review. This review of past learning is in addition to using the first four steps of SQ3R for any reading assignment in this course. Each student keeps a record of grades earned during the month. If a student makes the decision to do better in a course, frequently performance automatically improves.

At the end of the month ask each student to respond to the following questionnaire: What changes have you made in your study procedure? How have the changes affected your learning? What are your reactions to having an organized approach to study? Have your grades improved in this course? Before giving their evaluations to the teacher, the students discuss their experiences with each other in small groups.

What are the results? In our experience, grades do improve as a consequence of this approach. Proving the value of *frequent review* stimulates a behavioral change so that SQ3R becomes a habit.

3. Invite high-school graduates to visit your classes when they are home from college during vacation time. As these college students display their textbooks and discuss all the information to be remembered, high-school students see the need for efficient study methods. When a college student reports less anxiety and less study time needed for major tests because of frequent review, high-school students are motivated to become efficient learners. Videotape or film these presentations by college students to use in all your classes. Our students claim that the sessions with college students really motivate them to become skilled in using SQ3R.

ASSESSING ACHIEVEMENT OF OBJECTIVES

To assess their knowledge and use of SQ3R, ask the students to do the following:

1. Write an explanation of the SQ3R study approach, defining the purpose of each step.

2. Begin studying the next textbook chapter. (Through observation, determine which students survey the material before they begin reading.) Remember to record questions that may be answered in the chapter.

3. (Distribute a reprint of a short, well-organized article without headings, and give the following directions:)

   • In four minutes survey the article and underline the clues to the organization of ideas.

   • Predict and record in the margin questions that may be answered in the article.

   • Read the article.

   • Mentally review what was learned. Answer major questions or list the major concepts in the article.

4. List what you perceive to be the advantages and disadvantages of this organized approach to study.

5. Briefly summarize where you are applying SQ3R in your school day.

RESOURCES FOR TEACHING

Below is a selected list of resources for teaching the concepts and topics of this chapter. It is divided into two categories: "Books, Pamphlets, and Articles" and "Other Resources." Addresses of publishers can be found in the alphabetical list in Appendix A

Books, Pamphlets, and Articles

Andre, M. E. D. A., and Anderson, T. H. "Development and Evaluation of a Self-Questioning Study Technique," *Reading Research Quarterly* 14 (1978–1979): 605–623. "Two studies attempted to determine whether or not generating good comprehension questions while studying prose material was an effective study technique. . . . Results from both studies indicate that student generation of questions during study is more effective for lower than for higher verbal ability students." Write to the International Reading Association for further information.

Davis, J. Kent, and Annis, Linda. "The Effect of Study Techniques, Study Preferences, and Familiarity on Later Recall," *Journal of Experimental Education* 47 (Winter 1978–1979): 92–96. Although this article does not discuss the SQ3R process directly, it does give recommendations for good reading-study techniques. Write to the Helen Dwight Reid Education Foundation for further information.

Driskell, Jeanette Lynn, and Kelly, Edward L. "A Guided Notetaking and Study Skills System for Use With University Freshmen Predicted to Fail," *Journal of Reading* 23 (January 1980): 327–331. Instruction in note-taking and SQ3R was given to college freshmen. A study made at the end of the first semester of college revealed that this approach "appears to be broadly beneficial to entering students with dangerously low SAT scores. Training in how to select and organize material during study apparently helps many students succeed." Write to the International Reading Association for further information.

Johns, Jerry L., and McNamara, Lawrence P. "The SQ3R Study Technique: A Forgotten Research Target," *Journal of Reading* 23 (May 1980): 705–708. The authors of this article advocate continued research on study techniques and their value. Write to the International Reading Association for further information.

Karahalios, Sue M.; Tonjes, Marian J.; and Towner, John C. "Using Advance Organizers to Improve Comprehension of a Context Text," *Journal of Reading* 22 (May 1979): 706–708. This article discusses the value of advance organizers in content-area studies (middle and high schools) and describes one study that demonstrated the effectiveness of the technique. Write to the International Reading Association for further information.

Lazarus, A. "Reading-Study Strategies," *High School Journal* 63 (October 1979): 42–44. This is an excellent article for content-area teachers; it surveys research in the area of reading-study strategies and emphasizes the value of the results of using SQ3R, PQ4R, or similar strategies. Write to the University of North Carolina Press for further information.

Lewis, Jill Sweiger. "Directed Discovery Learning: Catalyst to Reading in the Content Areas," *Journal of Reading* 22 (May 1979): 714–719. The article discusses the need for a study-skills approach to reading in the content areas and outlines a Directed Discovery Learning approach. Write to the International Reading Association for further information.

Pauk, Walter. *How to Study in College*. 3rd ed. Boston: Houghton Mifflin, 1984, "Learning from Your Textbook," pp. 156–174. Presents study skills, techniques, and principles for studying a chapter including SQ3R.

Robinson, Francis P. "Survey Q3R Method of Reading," in *SR/SE Resource Book*, ed. Frank L. Christ. Chicago: Science Research Associates, 1969, pp. 35–40. The SQ3R method is defined and outlined in this article. Discussion questions follow.

Spache, George D., and Berg, Paul C. *The Art of Efficient Reading,* 3rd ed. New York: Macmillan, 1978, "Reading for Study Purposes," pp. 78–108. This chapter reviews the PQRST technique and provides exercises for achieving proficiency with the method.

Starks, Gretchen A. "New Approaches to Teaching Study Skills in High School and College," *Journal of Reading* 23 (February 1980): 401–403. Through interviews, survey projects, and study files, students at the University of Minnesota Technical College Reading Center were motivated to learn better study skills. Write to the International Reading Association for further information.

Tadlock, Dolores Fadness. "SQ3R—Why It Works, Based on an Information Processing Theory of Learning," *Journal of Reading* 22 (November 1978): 110–112. "SQ3R compensates for inherent deficiencies in the information processing system and forces readers to use their processing systems in a productive manner. If . . . students are made aware of this, they may be more likely to use SQ3R and . . . to profit from it." Article reviews the SQ3R method also. Write to the International Reading Association for further information.

Other Resources

School Survival Skills: How to Study Effectively. White Plains, N.Y.: Center for Humanities. Three sound-slide parts (or sound filmstrip and video cassette format) teach students to become more active readers by prereading, reading with a purpose, note-taking, and summarizing.

7

Mapping:
Discerning the Design

What one study technique enables students to understand, visualize, and remember the organization of ideas as they—

- SQ3R?

- Study lecture notes?

- Synthesize information gleaned from texts, articles, tapes, films, demonstrations, and lectures?

The answer? **Mapping.**[1]

We realize that this may sound a little like Dr. Keystone's all-purpose educational medicinal, but there is so much potential for using mapping to record and to "picture" thinking, thus heightening recall, that this study method deserves our undivided attention.

Precisely what is a map? It is a word picture of ideas that the student organizes and designs. It is an alternative to conventional notes and outlines and extends far beyond their scopes.

Being adept at SQ3R (Chapter 6) is a great aid for learning to map. Once students are able to detect the author's major concepts through surveying, mapping is the secret to having a one-page visual record of those key thoughts for future study and review.

Since the mapping procedure necessitates evaluating the relative importance of ideas, students need a keen sensitivity to transitions—guideposts such as *and, however, in conclusion,* that link meaning. Thus, the first topic in this chapter provides a variety of ways to create student awareness of transitions and their functions.

---

1. M. Buckley Hanf, "Mapping: A Technique for Translating Reading into Thinking," *Journal of Reading* 14 (January 1971): 225–230.

Next, the definition of mapping is carefully explored with the students, and the step-by-step procedure for designing a map is presented. Finally, after they have had a number of opportunities to practice mapping, students will determine the unique features of mapping.

How much class time should be spent on mapping? Each teacher is the best judge, knowing the students' abilities and the subject matter. A broad recommendation is initially to spend two class periods on instruction and immediate application of this study technique; follow that with much reinforcement. For example, request that students map their reading assignments. In this way, students discover that the discriminating thinking required while reading, then designing a map, ultimately enhances both their understanding and remembering the content.

PERFORMANCE OBJECTIVES

After the learning experiences in this chapter, students will be able to:

1. Demonstrate knowledge of transitions and their role in revealing relationships of ideas.

2. Define mapping.

3. State the three components of a map.

4. List five special benefits of this technique.

5. Design a map.

LEARNING EXPERIENCES

Topic 1: Transitions: Guides to Relationships of Ideas

An essential element for students' remembering is their finding the *organization of ideas* in study materials. Students can most effectively accomplish this vital step by surveying and questioning before study-reading and by watching for *transitions* (guideposts that link ideas) along the way as they read.

However, most students are rather oblivious not only to transitions per se, but also of the strategic role that they play in guiding the reader through the author's thinking. The following activities may help sensitize students to those invaluable aids to comprehending and remembering, transitions.

1. To demonstrate the power and the purpose of transitions, ultimately you will hand every student in your class three envelopes labeled *A, B,* and *C* respectively.

   To arrive at that end, first use Reproduction Page 25, "Sentence Scramble," which contains the individual sentences from three distinct paragraphs. The first five sentences constitute paragraph *A,* the next group of sentences constitutes paragraph *B,* etc. After duplicating this material, cut it apart sentence by sentence; then have a few students help place one of each of the *A* sentences into a business envelope labeled *A*. Prepare enough envelopes for every student in your largest class, plus ten or so extra. Repeat this procedure for paragraphs *B* and *C*.

Next, hand an *A* envelope to each student and have him or her reassemble the paragraph in its proper order. After students accomplish this, write the various "answers" (by sentence number) on the board and insist that students use evidence to justify their responses. Answer Key—Appendix B. The evidence will be the transitions; be certain that students understand this and, thereby, note how ideas are logically organized. Their perceiving this logic, then, spurs them to capitalize on transitional clues to organization for comprehending and remembering study material. Repeat this process using the *B* and *C* paragraphs. This activity receives "bravos" from students!

2. Have students use paragraphs that they themselves have written for assignments as a source for this work on transitions. Each student scrambles the sentence order of his or her paragraph, then records each sentence on a separate line of a sheet of paper.

After cutting the sentences apart and placing them in an envelope, students pair off and exchange envelopes to see whether they can properly reorder the sentences in their partners' paragraphs. Have students pair off with several different partners. Once again, students cite the specific clues that aid them in accomplishing this task. Students enjoy this "test" of thinking which reinforces the key role transitions play in coherently conveying the students' own thoughts as well as revealing the author's ideas in study materials.

3. Mention to students that the map of transitions you are about to hand them, Reproduction Page 26, "Transitions Make the Connection," is meant to raise their consciousness of the great power of little words and phrases. These are students' mental guides as they study. Even universities are concerned that students realize this; specifically, at the University of Wisconsin-Madison the study-skills book for incoming freshmen, *Preparation for College*, contains a section devoted solely to transitions. It begins, "No words are so helpful while reading as the prepositions and conjunctions that guide your mind along the pathways of the author's ideas."[2]

We do not recommend that students sit down to memorize every word on this map of guideposts to organization. Rather, have them think through each heading, then write additional, appropriate words or phrases in the blanks. Next, hand out Reproduction Page 27, "Transitions Make the Connection—Additions," to show a more thorough list of transitions and the relationships that they indicate. Thereafter, relate this to the students' classwork.

4. Make a transparency of a page in your textbook chapter, but ink out many of the transitions. Have the students read this material, and ask them to replace the missing "links." This might be done individually or as a total class.

---

2. University of Wisconsin-Madison High School-University Curriculum Liaison Committee, *Preparation for College* (Office of Undergraduate Orientation: 432 North Murray Street, Madison, Wis. 53706), p. 24.

5. Several materials (Resources for Teaching—this chapter and Chapter 8) offer instructions on transitions and organizational patterns which clarify the process for students without taking much class time. In addition, these materials provide specific practice so that students can immediately apply their new knowledge to study assignments.

6. Use the envelope format (Activity 1), but this time cut apart, paragraph by paragraph, a well-organized section of a reprint article, and have students reassemble it. Then cut apart, major concept by major concept, an entire reprint article, and have students reconstruct the proper thought sequence.

7. Work on transitions relates to all the communication skills: reading-writing, speaking-listening. Since continuous reinforcement is essential if students are habitually to utilize transitions as clues to the relationships of ideas, some simple approaches can serve as reminders. For instance, have students record ten transitions from one section of a reading assignment and designate what each clue reveals (cause-effect, simple listing, etc.). Also, have students underline transitions as they write essays for assignments or exams. In addition, have students incorporate obvious transitions when giving speeches since listeners especially need such directional clues. Finally, have students record and discuss the function of five to ten transitions as they hear you or each other give oral presentations.

Topic 2: The Mapping Process

1. Ask students to give a description of a map. Usually they emphasize that a map is a drawing or a representation of an area. Continue by asking what purpose a map serves. Students typically suggest that a map—

   • Provides an overview of the territory.

   • Saves time for a traveler by indicating possible routes to a destination.

   • Diminishes a traveler's frustration.

   • Increases a traveler's feeling of security.

2. To allow students to discover inductively what a cognitive or mental map is and what it can do, hand out "A Chapter Map," Reproduction Page 28. Inform students that this one sheet contains all the most significant information from an entire biology chapter. Ask them specifically what they can learn from it. In small groups or with partners, have students discuss the answer to this question. Answer Key—Appendix B. Then have the entire class share specific information from the map as well as their impressions of the map's usefulness. Students are generally amazed at how much they can learn from this one-page visual summary.

   Based on this firsthand experience, request that students redefine a map. Any response that closely resembles the following is acceptable: *a word picture of ideas that the student organizes and designs.* Tell students to turn to the study-skills section of their notebooks (Reproduction Page 36). In a three-page section they might designate "Mapping: Discerning the Design," have them write the mapping definition.

3. Reproduction Page 29, "How a Map Is Born," delineates the progression in designing a map. Use it as a prelude to an actual application of the mapping study method. Also, inform students about the workings of the brain (Chapter 4, Topic 5, Activity 3), since mapping combines both the logical and the imaginative dimensions for a dynamic, whole-brain approach!

After they have read the handout, ask students when the mapping technique can be applied. As a companion to SQ3R, as an aid in organizing speeches and essays, as a review method to synthesize notes of all kinds are some possibilities. (Supposedly, mapping can be used during lectures, but unless the lecturer is extremely organized and states the major concepts at the outset of each lecture, our students have been frustrated with this kind of application.)

Topic 3: Applying Mapping

1. Hand out and map together the "Lumberjills" article, Reproduction Page 30, as if it were an assignment. This is a good opportunity to reinforce all the aids to finding structure: surveying and using transitional phrases, for instance. Your using a transparency on the overhead projector allows students simultaneously to watch you map and to draw their own maps, too. "Talk through" the entire procedure, from surveying through the reciting and reviewing stages.

One way of organizing the article follows, by paragraph number:

1–3. Introduction: Wisconsin logging-camp history

4–7. Women come to the camps

8–11. The cookshack—hub of the universe

12–16. The cook—highest camp status

17–19. Leisure time

20–21. History and conclusion

This content can then be categorized into the major concepts of (1) camp history, (2) cookshack—hub, (3) cook, and (4) leisure. If you were presenting this reading as a lecture and students were note-taking, the major concepts just cited would be the principle points selected at the noteSHRINK, or reducing, stage (Reproduction Page 35). Help students to see this connection.

Following the article is a sample map, Reproduction Page 31, that you may wish to use as a reference or as a student handout.

2. Hand out to each person in your class a reprint article, preferably one from your subject area, or have the class use instead a chapter from your textbook. Now map it together, section by section, involving students in the decision making and having them concurrently design their own maps. You or a student with legible writing can demonstrate using a transparency or the black-

board. Since a text chapter or reprint article with headings is easier to analyze than one without headings, we strongly recommend using material with headings at first. However, students need mapping experience with both types of material; therefore, later map together material with no headings.

An alternative is to have students perform this task in pairs or small groups: their discussing and arguing about what goes on the map can provoke thought. At this early stage do provide a guide to the thesis and the major concepts of the study material; then gradually wean students from this kind of aid.

To illustrate that mapping is applicable to all subjects, one student's algebra trigonometry map is included. See Figure 7-1.

3. As a pretest review for a chapter exam, divide the class into small groups and assign each small group a major section of the chapter to map. Have the total group decide on the topic or thesis of the chapter and its major sections; then provide a large sheet of colored construction paper or tag board and a marking pen to each group and set them to work.

   Students will enjoy posting their segments of the map and seeing the chapter gradually spring to life! The resulting "class map" will clearly spotlight the major concepts of the chapter and the important supporting information, categorized for easy recall.

4. Incorporate mapping into the study of novels. Depicting the development of the plot or of major characters is a possibility. With this kind of application, instead of determining the theme at the outset, however, the theme will gradually evolve as students become more knowledgeable about the characters, the plot, the setting.

5. Frequently speech teachers are frustrated by their students' inability to organize ideas. Therefore, one speech teacher has his ninth-grade students map a chapter from their social-studies texts, then a chapter from their science texts, and finally, the speeches they are about to deliver. Consequently, he is particularly happy with the students' increased sensitivity to organization, since that is a critical component not only of effective speaking, but also of effective listening, writing, and study-reading.[3] Try variations of this procedure to aid your students.

6. Maps are helpful "essay planners." When you assign an essay, ask students to decide on the thesis statement and major concepts, and work out essay details using the mapping format. Tell students that neatness should not be a consideration as they "sketch"; rather, they should let their thoughts on the subject flow as freely as possible. A more discriminating organization can then be determined by reworking the map as the student begins the actual writing.

7. Inundate students with maps! Fill every available inch of bulletin board and wall space with the infinite variety of students' handiwork; then resort to the ceiling to suspend maps from thumbtacks and strings. Make map mobiles of coathangers taped in tiers with maps hanging from each layer. Hence, students will capture not only the method of mapping, but the spirit as well!

---

3. Thomas Chritton, speech teacher at LaFollette High School, Madison, Wis. Remarks to Bragstad, May 1977.

Figure 7-1. A sample math map by Paul Clayton, a LaFollette High School student, Madison, Wisconsin.

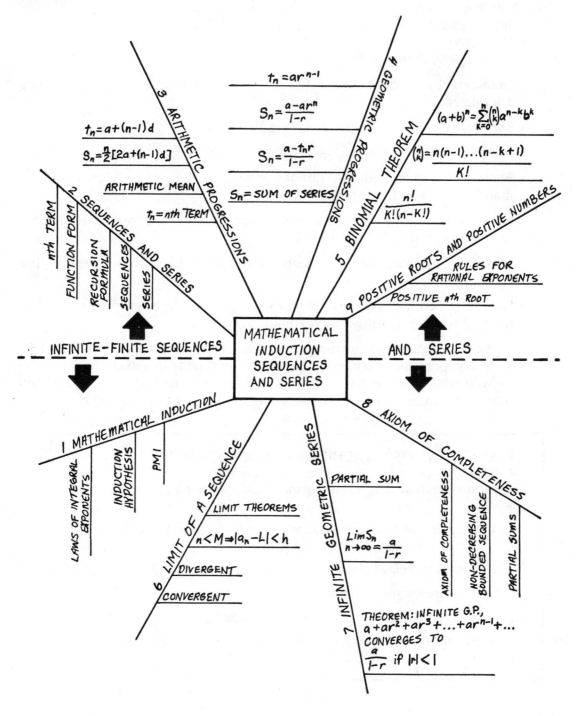

Topic 4: Unique Features of Mapping

1. Now that students have engaged in mapmaking, ask them to identify the unique features of the mapping process, which they might record in their notebooks.

   Mapping, then—

- Demands that students think critically to discern how ideas in the reading are related.

- Shows vividly the relationship among those ideas.

- Allows for individuality and creativity in recording the content.

- Allows for easy addition or subtraction of ideas, since it is freeform rather than linear (i.e., conventional notes).

- Gives prominence to the topic or thesis and major concepts, which trigger knowledge of details.

- Provides for perceptual rather than verbal comprehension by revealing the Gestalt (whole).

- Encourages compression of the study material (a one-page map can "illustrate" the contents of twenty textbook pages!).

All of the above enhance concentration, understanding, and remembering. In addition, many students appreciate the fact that a map can easily be reviewed while waiting for a friend or for class to begin. This streamlined study results in improved grades, another welcome bonus of mapping!

ASSESSING ACHIEVEMENT OF OBJECTIVES

To see if students have adequately met the stated objectives, you might use the following:

1. Underline and explain the function of each of the transitions in the following paragraph. (Provide a paragraph.)

2. What is mapping? Define it.

3. What are the three components of a map?

4. List five unique benefits that mapping offers.

5. Map the following material. (Use an article reprint or a textbook selection.)

RESOURCES FOR TEACHING

Below is a selected list of resources for teaching the concepts and topics of this chapter. It is divided into two categories: "Books, Pamphlets, and Articles" and "Other Resources." Addresses of publishers can be found in the alphabetical list in Appendix A.

Books, Pamphlets, and Articles

Buzan, Tony. *Use Both Sides of Your Brain.* Rev. ed. New York: E. P. Dutton, 1983, pp. 86–116. Refreshing, not-to-be-missed material. Contains multicolored maps. Develops the mapping idea through directly involving the reader. Exciting information on the brain's functioning and on creativity.

Hanf, M. Buckley. "Mapping: A Technique for Translating Reading into Thinking," *Journal of Reading* 14 (January 1971): 225–230. An explanation and step-by-step illustration of the mapping process. Contains a well-considered rationale. Write to the International Reading Association for further information.

Hansell, Stevenson T. "Stepping Up to Outlining," *Journal of Reading* 22 (December 1978): 248–252. Discusses the value of outlining as a learning tool and describes "array tasks" (similar to mapping) that can be used as an effective means for enhancing learning and memory. Write to the International Reading Association for further information.

Other Resources

Niles, Olive Stafford; Bracken, Dorothy Kendall; Dogherty, Mildred A.; and Kinder, Robert Farrar. *Tactics in Reading II.* Glenview, Ill.: Scott, Foresman, 1964. A kit with class sets of exercise cards on a variety of skills, including "Relationships" (time order, simple listing, comparison-contrast, cause-effect).

8

Note-Taking:
Listening, Writing, Learning

"But they should know that already!"

This may very well be our reaction to teaching the skill of note-taking from lectures to our students. Yes, perhaps they should know it; in fact, they probably have been taught it; and, certainly, they do have adequate opportunities to practice it during a typical school day.

But what is the reality?

To discern quickly the answer to this question, collect your students' notes (without advance notice) at the end of your next lecture. Then spread out the notes and feast your eyes on the "banquet" before you: everything from undercooked to overcooked! One or two words plus doodlings by Dave. No notes at all from Joan-by-the-window. A painstaking, blow-by-blow account from diligent Tom. Perhaps not many "choice dishes" on the banquet table. So the need for addressing the subject of note-taking is clear to you. But how clear is it to students themselves?

Mixed reviews—the subject of note-taking on lectures has received that reaction in our classes. A sprinkling of students have been enthusiastic or at least receptive; however, the majority of college-bound seniors have touted themselves as already adept at taking notes. To our dismay, more than half the sophomores and juniors with serious skill deficiencies displayed the same attitude, until they examined convincing evidence to the contrary as a consequence of activities in this chapter.

Action is the key word for students' learning to take notes effectively. A student could collect all the handouts from this chapter and still not improve one iota; implementing the suggestions in these handouts, however, will produce results. And the myriad of activities to engage students in advancing their note-taking facilities apply not only to lectures but also to other listening experiences, such as tapes and documentaries. To beckon students to be actively involved, Reproduction Pages 32–37 include personal analysis columns.

In teaching students how to take notes, we do not advocate a two-week vacation from course content. On the contrary, how to learn (process) should be tightly linked with what to learn (content). In this chapter you will find many note-taking tips within the activities, plus suggestions for practice and more practice. Give an initial "shot" of these note-taking tips, then have students immediately apply them to whatever content you concentrate on that week. Since reinforcement is important, thereafter, intermittently reserve a few final minutes of class time to project on a screen some samples of notes that students have made that day. Then ask students to examine each other's notes on the lecture.

This chapter on note-taking centers on detecting student needs; on the rationale for note-taking on lectures; and on prelecture preparation, which spotlights listening. Then what to do at the lecture is explored, followed by postlecture essentials that facilitate the students' mastering and remembering the lecture content.

PERFORMANCE OBJECTIVES

As a result of the learning experiences in this chapter, students will be able to:

1. List four reasons why note-taking is important.

2. Enumerate the three primary causes of listening difficulties, then add any additional causes from their personal experiences.

3. Take notes using a highly effective five-step system.

4. Analyze a set of notes, commenting on all facets of the process, i.e.,

   a. the presence of central thoughts and significant details,

   b. the adequacy of the quiz column,

   c. the use of abbreviations.

5. Share with the class their most successful note-taking tips.

6. Compare and contrast both the purpose and the procedure of note-taking with those of SQ3R (Chapter 6).

LEARNING EXPERIENCES

Topic 1: Detecting Student Needs

1. Before teaching how to take notes from lectures, we strongly suggest teaching and reviewing at least one of the study skills that center on how to determine the organization of ideas in written material: SQ3R (Chapter 6) or mapping (Chapter 7). Why? A text bears repeating, but a lecture is fleeting! Gleaning the essence from a printed source is simpler than gleaning the essence from a lecture. With a text the student has a tangible aid to read and reread if necessary, which provides more control than with a lecture. For one thing, a student can survey a text assignment to find highlights before study-reading; in a

lecture the student is at the mercy of the lecturer and may gain no overview before the content is presented. For another thing, with a text or article, the student sets the pace; at a lecture the student adapts to the pace—generally a keep-it-rolling situation. Consequently, the student's thinking must be keener and quicker to perceive the most significant content of a lecture as compared to that of a printed source. Since we know that success motivates, giving students time to warm up by sifting major concepts from written material results in their feeling more confident as they encounter the challenges of a more fleeting lecture.

Ask students themselves to discern the differences between taking notes on text material versus a lecture.

2. You might introduce note-taking to your classes with a presentation like this: "As you're headed into a class, the bell rings. Suddenly you realize you've forgotten your notebook. How do you feel?"

   a. Just fine—you never use it anyhow.

   b. Distressed—you keep good notes for study and test review.

   c. Relieved—if you had it you might use it, but since you don't, you'll just relax.

   d. Anxious—your teacher rages at non-note-takers.

   Ask students which option is most likely to lead to learning success. Clearly, option *b* is the answer.

   Mention to students that today they will have an opportunity to diagnose their competence with a fundamental skill of student life—note-taking from lectures. We suggest a two-pronged diagnosis: (1) analyzing a *sample* of each student's notes and (2) analyzing each student's personal note-taking *procedure*.

3. For the first facet of the diagnosis, have each student actually make notes while you read a selection or play a tape. You may wish to read aloud "Unlucky Strikes," Reproduction Page 32, while class members take notes in their typical styles. (Introducing students to the term *carcinogenic,* meaning cancer-producing, may be necessary before you lecture.)

   After the diagnosis:

   • Display on the overhead projector a transparency of the "Sample Notes" on this article (Reproduction Page 33).

   • Request that students compare the content of their notes with the content of yours.

   • Ask students what distinctive characteristics they notice in the format of your notes. Answers: spaces between central thoughts; margin drawn down the page; a box surrounding the thesis, the statement of the author's subject and purpose; questions in the left-hand margin that summarize the author's major concepts; paragraph format. Reproduction Page 35 details this particular procedure.

   We suggest that you also produce a transparency of Reproduction Page 32 to exhibit to the class. In this way students get a quick review of how to mark an article (a box frames that all-important thesis statement) as well as an opportunity to see notes taken in a new style that demands their concentration and critical thinking, particularly when determining the questions for the quiz column on the left. Once students compare what they could gain from notes with what they presently are getting from them, they sell themselves on the need for improving their lecture note-taking skills.

4. When handing out Reproduction Page 34, "What's Your NQ (Note-taking Quotient)?", mention to students that this diagnosis is designed to help them analyze their total note-taking methods—preparation, actual note-taking, use of the notes thereafter. Tell students to jot their answers in the *before* column.

   Upon completion, these assessments reveal your students' self-perceptions of needs as well as the reality. In your grade book write some general headings from the diagnosis above the graph, then checkmark appropriately under these for each student. The resulting class profile allows you to see at a glance each student's needs and the entire group's needs so that you can design your instruction accordingly. Reading across the row indicates how one particular student is doing, whereas reading down the column shows how the class as a whole is doing. For example, Kathy Mueller is basically doing well, while most of the students need to develop the review habit. See Figure 8-1.

5. If you have not already done so, ask students to designate about the last twelve pages of their notebooks as a special "How to Study" section (Reproduction Page 36). Tell them to reserve a few of these pages, titling them

Figure 8-1. A partial class profile of some note-taking procedures.

Name	BEFORE lecture: read ass't	review notes	recall relevant lrng.	have pen, notebk.	section for each course	no. pp. + ass't pp.	2½" recall col.	DURING lecture: get inter.	ignore distractions	listen for cues	record legibly	record c. thoughts,*details	match nt. style
Christian, Aaron	✓		✓	✓							✓	✓	
Kelley, Chanda Michelle				✓	✓					✓	✓		
Marcs, Greg	✓		✓					✓	✓				
Michaels, Katie	✓	✓		✓	✓		✓	✓		✓		✓	
Mueller, Kathleen	✓	✓	✓	✓	✓	✓	✓	✓			✓	✓	
Muench, Collen	✓				✓			✓			✓	✓	
Torstenson, Tanya J.	✓	✓		✓							✓	✓	

"Helps for Lecture Note-takers." Each student should then copy any suggestions gleaned from the diagnosis (Reproduction Page 34) under a heading such as "I'm going to try. . . ." Of that list have students asterisk just two items to implement that week so the students do not feel overwhelmed.

To ensure a follow-up, tell students that in one week they will assess their progress in applying the two changes. Immediately note the date of that follow-up in your lesson plan book—a safeguard against retroactive inhibition and other misfortunes!

Topic 2: Rationale for Note-Taking on Lectures

1. Collect students' notes from a class lecture presented three or four weeks ago or use notes from former students to assure anonymity. Then select some poor and some good note samples to display on the opaque or the overhead projector. Challenge the class, either individually or as a group, to recall the essence of that lecture, based on the notes.

   Present the inadequate samples first, then the ample ones, to underscore the value of the latter. Next, ask students which note sample they would feel most confident about utilizing for study and review. Finally, mention that you intend to provide instruction and practice opportunities for students to advance their note-taking proficiencies, thus facilitating long-term learning and remembering.

   An alternative is to have students break into small groups of five or six, then exchange notes with one another.

2. Without explaining why, request that half your class take notes, the other half just listen as you give a lecture. Two weeks later, distribute a quiz on that same lecture material. What is the average score of the note-takers versus non-note-takers? Let this fact speak for itself!

3. Ask students to imagine that they are sitting near John during a lecture; John never sets pen to paper during the entire period. How much lecture material do students think that John will forget after fourteen days? Jot speculations on the blackboard before reporting the evidence: in Pauk, a study of *non-note-takers* reveals that they *forget 80 percent* of a lecture within *two weeks!*[1] Often tests are not given within that time frame. Therefore, ask students whether they are willing to take this great risk.

4. Ask students, "If someone who had never before seen a school asked you why you scribble notes all during a class lecture, how would you explain your behavior?" Students may list their responses in their notebooks. For example, note-taking

   • Piques concentration and necessitates discriminating listening.

   • Is an aid to learning the essence of a lecture.

   • Reveals the purpose and the underlying structure of a lecture.

---

1. Walter Pauk, *How to Study in College,* 3rd ed. (Boston: Houghton Mifflin, 1984), p. 122.

- Enhances memory. *Hearing* the material, *recording* the essence, *reading,* then *reciting* provides four avenues for learning instead of just one, hearing.

- Provides a readily available written record of important information (possibly unavailable in class sources) for future reference and test review.

Since altering study habits requires effort, this list invites students to improve by reminding them of concomitant rewards.

5. Ask three students to wait outside your classroom as you tell a three-minute story to the remaining students. The students in class may take notes as you story-tell.

   Then invite one of the students outside your room to return. Repeat your story. The "newcomer" may not take notes while listening. Next, invite the second student waiting outside to return and have the first student relate your story to the second student. As the third student returns, have the second student repeat the story to that student.

   As each student reenters and retells your tale, have the other class members record any deviations from your original story. Finally, relate the findings of this experiment to students who say they do not need to take notes because "just listening is enough."

6. Students frequently act as though merely *recording* notes is the goal of note-taking. Therefore, ask students what they think of someone who purchases a new hockey stick, then expects to be a superstar without practicing. Just as this hockey enthusiast must actually take to the ice and use his stick to develop skill and finesse, so the students must regularly *use* their notes—*reciting,* and *reflecting* on them—to skillfully master the content and to integrate it into their thinking and living. In fact, students who study their lecture notes by *reciting* remember *one and one half times more* after six weeks than students who do not review![2]

   Taking notes, then, is a step in the learning process, but actually studying those notes is essential to achieve the ultimate goal of note-taking—absorbing and applying the note content. Distribute Reproduction Page 35, "Gaining the Most from Lecture Notes," which underscores how to capitalize on notes in order to learn. Since the NoteSHRINK step is the most challenging, you may wish to use students' class notes as the focal point in discussing the thinking process for this stage.

Topic 3: Prelecture Preparation

1. Ask students to evaluate the "Prelecture Prep" material, Reproduction Page 36. The suggestions it contains have been effective for other students; however, stress the fact that each student needs to experiment to ascertain which learning procedures are best suited to him or her.

   Since transitions play a key role in revealing the significant content of a lecture, you may wish to review with your students the transition material (Chapter 7, Topic 1, and Reproduction Page 27).

---

2. Ibid.

2. Ask the class, "What is the most critical element in successful note-taking from lectures?" The answer—listening. Next, ask students to recall and write in the note-taking sections of their notebooks three instances when they have had trouble listening. Then ask students to analyze and record the cause(s) of their difficulty. Discuss.

3. To underscore the necessity and importance of developing listening skills, have students record the amount of time in a single day that they spend listening in their classes—to discussions, instructions for assignments, questions. Request that the students then calculate the total percentage of time in class that they must devote to this vital communication skill.

4. According to Dr. Ralph G. Nichols, former head of the University of Minnesota's Department of Rhetoric and renowned authority in that field, listening problems occur for three primary reasons:

   • The erroneous notion that one can listen and relax simultaneously.

   • The urge to interrupt with one's own ideas or words.

   • An emotional reaction triggered by hearing words or ideas (i.e., abortion, conflict issues in school) so that one misses the message.[3]

   Request that students compare their own perceptions to the above causes. Students might add disinterest or boredom as a chief contributor to listening difficulties, for example. Further, have students compile a list of these obstacles in one column of their notebooks, possible remedies in an adjacent column. This list might then be published in the school newspaper.

5. Mention to students that listening is hard work for everyone. In fact, our bodies react to the effort of listening: our hearts beat faster, our blood circulates more quickly, and even our body temperatures increase slightly.

   Another fact that sheds light on our listening problem is that the average person speaks about 125 words per minute; however, we can think at many times that rate.[4] This discrepancy poses an interesting challenge to the listener. Ask students their suggestions on how to fill all that vacant mental space. Possible answers: summarize what the speaker has already stated, jot down any pertinent questions that come to mind, anticipate the next point, relate what one is hearing to previous experiences and learnings.

6. An engineer in a management position and a fire chief both report that, of their employees having job difficulties, the greatest cause is not listening carefully to and following instructions. The importance of listening reaches far beyond the school walls to all of life. Hence, invite to your class a variety of people—a physician, pharmacist, secretary, auto mechanic, bank teller, waiter, police officer—to discuss the necessity of attentive listening while at work and the implications of not doing so.

   Alternatives are to tape-record interviews with these people and play the tape to the class, to have each student interview two adults or employed

---

3. Ralph G. Nichols, "Listening Is a Ten-Part Skill," *Nation's Business* (July 1957).
4. Ibid.

classmates and share the results in class, or to have students with part-time jobs report on their own experiences with the necessity of attentive listening at work.

7. To illustrate that listening is crucial in personal relationships, too, have students write in their notebooks one instance when not listening had serious consequences. This may have occurred with anyone—a teacher, a parent, a friend, for instance. You and student volunteers might share experiences of this kind.

Topic 4: At the Lecture

1. As an opening ask people in your class how they currently do record notes. They may mention the following styles: paragraph form, block form, outlining, eclectic. If no one cites the more dynamic methods, suggest that students "freestyle" in recording some information. Be prepared to use the blackboard or a transparency to illustrate the following techniques. For instance, if the speaker announces, "Now let's consider the pros and cons of solar energy versus nuclear energy as a heating source," the creative student may set up a chart as follows:

	Solar Energy	Nuclear Energy
Pros		
Cons		

If a social-studies teacher states, "A number of factors influenced the development of the railroads over a fifty-year period," the student might well choose a time line (typical of social-studies material, for example):

The procedure for a chemistry experiment or the steps for constructing a cabinet or sewing a skirt simply need to be listed: 1.

2.

3.

If the teacher cites a chain of cause-effect relationships, the student should feel free to draw ◯ or ⟶ ⟶ (typical of social studies, chemistry and physics material.)

2. So that your students gain experience with a variety of note-taking techniques, you might employ diverse note-taking forms as you lecture, create study guides for assignments and readings, or construct exams. For instance, after delivering a statement such as, "There are both advantages and disadvantages

to a representative democracy form of government," you might pause to ask the class members what method would be most logical for recording the information you are about to convey. The answer: parallel columns headed *advantages* and *disadvantages,* which you may wish to draw on the board or a transparency. This modeling enables students to observe how to mix and match content with the most appropriate note-taking technique. Thus, students will experience that the content suggests a note-taking form to be used, and, in turn, the form of the notes expedites their learning of that content.

Hand out Reproduction Page 37, "At the Lecture," which contains more note-taking fundamentals. In addition, a specific example of how two teachers apply note-taking to biology is featured later in this book (Chapter 12—Science).

3. Concerning the specifics of how to record notes, we, the authors, do not find writing complete sentences a boon, except for central thoughts and major concepts. Generally we advocate that students experiment to discover what works well for each of them; we do insist, however, that students (1) skip a line or two between each central thought of a lecture (a little breathing space for additions and a way of accentuating diverse aspects of the topic) and (2) use a quiz column on the left of each page.

How much to record is also a note-taking consideration. What factors affect this decision? After inviting students to tell how they determine what to include in their notes, you may want to discuss briefly at least the following criteria:

• The note-taker's background of knowledge and life experience.

• The lecture content.

• The note-taker's purpose.

4. Tape-record a lecture you are about to give to your class. When you play this tape during class, actually take notes on a transparency so that students witness you listening and thinking intently, then recording *selectively.* Discuss. Inform your students that some study-skills experts recommend that the ratio of listening to note-taking be nine to one!

An alternative is to use prepared tapes, a student presentation, a documentary, as you take notes.

5. Provide for your students a *note guide* that contains all the important information on the first major concept of your lecture for that day. Then provide less information under each successive major concept. (Do not forget to use flow charts, listing, parallel columns, etc., when appropriate so that students grow comfortable correlating their note-taking techniques with the content.) See Figure 8-2.

After each major concept of your lecture, stop to review what should have been recorded to that point. Use the opaque or overhead projector or the blackboard so that students see what you mean. Then be certain that

Figure 8-2. Note guide.

Biology

August 27

Alcohol and Its Effect on the Brain

Brain – 3 sections

medulla, cerebellum, cerebrum

Alc. affects first cerebrum.

affects memory, decision-making,

_____ , _____ ,

_____ .

Alc. affects next the _____ ,

_____ , _____

_____ , _____ .

Alc.

students noteSHRINK. (For their eventual success in college note-taking, some of our alumni credit their former social-studies teachers who used this note-taking approach.) Gradually wean students by giving only major concepts at the start of the lecture; later, reveal major concepts at the end of the class instead.

For students with serious skill deficiencies, you might introduce this procedure by presenting brief, clearly structured lectures.

An alternative is to let individuals choose content-related newspaper and magazine articles to present as lectures to the class, using accompanying note guides. Check these articles for clear organization, however. (*Scope* magazine, *Seventeen, Runner's World, Reader's Digest,* and the school newspaper are rich sources for short lecture material.)

6. Especially for students with serious skill deficiencies, we suggest handing out a transcript of a short lecture after they have heard it and taken notes on it. Alone, in small groups, or with the entire class, students then underline the transitional clues and key words that indicate how the lecture is organized: by simple listing, chronological order, cause-effect, comparison-contrast (Reproduction Page 27). Build in as many success experiences as possible for the students.

7. The primary goal of this activity is to sensitize students to the structure of a lecture. Write on the board or a transparency the first two major concepts of a

lecture that you are about to give. Tell students that you want them to record not only the notes but also the organizational clues that lead to those two major concepts (Reproduction Page 27). Stopping after each point to ask students to cite these specific clues takes only moments.

After the lecture, use an opaque or overhead projector to show your own or several students' notes of each section. Especially for very challenging lectures, this aids students in experiencing that, regardless of the specific content, the process in note-taking from lectures is always the same: *search for structure*. Then have students noteSHRINK.

An alternative is to ask students how else you could have moved from one facet of the topic to another, and let them substitute new transitions and clues.

8. Assign students to take notes on the information from commercially available tapes, TV documentaries, or educational radio or TV lectures. Have one or more students take notes on a transparency so that the entire class can later critique them. Using the capitalized items from "What's Your NQ (Note-Taking Quotient)?," Reproduction Page 34, as a guide, request that students evaluate how well the note-taker met each criterion. Having the class interview the note-taker is another option; several other items on Reproduction Page 34 could be springboards for this.

9. The sound-slide presentation *How to Survive in School: Note-taking and Outline Skills* (Resources for Teaching) informs students of various methods of note-taking and provides practice with lecture material developed specifically through simple listing, chronological order, cause-effect, comparison-contrast. Further, requesting that your students noteSHRINK after each lesson enhances their opportunities to practice organizing ideas.

Topic 5: Postlecture Essentials

1. We heartily recommend that at least one set of study-skills books be available in your instructional materials center or school library as a resource for students and teachers alike. As a general study-skills text, we suggest either Pauk's *How to Study in College* or Spargo's *The Now Student* (Resources for Teaching).

Reserve some class time for students to peruse study-skills books, garnering more note-taking pointers as they go. Have them add to the note-taking sections of their notebooks any helpful suggestions they discover. In particular, *How to Study in College* affords numerous fine illustrations of diverse note-taking styles. This material helps students see that different types of content dictate varied styles of note recording. Despite this variety, the four steps after the lecture remain constant.

Students may enjoy writing on the blackboard any new note-taking discoveries that might benefit their classmates.

2. Allot time for some general note-swapping so that students can pick up from each other new methods of getting lecture thoughts on paper. Have students record any new insights in the "Helps for Lecture Note-takers" sections of their notebooks. Occasionally request that students share aloud the hints they have experimented with and their evaluations of them.

3. In their notebooks and on a special page entitled "Tips for Improving Note-taking," ask students to evaluate each other's notebooks based on (1) adequacy of the notes and (2) organization. Have students exchange note-taking advice on these sheets as well. The physics teacher who devised this technique observes that students become more keenly aware of the value of good notes. Through this approach, everyone benefits. For example, low-achieving students see specifically how others take notes and can often improve as a result, while the students making the suggestions enjoy helping classmates improve their learning skills.[5]

4. Distribute to students a set of notes that is poorly done: no abbreviations, complete sentences, minor details, misplaced spaces (no new topics follow them), no quiz column. Alone, in pairs or trios, ask the class to perfect the notes by applying all they have learned in this unit.

5. Because a teacher's directive to review each subject for five to ten minutes once a week often elicits innumerable moans, chuckles, and sighs, tell students that you will earmark class time for such review. For one entire quarter, allot ten minutes on a designated weekday for reviewing class notes. (*Reading teachers:* You might have students target the notes from one subject during this review time.)

   This arrangement convinces students that you truly believe that review pays dividends, and, more important, the success that students will experience after such concerted review in one class can spur them to employ this approach in all other classes. Mission accomplished!

6. You may find, as we have, that in every class some students feel that they need more guided note-taking experience than the majority. To meet this need, recruit student volunteers or people in speech classes to tape selections from a range of magazines (*Newsweek, Time, Harper's Bazaar, Psychology Today, Human Nature, Reader's Digest, Scope*). This tape-bank resource might be kept in your instructional-materials center. You will need to write accompanying notes including the noteSHRINK step, and we recommend keeping these in your file cabinet. After listening to a tape and making notes, students should personally sign out your notes. Insist that these be returned to you as soon as students have made their comparisons. If several students listen to the same tape, suggest that they compare notes with one another before comparing with your notes.

---

5. Paul McIntosh, physics teacher at LaFollette High School, Madison, Wis. Remarks to Bragstad, January 1980.

ASSESSING ACHIEVEMENT OF OBJECTIVES

To determine whether students have accomplished the objectives for this unit of study, you might use many activities in this chapter and/or give an evaluation like this one:

1. Why take lecture notes? List the four reasons we discussed.

2. Enumerate the three primary obstacles to good listening; then list any additional obstacles from your personal experience.

3. Listen to a lecture and take notes, applying everything you have learned in this unit.

4. After you have finished with the entire note-taking procedure, analyze your notes. (Or, have students exchange and analyze each other's notes, in writing. To accomplish this, you may wish to use only the capitalized items from "What's Your NQ?" Reproduction Page 34.)

5. What are some note-taking secrets you have found especially helpful? List them. (Publish this information for all your students and for the entire school, if you can.)

6. Retake "What's Your NQ?" (Reproduction Page 34) and compare your pre- and post- results. The differences between the two columns are indicators of your learning.

7. Compare and contrast the purpose and procedure of note-taking with those of SQ3R. (Answer Key—Appendix B.)

RESOURCES FOR TEACHING

Below is a selected list of resources for teaching the concepts and topics for this chapter. It is divided into two categories: "Books, Pamphlets, and Articles" and "Other Resources." Addresses of publishers can be found in the alphabetical list in Appendix A.

Books, Pamphlets, and Articles

Butler, John H., and Jacoby, Theresa J. "Efficient Note Taking," in *SR/SE Resource Book,* ed. Frank L. Christ. Chicago: Science Research Associates, 1969, pp. 47–53. A discussion of efficient note-taking procedures is presented with examples and follow-up questions.

Duker, Sam, ed. *Listening Bibliography.* 2nd ed. Metuchen, N.J.: Scarecrow Press, 1968. Lists about 1,140 articles in education and speech journals about listening and the teaching of listening in the K-12 classroom.

Ladas, H. S. "Notetaking on Lectures: An Information-Processing Approach," *Educational Psychologist* 15 (September 1980): 44–53. Using an information-processing model, researchers are better able to understand the values of note-taking. Implications for lecture strategies to enhance learning and memory are discussed.

Norman, Maxwell H., and Norman, Enid S. Kass, eds. *How to Read and Study for Success in College.* 2nd ed. New York: Holt, Rinehart & Winston, 1976, "Organizing Textbook Notes" and "Organizing Lecture

Notes," pp. 156–195. Formats for organizing one's textbook materials and lecture materials are presented. Also an evaluation form to assess lecture classes is included.

Pauk, Walter. *How to Study in College.* 3rd ed. Boston: Houghton Mifflin, 1984, "Listening and Taking Notes," pp. 117–142. Students are advised of the best methods for taking lecture notes and using those notes for test preparation.

Spargo, Edward. *The Now Student.* 2nd ed. Providence, R.I.: Jamestown, 1977, "Listening Effectively," pp. 151–168. Part of this material centers on poor and sound listening habits, and part of it on pointers for note-taking. Each topic is followed by two cloze comprehension tests and several practice exercises.

Other Resources

Brown-Carlsen Listening Comprehension Test. New York: Harcourt Brace Jovanovich. Tests immediate recall, following directions, recognizing transitions, recognizing word meaning, and lecture comprehension. For grades 9–12.

How to Study Effectively. White Plains, N.Y.: Center for Humanities. Three sound-slide segments (or sound-filmstrip and video cassette format) teach students to become more active readers by prereading, reading with a purpose, note-taking, and summarizing.

How to Survive in School: Note-taking and Outlining Skills. White Plains, N.Y.: Center for Humanities. Excellent three-part sound-slide program. Part One presents a variety of approaches to note-taking, with students' involvement. Part Two presents the skill of organization as basis for outlining and includes exercises in listening for main ideas and supporting details. Part Three synthesizes what students have just learned, including cause-effect, comparison-contrast, and simple lists. Examples from science, social studies, and English are used. 240 slides in 3 carousel cartridges, 3 tape cassettes.

Note-Taking and Outlining Skills. White Plains, N.Y.: Center for Humanities. Three sound-slide segments (or sound-filmstrip and video cassette format) teach students practical systems for note-taking and classifying many different kinds of materials. Explains that notes may take the form of simple lists, comparison-contrast, or cause-effect.

Working with Main Ideas. New York: Guidance Associates. This program (2 filmstrips, 2 cassettes, 2 records, Library Kit, Teacher's Guide, Ditto Masters) helps students grasp main ideas in reading by illustrating common ways in which writing is organized.

9

Taking Tests:
Meeting the Challenge

What is more omnipresent in the life of a student than tests? Most weekly schedules include at least one exam in addition to class quizzes. Although students have been taking exams for most of their lifetimes, they are not necessarily as accomplished at it as they could be, if instructed in the art of test-taking.

When asked their standard operating procedure for test preparation, students usually respond with comments such as "I look over my notes," "I listen hard when the teacher reviews in class," or "I trust to luck." To hone their test-taking abilities, in this chapter we offer students a sound plan for physical, emotional, and intellectual readiness that will help them feel less anxious and more eager to reveal what they know when taking tests.

One can hardly hear the word *test* without also thinking about questions. In this chapter the term *question* refers to any intellectual activity, including problems and projects, that necessitates a response. This chapter opens by focusing on the lively art of questioning—first on basic questioning guidelines, then on levels of questions per se.

In our experience, students have little or no background in analyzing the levels of questions that they are asked. How could this knowledge help students? In school they are bombarded with questions—on assignments, during class sessions, and on exams. If they understand the level of the question they are being asked, they also hold the key to *how to think through* to the answer. Once again the focus is on teaching students process. To accomplish this, Reproduction Pages 38–42, containing definitions and examples of each level of questioning, plus numerous related activities, are included in this chapter.

After introducing students to levels of questioning, teaching students how to prepare emotionally and mentally for taking tests is the next natural step. Reproduction Pages with personal-analysis columns contain fundamentals that students can easily apply to upgrade their test-taking performances.

In this chapter on test-taking, then, you will find information and activities concerning general questioning guidelines, levels of questioning, and test-taking procedures.

PERFORMANCE OBJECTIVES

After the learning experiences in this chapter, students will be able to:

1. Analyze and identify given questions on all levels.

2. Note any changes in their attitudes toward tests and in their test-taking procedures and performances.

3. List the steps in preparing for an exam and analyze their applications of these steps.

4. Enumerate the procedures for taking both objective and essay tests and analyze their individual applications of these.

5. Analyze their test errors to discern patterns.

LEARNING EXPERIENCES

Topic 1: General Questioning Guidelines

1. One key strategy for improving study-reading is asking questions to set purpose prior to students' reading. Also, the "students need to be helped to analyze the questions and plot out their reading strategies. . . ."[1] To prepare students for a reading assignment, lab experiment, tape, or movie, asking questions before the activity increases students' remembering of relevant information.[2]

2. In general, to foster their improved thinking, provide students with as much time as they need to answer your questions. This may sound simple, but in fact it may not be. How much "think time" do you typically give students? That is, how much time to think do students receive after you ask them a question? The average amount of this precious commodity afforded younger students—one second![3] High school teachers, too, experience this dilemma. Yet, when think time is increased to at least three seconds, the following occurs:

   • Students give longer responses.

   • Students cite more evidence both before and after making inference statements.

---

1. H. Alan Robinson, *Teaching Reading and Study Strategies: The Content Areas* (Boston: Allyn and Bacon, 1975), pp. 40–56.
2. J. R. Sanders, "Retention Effects of Adjunct Questions in Written and Oral Discourse," *Journal of Educational Psychology* 65 (October 1973): 181–186.
3. M. B. Rowe, "Wait-time and Rewards as Instructional Variables," *Journal of Research in Science Teaching* 11, no. 2 (1974): 81–94.

- Students ask more questions and suggest more activities.

- Students volunteer more appropriate responses.

- Students offer a greater variety of responses.

- More speculative, creative thinking occurs.

- Student-student interaction increases.

- Students' failures to respond decrease.

- Slow students make more contributions.

- Students' confidence in themselves increases.

- Student-centered teaching increases.[4]

From the very outset of your course, we suggest waiting even longer than three seconds for students to respond to questions. Explain to students that, after you make an inquiry, you will give them as much time to think as they need. In other words, if they require five minutes to formulate a response, so be it. This action necessitates students' assuming greater responsibility for their own learning and also underscores your conviction that they can handle the challenge.

3. In addition to knowing when to ask questions and increasing the think time after asking them, you can advance your students' intellectual and emotional growth through your personal interest in them (Chapter 1) and in their responses. Calling students by name and listening intently to what they have to say lets students know that they count. In this kind of caring atmosphere everyone can enjoy taking risks to learn and grow. If a student seems unsure of herself while answering a question, a supportive remark, for example, "That's a good start, Barb. Now can you elaborate on . . . ," increases the student's willingness to risk further. And instead of responding to a student's comment with vague *uh huh*'s or *mmm*'s, stating "So then, John, you agree with Martha when you contend that . . ." contributes to students' motivation to learn since they perceive that you hear and value their ideas.

Topic 2: Levels of Questioning

1. You might wish to introduce the kinds-of-questions concept by walking around the room, asking students questions about their eye color, date of birth, home address, skirt color.

Then inquire, "What's your opinion on abortion, Tom?"

Next, ask the class, "Which one of the questions I have just asked requires you to think in a different way from all the others?" The last question, of course. Capitalize on the fact that people in class already have a "sense" about various levels of questioning even if they do not have labels for each of them.

---

4. Ibid.

Figure 9-1. Levels of questions.

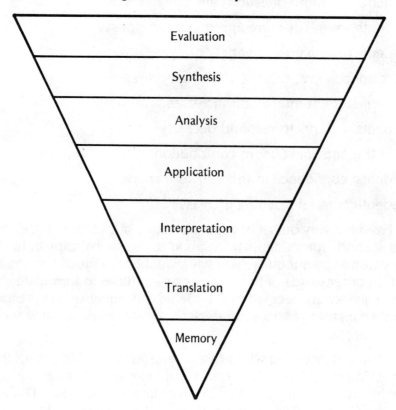

According to Norris Sanders's taxonomy, there are seven levels of questions: memory, translation, interpretation, application, analysis, synthesis, and evaluation.[5] See Figure 9-1. The inverted triangle symbolizes that each step up is inclusive (e.g., an evaluation question demands thinking on all the previous levels as well) and, therefore, challenges students in new ways. You might draw Figure 9-1 on the board so that students get the benefit of it.

2. In teaching about the levels of questions, distribute copies of Reproduction Page 38, "Synopsis of Taxonomy of Questions." This material defines and illustrates each level of question. We suggest introducing this subject, then dealing with only the first three levels during the initial class period; save the last four levels for a second day. This gradual introduction minimizes student confusion. Since the entire concept of thinking levels is abstract, students need time and much practice to ground this in their own reality.

We recall feeling some initial reluctance to teach students the taxonomy because it seemed to remove a bit of mystery and magic from the art of teaching. Now, however, we enjoy great satisfaction when a student confidently states that her geometry tests involve primarily application and analysis, or that his psychology exams consist of mainly memory, synthesis, and evaluation questions.

---

5. Norris M. Sanders, *Classroom Questions: What Kinds?* (New York: Harper & Row, 1966).

3. Have students read the "Wife Wanted" newspaper article, Reproduction Page 39, and, in groups of four, analyze the level of each question adjacent to it. Answer Key—Appendix B. Remind students to refer to Reproduction Page 38, "Synopsis of Taxonomy of Questions," so that they begin to understand the different kinds of thinking demanded by each question. To heighten critical thinking, request that the small groups attempt to agree on each answer. Also, tell students that analyzing the level of each question does not entail answering any of the questions themselves.

4. Using Reproduction Page 40, "Getting Test-Wise: Profile of Test Questions," have students analyze two tests from your class. After students fill in their own charts, they will have a handy guide for deciding what their overall study emphasis might be for your course. Stress that the more one knows about *how to think,* the more efficiently one can study. Discerning the kinds of questions a teacher usually asks helps students to know whether their study efforts must focus primarily on memorizing details or on that, plus arriving at a position with supporting logic or information (evaluation), for example.

　　For each exam, initially have students classify the level of every exam question and write that determination in the left-hand margin of the test. After analyzing the first test, ask students to (1) write the course title of that exam in the square after the word "course" and (2) tally the results of the question analysis by referring to the classifications in the margin: for example, if 20 matching items plus 6 other items dispersed through the exam are on the memory level, simply write 26 in the square after memory. See the following sample:

Level of Question	*Course*	Biology			
Memory		26			
Translation		4			
Interpretation		6			

Repeat this process for the second test.

　　Finally, fill in the Course Profile at the bottom of the page. To do this, glance over the entire column for the first test and notice which levels of questions are asked most frequently. Record these trends and repeat the process for the second test. The following example may help you explain this procedure:

Course	*Results of Test-Question Analysis*
1. Biology	heavy memory; interpretation, analysis
2. English	some memory; heavy analysis and evaluation
3.	

Encourage students to use this same analytical procedure in all their courses so that they have a complete profile to help them in preparing for exams.

Analyzing test questions is a beneficial activity not only for students but also for teachers. Just as athletes need more than jumping jacks to be in top-notch physical condition, so students require more than memory- and translation-level questions to be in peak mental form. Since research indicates that the most prevalent level of thinking required in the classroom is recall,[6] classifying the range of intellectual challenges we offer our students, not only at test time but also during class each day, is a wise decision.

To analyze classroom questions, then, simply tape-record one or two of your class sessions and later replay the tape(s), with pen in hand. Using Reproduction Page 40, determine and chart the level of each question you asked.

You may find the resultant profile of your questions to be very illuminating. When completed, it suggests both the range and the planes of intellectual challenges students experience in your course. If a discrepancy exists between what you have intended to demand of your students and what you actually are demanding in this respect, perhaps the aids suggested in Activities 5 and 6 can assist you in bridging the gap.

5. Reproduction Page 41, "Levels of Questioning 'Activator'—The Web," is a practical aid to facilitate analyzing and/or developing questions on all levels. Each pie-shaped piece represents one level of thinking. The entire web consists of three components: (1) the levels of thinking (center), (2) the process words, and (3) the products and possible outcomes (outer ring).

If you or your students wish to devise a synthesis question for a social-studies unit on the turbulent 1960s, for instance, first locate the synthesis segment of the web and follow the arrow outward. Next peruse the process words to see which one might suit your purpose, for example, the word *compose*. Again, follow the arrow outward and select some product(s), e.g., news article, song, movie. Ultimately, then, your activity might be that, after studying this unit, "The students shall compose a news article, song, or movie that captures the prevailing mood of the 1960s." (Note: This web is suggestive rather than definitive. Also, using a process word such as *judge* in your inquiry does not guarantee that you will be asking an evaluation question. Since students' experiences vary, a student who has read an editorial based on the topic he is to evaluate could merely operate at the memory level as he responds to that question.)

Both teachers and students can use this guide to analyze or formulate questions for subsequent activities in this chapter and for class assignments and exams. However, some teachers reserve this guide solely for their own uses. Each teacher makes this judgment.

6. After reading several pages of a textbook chapter, have students break into pairs or trios. Their task, based on the reading, is to devise one question on each level of thinking. They may record these on Reproduction Page 42, "Thinking Skill Grid," which contains an illustration. To use this tool,

• Decide upon two concepts from the textbook that you wish to emphasize. Have students write each concept in the appropriate column of the grid.

---

6. U. S. Chaudhari, "Questioning and Creative Thinking: A Research Perspective," *Journal of Creative Behavior* (January 1975), pp. 30–34.

- Use the web, Reproduction Page 41, to assist students in designing one question on every level for each concept.

- Have students record their questions in the appropriate spaces on the grid.

The Thinking Skill Grid facilitates not only the students' work but also the teachers'. In addition to being beneficial to you in planning your units of study, this grid affords a concise, organized record for your future reference.

7. Our affirmation of the *student's right to question* certainly facilitates students' growth toward becoming confident, independent, lifelong learners. Inquiry skills are elemental to that end. Therefore, encourage students to ask questions—even insist that they do. You may wish to designate, as an integral part of assignments, that each student write on paper several relevant questions that are at or above the translation level, to be used for class discussion or as projects.

Topic 3: Test-Taking Procedures

1. "Imagine that you are just walking into your classroom on the morning of an exam. How do you feel? Jot down your answer on a sheet of paper." Continue by asking students whether they feel differently about taking tests in various courses. Why or why not?

   Next, allot time for small-group and large-group sharing of this information. You might jot some of the students' reactions on the board, then poll the students on each item. Or you might have a few students tabulate the results and report them to the class.

   Students are sometimes unaware of the great impact that their emotions and mental attitudes can have on their exam performances. For instance, students' knowing that everyone has some fear of the unknown—whether in the doctor's waiting room or the classroom on the day of a test—helps them feel more relaxed about their own anxieties. Remind students that great athletes and renowned stage and screen performers suffer from pregame or preperformance jitters. This kind of edge actually contributes to a better performance, if the stress is manageable. Also, tell students that you will present preventive measures to help alleviate unproductive levels of tension.

2. Students often do not realize how negative emotions interfere with their preparing for and performing on exams. For students who cited largely *negative self-talk* in the previous activity—"I know I'll fail," "I just can't do it!"—combating this destructive habit is not only necessary but also possible. For example, when confronting a stressful situation such as an exam, students can override negative self-talk with *coping, positive self-statements:* "Don't think about fear—just about what I have to do," "Stay relevant," and "One step at a time; I can handle the situation."[7]

   For each negative comment students wrote in the previous activity, then, request that they write a counteracting positive assertion that will help

7. S. A. Bower and G. H. Bower, *Asserting Yourself: A Practical Guide for Positive Change* (Reading, Mass.: Addison-Wesley Publishing Co., 1976).

them alleviate undue anxiety. Thus, rather than worrying about their poor test performance, students can convert that energy to prepare for and focus on mastering the test itself.

3. To help students avoid anxiety because of eleventh-hour test preparation, one week before your exam, give them a handout labeled with the following

TEST PREP LOG

DATE/TIME?	GOAL?	OUTCOME?	REWARD?
Mon. 8–8:45	review ½ of class notes	finished!	call Ann

Each day request that students fill in the first line with their intended goal for that day (sample above). Consequently, what could seem an overwhelming task becomes instead a series of bite-size, manageable chunks.

4. We have discovered that students gain confidence in their test-taking abilities by following this advice: after mastering the material, review for ten extra minutes; at the exam consciously relax by taking several slow, deep breaths; survey the test before beginning. After trying these suggestions, a few students dropped notes of appreciation in our mailboxes—proof of a real breakthrough!

5. Ask students to reflect on the last test they took. Have them trace all the steps they followed from the moment they entered the classroom until the end of the test period, for example, (1) "asked friends to clarify two points I didn't understand, (2) put my name on the paper, (3) started working on the first question and worked straight through the test, (4) ran out of time before answering the last ten-point question."

   Then ask students to speculate: If they could retake this exam, how would they alter their procedure in order to (1) feel more at ease during the exam and (2) improve their scores? Emphasize that assessing the effectiveness of one's personal test-taking approach is the initial step toward upgrading it.

6. Do students view the errors they have made on exams as opportunities to learn, as temporary gaps in understanding that can be remedied? To determine this, ask your students, "Do you examine what you get wrong on a test?"

   In a study-skills survey of 467 freshmen, we asked students that very question. The outcome?

Almost always	13 percent
More than half the time	19
Half the time	31
Less than half the time	21
Almost never	16

Of these students, 319—that is, 68 percent—ignored their test errors half or more than half the time!

   Finally, ask your students how they can benefit from examining the nature of their test errors.

7. Analyzing their test errors is essential if students are to improve upcoming performances; therefore, ask each student to bring to class five tests that he or she has taken recently. Then hand out Reproduction Page 43, "Becoming Test-Wise: Exam-Error Checklist." Have students (1) record the course title of the first test after the word "course," (2) analyze every error made on that exam, and (3) record the error type (X) in the square next to the appropriate kind of mistake. Students repeat these three steps for each of the exams.

   The end result? Ask students to search for trends in their errors, both according to subject (read down each column), and according to error type (read across each row). When students do discover trends, they become aware of what to alter as they prepare for and take future tests. (For a more detailed assessment of essay test responses, see Reproduction Page 47.)

8. In this activity students will assess their "Perceived Causes of Success and Failure."[8] "After students receive grades on one of your course examinations, ask each of them to describe the causes of his or her performance on four scales: ability, effort, task difficulty, and luck. Here is an example:

   How important was each of the following factors in determining your grade?

   a. *Ability* (intelligence, skill in this area or on this kind of test):

1	2	3	4	5	6	7

   not at all important   very important

   b. *Effort* (how much or how little you studied, how hard you tried to attend class and do the assignments):

1	2	3	4	5	6	7

   not at all important   very important

   Ask students to compare answers and to discuss the similarities and differences."

9. Have students imagine that their best friends are scoring very poorly on course exams. In small groups, students are to draw up a list of their finest test-taking recommendations to aid their friends.

   You might hand out to students the "Test Prep" guidelines, Reproduction Page 44, instead. Be certain students analyze their own applications of the hints in the personal-analysis column. This encourages their concentration on the contents and can facilitate their actual transition to more sound test-prep habits.

10. Write two headings on the blackboard—*Objective* and *Essay*. Have the class pool their knowledge of hints to take each kind of test.

    If you prefer a handout on the subject, Reproduction Pages 45, "Boot Camp for Test-Takers: At the Exam," and 46, "Essay Essentials," are summary sheets that contain personal-analysis columns so students can get involved as they learn this same material.

---

8. Teacher's Resource Manual for Virginia L. Hoitsma et al., eds., *Understanding Psychology*, 2nd ed. (New York: CRM/Random House, 1978), p. 35.

11. Allow time for students to search for additional test-taking pointers in a host of study-skill books (Resources for Teaching). Since students value variety, you might also utilize some of the excellent sound-slide materials focusing on intellectual and psychological preparation for objective, essay, and standardized tests.

12. When you return an exam containing an essay question, use the overhead projector to have the entire class analyze sample student essays (with prior student permission). Reproduction Page 47, "Sharpen Your Essay-Writing Skills," contains the criteria.

    Then ask students to compare the process of writing an essay with the processes of SQ3R (Chapter 6), of mapping (Chapter 7), and of note-taking at a lecture (Chapter 8). This allows students to discover that they must apply the same organizational principles whether writing an essay, reading a text, or listening to a lecture: that is, attending to an introduction with a thesis statement, transitional clues to the organization, a body of clearly stated evidence, and a conclusion. In brief, the process is the same! You may wish students to write this response so that each of them individually can arrive at this conclusion.

13. Using the "Sharpen Your Essay-Writing Skills" guidelines, Reproduction Page 47, have students analyze one or two of their own essay answers from exams. Then have students trade with two other classmates to gain additional evaluations. This kind of practice is essential for students to truly grasp what the essay principles mean when "activated."

14. As a component of test review, have each student formulate one essay question based on the unit material. Then have students pair off, exchange papers, and write a response to the one question each of them receives. The person who answers the essay question might use the checklist on Reproduction Page 47, "Sharpen Your Essay-Writing Skills," to analyze his or her own writing. Then ask the question-writer and one other person to critique the essay also. Repeat this process as often as you wish.

    Remind students that the more practice they get in writing essays, the more facile they will become at effectively organizing and expressing ideas when they cope with the tension of a test situation.

15. When preparing for essay tests, students can utilize notes and maps to predict questions. After having predicted some questions, students can practice writing (a) a specific thesis statement, (b) transitions and central thoughts, and (c) a conclusion for each question. (*Reading teachers:* Students may do this for one of your exams or for an exam in another course. If several students in class are taking the same test, have them compare thoughts.)

16. From essay answers that students have developed for an assignment or exam, choose two sample essays: one that is well organized and filled with relevant facts; the other, reasonably well organized with some pertinent facts, but a preponderance of irrelevant information. You might consider writing one or both of these essays if your students do not afford you this "raw material."

    Using an opaque projector, a transparency on the overhead projector, or copies of these essays, ask your students to evaluate both samples and assign a letter grade to each one. In addition, request that students jot down the reasons for their judgments.

This activity can be a revelation for some students, who notice that being selective about the data to be incorporated into an essay response is crucial. You may wish to conclude by having students apply "Sharpen Your Essay-Writing Skills," Reproduction Page 47, for a more thorough analysis of the essays. Ultimately, the general goal of this activity is for each student to gain insights into the thinking process involved in organizing a coherent essay answer; a more specific goal is to underscore the importance of utilizing only evidence that is relevant to the topic, when writing an essay.

This kind of critical-thinking activity is such a challenge that Harvard University employs it to diagnose the reading-thinking skills of every incoming freshman.[9] Your students might enjoy knowing that fact!

ASSESSING ACHIEVEMENT OF OBJECTIVES

Many activities in this chapter can be used for evaluating student achievement. In addition, the following suggestions may be used for evaluation or as learning activities:

1. Determine the level of each question below and tell why you decide as you do. (Three sample questions follow.)

   - What idea that we have studied in this unit is depicted in this cartoon? (Translation)

   - Eleven people find themselves in a bomb shelter after a nuclear attack, with oxygen and other supplies for only six people. A description of each individual is offered. You, the owner of the shelter, must decide which five people should leave in order to save the others. (Evaluation)

   - Using the criteria that you have learned in class, compare and contrast the musical styles of any two of the following:

     a. Beethoven

     b. Bach

     c. Haydn

     d. Stravinsky   (Interpretation)

2. What changes have occurred in your attitude toward tests, your test-taking procedure, and your test scores because of applying your new test-taking knowledge?

3. Delineate how you studied for this exam. How does your approach compare with the suggestions that we have studied?

4. Hand in sheets on test preparation and test-taking, with personal-analysis columns completed.

5. Write a personal profile entitled "Things to Zero in on during Exams," based on "Becoming Test-Wise: Exam Error Checklist" (Reproduction Page 43).

---

9. William Perry, Bureau of Study Counsel, Harvard University Reading Test (Test material, unpublished, Harvard University).

RESOURCES FOR TEACHING

Below is a selected list of resources for teaching the concepts and topics of this chapter. It is divided into two categories: "Books, Pamphlets, and Articles" and "Other Resources." Addresses of publishers can be found in the alphabetical list in Appendix A.

Books, Pamphlets, and Articles

Devine, Thomas G. "Remembering, Relating, and Test-Taking," in *Teaching Study Skills: A Guide for Teachers*. Newton, MA: Allyn and Bacon, Inc., 1981, pp. 291–304. Offers many concrete suggestions on how to help students prepare for and take exams.

Farquhar, William W.; Krumboltz, John D.; and Wrenn, C. Gilbert. "Prepare for Examinations," in *SR/SE Resource Book*, ed. Frank L. Christ. Chicago: Science Research Associates, 1969, pp. 63–69. A six-step approach to taking examinations is presented with several related activities as a review.

Henry, J. H. *Teaching Reading as Concept Development: Emphasis on Affective Thinking*. Newark, Del.: International Reading Association, 1974. An idea book for secondary English teachers that suggests diverse ways of teaching thinking skills through literature.

Jones, John A. "How to Write Better Tests," *Instructor* 89 (October 1979): 66–71. Jones, supervisor of assessment in the Missouri Department of Elementary and Secondary Education, developed teacher guidelines on how to construct better tools for evaluation. Contains several pages of suggestions and examples.

Lange, Roger. "Flipping the Coin: From Test Anxiety to Test Wiseness," *Journal of Reading* 22 (December 1978): 274–277. Discusses the research on test anxiety and gives examples of how people are alleviating test anxiety, either through systematic desensitization or by teaching test-taking skills. Write to the International Reading Association for further information.

Millman, Jason, and Pauk, Walter. *How to Take Tests*. New York: McGraw-Hill, 1969.

A thorough, clearly organized guide to emotional, physical, and intellectual readiness for taking teacher-made and standardized tests. Includes strategies and practice exercises for taking a host of test types, including objective, essay, open-book, oral, and others.

Norman, Maxwell H., and Norman, Enid S. Kass. "Organizing for Tests," in *How to Read and Study for Success in College*. 2nd ed. New York: Holt, Rinehart & Winston, 1976, pp. 252–263. Succinct presentation of test preparation for essay, objective, and standardized tests. Includes a form for students to use for analyzing both lecture and lab courses.

Pauk, Walter. *How to Study in College*. 3rd ed. Boston: Houghton Mifflin, 1984, pp. 227–266. Emphasizes strategies to use when reviewing and preparing for essay and objective exams.

Sanders, Norris M. *Classroom Questions: What Kinds?* New York: Harper & Row, 1966. An invaluable guide. General format: one chapter of explanation plus examples on each of the seven levels of questions, followed by a quiz for the reader on the content.

Spargo, Edward. *The Now Student*. Rev. ed. Providence, R.I.: Jamestown, 1977, "Reviewing for Examinations," "Taking Objective Exams," and "Taking Essay Exams," pp. 187–209. Pointers for becoming test-wise on objective and essay tests are presented and are followed by practice exercises and comprehension questions.

Weaver, Gail Cohen. "Teaching Children How to Take Standardized Tests," *Reading Teacher* 32 (October 1978): 116–119. Discusses and cites current research in the area of "test-wiseness" and the teaching of test-taking skills. Valuable suggestions and references to many relevant studies are included. Write to the International Reading Association for further information.

Other Resources

Test-Taking Skills: Effective Study Techniques. White Plains, N.Y.: Center for

Humanities. A sound-slide program in two parts designed to teach students skills that will help them prepare for answering both objective and essay test questions. Students learn techniques for coping with test anxiety and participate in exercises reinforcing test-taking skills. Excellent for class application. 160 slides in 2 carousel cartridges, 2 tape cassettes.

Test-Taking Skills: How to Succeed on Standardized Examinations. White Plains, N.Y.: Center for Humanities. Program in two parts focuses on practical and psychological preparation for taking standardized tests, with special emphasis on Scholastic Aptitude Test (SAT). Sample questions on verbal and mathematical skills demonstrate techniques for improving scores. Excellent for college-bound students. 160 slides in 2 carousel cartridges, 2 tape cassettes.

Farrar, Mary. "Studying for and Taking Examinations" cassette from *Listen and Read MN*. New York: Educational Developmental Laboratories. Presents general test-taking principles and essay exercises. This college-level material involves students in judging which essay outline is most appropriate for each sample essay question. Requires critical thinking and affords a good model for *how to think* when taking essay exams.

10

The Research Paper: Mastering the Process

Charles Carlson
Karen Carlson

It is Friday afternoon, the last hour of the day. You have just sent your class to the media center to begin a semester term paper. Your instructions to the class were to "write a ten-page paper on a topic of current interest." Of the twenty-eight students in the class, seven chose abortion as their topic, six chose child abuse, eleven chose drug abuse, and four don't intend to do anything but copy something from somewhere. When the class arrives in the media center, the media specialist is helping a freshman health class find materials for a unit on drug abuse. The media aide has just finished pulling together a cart of materials on child abuse and abortion for the contemporary women's issues class. The material will be on reserve for four weeks. Not surprisingly, your hoped-for planning time is interrupted by your returning students who tell you that there is nothing in the stupid library and that the librarian is a grouch who hates everyone under nineteen. Your first attempt at teaching research writing has somehow gone awry.

While the above scenario is an obvious exaggeration, it borders dangerously on the reality rather than the absurd in far too many schools. To avoid such a situation in our classrooms, we must make the research paper a meaningful learning experience, and not an end in itself. Simply assigning a ten-page paper does not guarantee that our students will do any original research. Cooperation with the school media special-

Charles Carlson is an Instructor of Social Studies at LaFollette High School, Madison, Wis.
Karen Carlson is a Media Specialist at Stoughton High School, Stoughton, Wis.

ist, planning to incorporate the paper as a part of our class curriculum, and active guidance on all aspects of the paper are necessary if the research experience is to be educationally valuable to our students.

The goals of student research are exploration of a topic, utilization of information, and the production of an original research paper. If students are cognizant of these goals, and if we actively teach research skills, the research paper will be an integral part of our class, not just an afterthought.

This chapter is not a research paper style manual. Instead, specific suggestions are offered to help you integrate a research paper into your curriculum. Other how-to's include planning for and introducing the research project, helping students choose topics, teaching research skills, helping students utilize and evaluate information, writing the paper, and applying research skills to other situations.

The challenge to you, the teacher, is obvious. The information explosion is giving high-school students access to information sources that were previously available only to scholars or specialists. Because students must now learn to access and process all this new information, we can no longer be content with passing on the body of knowledge we learned in college. New challenges to our students demand appropriate responses from us as their teachers. In a world swept by change and flooded with information, arming our students with research techniques and skills may well be the best insulation against the frightening speed of the information explosion.

PERFORMANCE OBJECTIVES

As a result of the learning experiences in this chapter, students should be able to:

1. Understand the research process.

2. Understand the importance of choosing a topic.

3. State the topic choice in a thesis statement.

4. Retrieve information.

5. Process, utilize, and evaluate information.

6. Understand the process of writing a research paper.

7. Produce a paper that incorporates the skills taught and satisfies the principles of true research.

8. Demonstrate awareness of the value of research skills in other classes and life situations.

LEARNING EXPERIENCES

Topic 1: Beginning the Process

1. Ask the class to define situations where finding information has been important to them. Responses might range from how to fix a ten-speed bicycle to

finding out which brand of running shoe is best suited for running on a wet track. List their responses; then explain that these are all research problems and that the process they are about to undertake will help them find answers to questions of all kinds. Discuss the information explosion and the probable impact of technology on the way they will locate and process information in the future.

2. Why do a research paper? Display several historical political maps of Africa. Briefly show the disappearance and emergence of various countries. Show students what the map looked like twenty to thirty years ago. Hand out two diagrams of a cell, one labeled with all parts known when their parents went to school and one diagram with cell parts discovered within the last twenty years. Ask students to see if their parents remember studying or reading about many black, Native American, or women authors when they were in school. Could a mechanic fix an electronic fuel-injected engine with skills acquired twenty years ago? Ask the class to list more examples of change and information growth. After the students have developed an extensive list, add this question to their list: *Will you be able to stop learning when you leave school?* Encourage students to think of research as a *process* which they will use in the future to update their job skills and to help them understand a rapidly changing world.

3. When you first introduce a research paper, divide both research and writing tasks into components, such as topic choice, thesis statement, survey of materials, trial bibliography, outline, etc. This assures that the components are manageable tasks which, when put together, will produce a research paper. A list of suggested components is included on Reproduction Pages 48 and 52. Discuss all components during the introduction so that students have a clear idea of what is expected of them. Discuss each step briefly, but stress that all issues do not have to be dealt with immediately. Help students realize that organization is vital to the accomplishment of a large research project.

4. Distribute the grading criteria during the introduction. Reproduction Page 51 might be used for your class, or draw up your own, or have the class itself help determine some of the grading criteria.

5. This is the best time to answer the inevitable question, "How long does the paper have to be?" Explain that length has very little to do with quality, and that a paper is long enough when a satisfactory answer to the research question has been reached.

6. Distribute a timeline to the class. Assure them that time will be given during class for research in the media center. Check with the media specialist and book your class into the media center well in advance.

Topic 2: Choosing the Topic

1. Ask students to state possible selections in the form of questions or problems. If your class believes that research questions can be answered by a quick check in the encyclopedia, spend some class time developing questions suit-

able for use as true research topics. Your brainstorming session might produce topics such as: Who should be responsible for cleaning up toxic waste sites—the government or industry? Is atomic energy a blessing or a curse? Do John Steinbeck's novels about the 1930s accurately portray the impact of the Great Depression on American life? Who was responsible for U.S. unpreparedness at Pearl Harbor? Was D-Day really the turning point of the war in Europe?

Notice that the list of topics does not include questions such as: What is acid rain? What was the League of Nations? These questions require only factual answers and utilize none of the higher skills such as synthesis, analysis, or evaluation. A good topic calls for the student to gather and use data to reach conclusions and/or to prove a point.

2. If students have difficulty choosing a topic, use the following activity. Have students list their interests, hobbies, or plans for the future. Transpose those ideas into the time span or subject area you are working with, and your indecisive students should now be able to formulate a topic that has personal interest.

3. Even if your students have had some research experience, their main problem might be stating the topic correctly. Stoughton High School's class in research writing is the culminating research experience for high school seniors who intend to go on to college, yet the teacher finds that students still need guidance in choosing a topic and writing a thesis statement. "Prod students into answering two questions: 'What are you trying to prove? What questions are you asking?' They will automatically formulate a thesis statement while they choose a topic."[1]

4. Approval of the topic and thesis statement must come from two sources. The classroom teacher must approve both components, and the media specialist should approve the topic to ensure the media center has adequate information available. Now research can begin.

5. Require a survey of literature and a trial bibliography to help combat the "I-can't-find-anything" blues. Depending upon the extent of the research project, a minimum number of sources should be identified and cited in correct form on the trial bibliography. Emphasize that this is only a test run to see if information is available. Inform students that they will be expected to explore all sources for their final bibliography (Reproduction Page 50).

The media specialist and teacher should observe these first attempts at research carefully so they can identify trouble areas for group skills instruction or individual attention. Offer immediate help individually and schedule sessions for group instruction with the media specialist.

Topic 3: Researching the Topic

1. Why teach students research skills? Students need instruction in the *how-to* before they can produce a paper that reflects individual research. As one

---

1. Conversation with Jeanette Carpenter, Language Arts Instructor, Stoughton High School, Stoughton, Wis.

student put it, "I spend five times longer on research than I do on writing the paper. If I find the right information, the writing is easy."[2]

2. Entice students with trivia! To promote reference skills familiarity, beyond solely encyclopedia usage, stage a trivia contest. Divide the class into teams and give each team a 3" × 5" card on which is written a trivia question. Tell students they are restricted to searching for answers in the reference collection, that media specialists and teachers are nonparticipants, and are therefore unable to help. Inform the teams their mission is to answer the question, cite their source, and then ask for another card. Appeal to their sense of competition; the more competitive the search, the more questions are answered, and with each answered question, students discover more reference sources.

Some groups are very adept at finding answers, so have at least ten questions per group on hand. If the media specialist and classroom teacher cooperate in writing the questions, a broad range of reference sources can be covered. Don't restrict questions to your subject area. Sample questions used at Stoughton High School include: What or who is Uncus? Find a formula which is said to fade freckles. Who is the "poor little rich girl" and what is her present occupation? What is Jodie Foster's real name? What is the OED? Does the Environmental Protection Agency have a speakers' bureau?

The team that answers the most questions is awarded a prize—rootbeer barrels or packages of gum. When this activity was first tried at Stoughton High School, both the media specialists and the teacher wondered if high school seniors would enter into the spirit of competition. "We needn't have worried. The excitement of the hunt infects the class, and soon students are shelf-crawling with surprising intensity."[3] The trivia search is the introduction to reference skills. Although it is tempting, don't offer help to your students during this exercise. A bit of frustration when all they have to lose is a rootbeer barrel is much better than experiencing frustration during their real research.

On the second day in the media center, ask the class to share their trivia questions and sources for answers. To complete the skills instruction, the media specialist need only elaborate upon the students' comments or highlight sources they missed. Without realizing it, students have absorbed two full periods of reference instruction, much of it self-taught.

3. Present instruction in other research skills on a need-to-know basis, one skill at a time. Plan with your media specialist to create a system of skills instruction that will guide students through an increasingly complicated maze of both print and nonprint information sources. Reproduction Page 50 is a sample checklist of sources. Distribute a similar list that emphasizes specialized bibliographic or information sources applicable to your subject area. Concentrate on one source or type of material at a time, and have students *utilize* each skill immediately after its introduction.

4. Your class will most likely possess such varying levels of ability in periodical research that there will be no one best method to teach that skill. If students

2. Erica Carlson, student at James Madison Memorial High School, Madison, Wis.
3. Marilyn Paull, Media Specialist, Stoughton High School, Stoughton, Wis.

demonstrate ability to use periodical indexes such as *Readers' Guide to Periodical Literature,* they should proceed with their research. However, classes that have trouble should be given group instruction, followed immediately by plenty of practice. The filmstrip *How To Use the Readers' Guide to Periodical Literature* is a valuable resource for large group instruction. (See Resources for Teaching.) It is also valuable as an individual learning lab when placed on the index table along with copies of the index.

5. The most basic research tool is the card catalog. Many teachers assume that their students can use a catalog effectively, but this assumption is often questionable. In the authors' experience it is not uncommon for high school seniors to wander around a media center searching for the location of a book with the number *478 p.* Because students often misunderstand a catalog card, both the media specialist and teacher should be on hand to handle individual problems. Walk the frustrated student through a search and stick with it until the material is found. Once the mysteries of author, title, subject cards, and classification numbers are understood, the entire research project seems easier.

6. Nonprint sources are becoming a large part of the reference collection in school media centers and public libraries. Students need to be introduced to the nonprint collection in a way that teaches them the unique qualities of microform. Familiarity with the microfilm and microfiche collection gives students access to current national newspapers, Civil War era periodicals, and a vast array of special collections, such as musical scores, scientific journals, and biographical information.

   As part of their research checklist, require each student to search the microform indexes. The media specialist should be available to help interpret these indexes, since each company or source seems to have a different indexing system.

7. The computer age is impacting upon high school research methods. On-line data base capability is available in some schools, and it will undoubtedly become more common in the next few years. How will the introduction of data bases affect our schools and our teaching? Some schools have already answered that question. Waunakee High School, Waunakee, Wisconsin, has been using on-line searches for several years. Research skills are an integrated part of the district's curriculum, and on-line research is used in many curricular areas.[4] It seems likely, then, that no matter what subject we teach, electronic information retrieval will affect us and our students. If your school is on line, work with your media specialist to utilize the data bases available to you. If you are in the planning stage, make sure your media specialist is informed of your anticipated needs and uses for an information retrieval system so that the data bases your school subscribes to will meet your students' needs.

8. For Stoughton High School's Biology I classes, the research tasks are smaller, but they receive as much attention from teacher and media specialist as do

4. Don Holmen, IMC Director, Waunakee High School, Waunakee, Wis.

the more advanced research assignments. The teacher divides research skills into steps which are introduced and taught by the media specialist. Each assignment reinforces the previous skill and adds one new element. In the first assignment (Reproduction Page 53), the *Readers' Guide* is the only source used. Because the teacher suggests subjects so that the student need only learn how to *use* the index, this assignment is adaptable to any classroom. Besides requiring students to use the *Readers' Guide,* subsequent assignments introduce the pamphlet file, reference collection, and microform indexes.[5]

9. Consulting an expert or interviewing an authority is a research step often ignored by teachers. Stoughton's advanced chemistry class utilizes the interview or consultation as the culmination of the research skills instruction begun in Biology I. The teacher asks the class to choose a general issue of current interest; acid rain, toxic waste, food additives, and carcinogens are among topics usually chosen. Students narrow the topic and find the most recent journal articles available in the media center. Then they formulate their topic based upon the latest information, identify an expert, and establish contact with their authority via telephone or letter. The teacher is anxious to get on-line data base capability because he feels the students would be able to identify an expert and tap into the latest research much faster. The final step in the research project will be to design an experiment that utilizes the expert's information. The time constraints of manual searching, letter writing, and waiting for replies impede the experimental design plan at present, but when on-line searches are possible, the students will design and carry out original research experiments.[6]

10. Have students become on-the-spot reporters. Interviewing is a valuable tool for research about subjects such as the "olden days." Students can usually find a family member or friend who remembers the Fabulous Fifties, the Great Depression, the Vietnam War, or what marriage was like decades ago. If your students are reluctant to get involved in a research project, send them out to interview someone as the first step; it is often a greater motivator for further research. Genealogical research is often based on interviews or the contents of an attic trunk, and it is always original. Turn your students loose on their family histories, and watch the dust fly. The American frontier teacher of LaFollette High School has received notes of appreciation from families whose youngsters suddenly became family historians. Families have even visited the areas or locales investigated by some American frontier students.[7]

Topic 4: Utilizing the Information

1. Have students write the thesis statement first so they can channel their research toward a specific goal. All the information they use should contribute

---

5. Tom Stokes, Science Instructor, Stoughton, Wis.
6. Phil Bednarek, Science Instructor, Stoughton, Wis.
7. Charles Carlson, Instructor of Social Studies, LaFollette High School, Madison, Wis.

something to the understanding or clarification of the thesis statement. Design a sample list of information about a famous person, such as Abraham Lincoln. At the top of the page, write a sample thesis statement: "Abraham Lincoln was faced with several major decisions that had a direct effect upon the outcome of the Civil War." List several facts about Lincoln. "He was born in a log cabin. He did not favor the extension of slavery. He decided to reinforce Fort Sumter. He had a son named Tad. His wife's family were southern sympathizers. In 1862 he issued the Emancipation Proclamation. He did not recognize a state's right to secede." List as many facts as you wish, including both extraneous and cogent issues. Have the students decide which statements are supportive of or clarify the thesis statement. Discuss relevancy of information and encourage students always to check their information against their thesis statement and their final goal.

2. Organize, organize, organize! To help your students make sense of their information, require a trial outline or map (Chapter 7) as a very early step in the research paper. An outline prevents wheel spinning during research and acts as a guide when the student begins to write. The teacher should approve both the trial outline and the final outline.

3. Note-taking (Chapter 8) is a skill that needs to be addressed. Too many students copy voluminous notes from their sources, only to find they have a completely unmanageable amount of unrelated information. Present two or three styles of note-making and let students choose one; reinforce that method early and often during their research periods in the media center. Collect notes from their first three sources and check them for relevancy and brevity. Teach students to synthesize the material they find and to avoid excessive note-taking. Share some student samples with the class and let students decide which are helpful and which could be improved.

4. Into each student researcher's life some rain must fall. Most students agree they are faced with a real monsoon when they begin a bibliography. Ease your students through this storm by encouraging them to take complete bibliographic citations from the very beginning of their research. Check their citations at several points along the way. Students who don't have to rush later to the media center to look up all the volume numbers of the periodicals they used will thank you.

Topic 5: Writing the Paper

1. A style manual is a necessary item for students writing a research paper. While there are several excellent guides published, some schools develop their own style manuals. LaFollette High School English, media, science, business, and social studies departments jointly developed a guide that is used schoolwide. Stoughton High School research writing teachers also wrote their own guide. Students should receive the style manual when the paper is first assigned. At each progress report, check the student's consistency with the manual. If students get used to using the correct format at each of their progress or

checkpoints, they will have less trouble following the correct style on their final draft.

2. The advent of word processors has changed the requirement of slavishly following a style manual. More and more students are writing their papers on word processors. If the required style is not possible with the specific program a student is using, encourage the student to maintain internal style control within the program's formatting capabilities.

3. The thesis statement has, of course, already been written and approved, so the beginning few lines of the paper should not be a problem. Have students include in the introduction the outline of procedure and justification of the paper. After your students write the introduction, collect it for approval. Throughout the entire writing process, stress that this is a learning experience. For high school students, the important outcome of the research paper is that they learn to write a good, solid paper. Remind them that the purpose of the paper is to teach them to be able to work independently in the future and that they are welcome to ask for as much help as they need.

4. The body of the paper is the next task. Teach footnoting techniques now. Explain the dangers of overly long quotations and overfootnoting. It is not uncommon for beginning research writers to overfootnote a paper. Reproduction Pages 54 and 55 are handouts students can use to guide them through the writing process.

5. Provide class time for proofreading so that students can ask questions about troublesome points. Hand out a sheet of standardized proofreading marks so that students will understand your corrections.

6. Emphasize that the conclusion is the most original part of the paper and is not only a summary of the paper but also an analysis of the material. The points proven during the body of the paper are driven home in the conclusion.

7. At all points during the actual writing of the paper, remind students to check their work against the grading sheet. Have students evaluate their own work before they hand it in.

Topic 6: Transfer of Learning

1. Once students have written a research paper as a learning experience, they should be able to reinforce and practice their skills in other classes. Cooperation between departments ensures there will be a developmental pattern implemented to teach research skills. While a single teacher can hardly instigate such a program, the beginnings of schoolwide cooperation can spring from a single English and a social studies teacher deciding to coordinate their research projects. Adopting a style manual and agreeing between departments to use the same style are important.

2. There are many opportunities to develop research projects within the curriculum of various classes. By integrating research skills within the structure of

our curriculum, we can meet the information explosion head-on by giving students the answer to a question that will always be relevant: "How do I find . . . ?"

ASSESSING ACHIEVEMENT OF OBJECTIVES

After completing the research project, students might assess their research IQs in the following ways:

1. Evaluate your own paper (Reproduction Pages 55–56).

2. Confer with your teacher regarding your research paper evaluation.

3. Prepare for the final exam by reviewing media and research skills along with course content material. A section on media and research skills will be included in the final exam.

RESOURCES FOR TEACHING

Below is a selected list of resources for teaching the concepts and topics of this chapter. It is divided into two categories: "Books, Pamphlets, and Articles" and "Other Resources."

Books, Pamphlets, and Articles

Baily, Edward P., Jr. *Writing Research Papers.* New York: Holt, Rinehart & Winston, 1981. Good advice on topic choice and developing a thesis statement.

Baker, Sheridan. *The Practical Stylist.* New York: Harper & Row, 1981. Excellent examples of stylistic qualities, punctuation, and paragraphing.

Condella, Janet S., and Johnson, Richard W. *Student Workbook for Learning Skills Program.* Madison, Wis.: University Counseling Service, University of Wisconsin, 1980, 181 p. A style manual for undergraduates at the University of Wisconsin.

Craver, Kathleen W. "An Introduction to On-line Bibliographic Searching for High School Students: A Successful Approach," *Educational Technology* 24, no. 6 (June 1984): 39–41. Outlines a successful integra-tion of on-line data bases and traditional research skills within a curriculum.

McKenzie, Jamieson A. "The Future Isn't What It Used To Be: Videotex Is on the Way," *Media & Methods* 21, no. 3 (November 1984): 8–11. Videotex, an interactive on-line data system, could radically alter educational processes.

Schuelke, David, and King, Thomas D. "New Technology in the Classroom: Computers and Communication and the Future," *Technological Horizons in Education* 10, no. 6 (April 1983): 95–100. Stresses the importance of emerging technology upon the classroom and what we teach our students.

Other Resources

How To Use the Readers' Guide to Periodical Literature. Sound Filmstrip, H. W. Wilson Co., 1983. A helpful resource for presenting research skills, this filmstrip is useful for large groups or individual instruction. Some adaptation may be necessary to tailor the information to your media center's periodical holdings.

11

Strategic Reading: Relating Rate to Purpose

Doug Vance

Most teachers would agree that the goal of education should be to help students become self-directed learners who are able to learn on their own. Just as the new employee cannot be expected to possess the skills and strategies necessary to be a company executive, our students cannot be expected to possess the skills and strategies needed for adult reading. Thus, content area teachers are in an ideal position to help students become strategic readers.

Think of yourself as a reader. How do you approach your reading? It depends, you say. It depends on what you are reading, why you are reading it, what you are going to do with it, and even how much time you have to read it. You read the newspaper at breakfast, scanning the headlines, skimming the articles, quickly reading the news that is important to you, saving the columns until you have more time. You read the morning announcements quickly before homeroom, eliminating those that are not relevant to you or your class, reading aloud those that are important. During your prep period you read a professional article, carefully underlining points you want to remember, taking notes. You reread a chapter in a textbook you will be teaching next week, trying to view it as your students will see it, anticipating problems students will have, noting difficult vocabulary, outlining the important concepts. In the evening you leaf through a magazine, decide which articles to read in depth and which to skip. Before bedtime you pick up a novel, quickly rereading the last page you read to remind yourself where you are, then settling back to enjoy the plot, character, and themes.

Doug Vance is a Reading Consultant at LaFollette High School, Madison, Wis.

Strategic readers know what they want out of reading. As adults we never read anything unless we have a reason, yet our students can seldom articulate a purpose for reading. The reader who can state a reading purpose is more likely to understand the material and how it fits into the overall purpose for studying. Strategic readers plan ahead. They choose the most effective strategies which will help them understand and remember what they have read. They first assess what they already know about the topic, and then determine what they need to learn, and how they can best go about learning it.

Planning also includes estimating how much time it will take to complete the reading successfully, along with where and when the reading will get done. Strategic readers can choose the reading rate that is appropriate to the task. When general understanding of main ideas is enough, strategic readers can read rapidly with good comprehension. When thorough understanding of details or difficult material is necessary, they can employ slower study reading rates. They can also use reference reading rates such as skimming and scanning to preview material, get the general ideas, and search for information.

Many students do not really know if they have comprehended what they read until they take a test. Strategic readers monitor their own comprehension as they read and make adjustments in their reading rates and strategies. When comprehension breaks down, they stop and figure it out. They set checkpoints in their reading when they will assess their own comprehension, and they take advantage of questions and activities in the text to check their understanding. Most important, they watch themselves as they read and are aware of how they do it. They can talk about what strategies they are using and how effective they are.

Once they have completed reading an assignment most students usually quit. They may have to complete a worksheet or answer questions, but then they are done. Strategic readers reflect about what they have read. They measure the outcome of their reading against their original purpose. They take some time to think about how the material fits in with what they already know about the subject and how it might change their thinking. They might question the qualifications of an author or the accuracy of the information. They will compare this reading with other reading they have done. They may take some notes about their reactions to the reading.

Setting purpose, planning, flexibility, self monitoring, and reflecting are the strategies of an effective reader. In this chapter we will show how you can teach your students to become strategic readers.

PERFORMANCE OBJECTIVES

As a result of the learning experiences in this chapter, students will be able to:

1. Describe what happens when they read.

2. Recognize the different purposes for their reading.

3. Increase their reading rate.

4. Be flexible in their reading rate.

5. Reflect on their reading.

LEARNING EXPERIENCES

Topic 1: How Do You Read?

1. In this activity the students will discover what happens when they read. Have them choose an article or reading that is two or three pages long from a textbook. Give the following directions:

   • As you are reading try to determine what you do as you read.

   • How do your eyes move?

   • Do you look back? If so, why?

   • Do you look at every word, or do you read in phrases?

   • Do you sometimes skip words or miss a line?

   • Does your mind sometimes wander? What are you thinking about?

   • Do you sometimes stop and think about what you have read?

   • Do you look at pictures and headings before or after you read?

   • Do you remember what you read?

   As soon as your students have finished reading, have them write down everything they have noticed. Have them share their discoveries in small groups and discuss ways to improve.

2. The purpose of this activity is to show students how they read different materials in different ways. Bring in examples of the following materials and have students discuss how they would read each one:

   • Newspapers

   • Magazines

   • Paperback novels

   • Short stories

   • Directions, recipes

   • Textbook from different content areas

   • Road maps, charts, graphs

   • Personal letters

   Have students suggest other types of reading materials and discuss how they could read each type.

Topic 2: Setting Purpose

To teach students how to set a purpose for their reading, go over the following suggestions for students and hand out "How Will You Read It?" (Reproduction Page 57).

Tell students that when they are preparing to read, they need to consider these questions.

- *What Is Your Purpose?* Why are you reading this? How will you use the information?

- *What Is This Material Like?* Preview before you read to determine how difficult the material is for you and how it is organized.

- *How Fast Should You Read?* You will need to adjust your rate to your purpose.

- *When Should You Speed Up or Slow Down?* Examine the material to know when you can go fast and when you need to slow down because the material becomes difficult or you need to read for details.

This activity could be followed by practice using real materials gathered by the teacher or brought in by the students.

Topic 3: Reading Rate

1. Most students read everything at the same rate. The reading selection "A Symbol of the Free Spirit," Reproduction Page 58, can help your students see how fast they read.

   Before they begin this exercise, have students estimate how fast, in words per minute, the average high school student reads, and then have them guess how fast they read. This will develop a mind-set for the students to become aware of their own reading rate.

   Tell your students they are going to read a story to find out how fast they read. They should read it at their normal speed, without racing, because at the end they are going to answer ten comprehension questions. Write the times and words per minute. (Answer Key—Appendix B) on the board. When the students have finished reading ask them to look up, so you can point to their time. When all have finished, have the students determine their comprehension. Answer Key—Appendix B.

   When the students have finished, have them look at their rate predictions and guess again how fast the average high school student reads. Is it higher or lower than their first prediction? In fact, the average high school student reads at about 230 words per minute. This, of course, varies with the type and difficulty of material.

2. In the last exercise you had students estimate how fast the average high school student reads. The following questions are designed to help students learn something about the reading process and show them how fast they might expect to be able to read.

   - *How fast do you think the average adult reads?*

     The average adult reads at about 230 words per minute. That is the same rate as high school students read. Why is that? The average person is not taught how to read faster.

• *How fast do you think the average sixth-grade student reads?*

Again, about 230 words per minute. In about fifth grade average readers attain the speed they will have for the rest of their lives, unless they consciously learn to read faster.

Why do people read at 230 words per minute? Consider the following questions:

• *How fast do you think you could talk if you talked as fast as you could, saying one word right after another?*

Research has shown that people can talk as fast as 220 words per minute, although most people talk normally at about 100 words per minute, and some fast talkers can reach 400 words per minute and still be understood.

• *What does this tell you about your reading?*
You read about as fast as you can talk. In other words, you are talking to yourself as you are reading. Faster readers do not say words to themselves as they read.

• *What is the fastest a person could read?*

Some commercial courses claim that they can teach people to read at thousands of words per minute.

John F. Kennedy supposedly read at 1200 words per minute. He read a book a day even while he was in the White House. He had all of his cabinet take a speed-reading course.

Teddy Roosevelt was known to read at 1200–1500 words per minute.

Some people claim to read at 2500 to 3000 words per minute. It is difficult to turn pages any faster than that.

The supposed record under laboratory conditions is 52,000 words per minute, achieved by a woman with "photographic memory."

Many researchers argue that these people are not really reading, but merely skimming over the material. See Ronald P. Carver, "Speed Readers Don't Read; They Skim," *Psychology Today* (October 1972), pp. 84–105.

3. To find out how fast the average person can read, it is necessary to look at what happens when we read. The following exercise will help students understand how they read.

Tell students to take the first page of the article "A Symbol of the Free Spirit" or any other reading material. Using a pen or pencil, poke a hole about halfway down the page, big enough to hold up to their eye to look through. Have each student pair off with a classmate and sit across from each other. One student should hold up the article and look through the peekhole to observe what the other person's eyes are doing as he or she reads. After the first person has observed, the pair should exchange roles.

Now have them answer these questions:

• What happens when they read? How do their eyes move? Do they move smoothly across the page, or do they jerk? Do they sometimes look back?

How many times did they stop on each line? About how long did their eyes stop?

Here are the facts:

- You only read when your eyes stop. This is called a "fixation." To prove this to yourself, move your head quickly around the room. What did you see? A blur.

- You can only make about four fixations per second. This would equal about 240 fixations per minute. What does this tell us about how fast we read? We make a fixation on every word.

- The most your eyes can pick up on any one fixation is about seventeen letters. How many words would this be? About three. To prove this to yourself, open a book up to any page, close your eyes, point to a line, and blink. How much did you see?

- If we can make 240 fixations per minute, and the most we can see during one fixation is three words, then that would indicate that the fastest we could read would be about 720 words per minute.

- Most psychologists agree that it is physically impossible to "read" at more than 800 words per minute. Those who claim to read faster are skimming, which is an important skill for getting main ideas, but is not really reading.

One last question:

- *How fast can a person think?*
  Psychologists say that the average person thinks at about 1200 words per minute. This means that when you are reading at 230 words per minute you are only using one-fifth of your brain's capacity. It also explains why your mind tends to wander when you are reading slowly. As you increase your reading speed, you are using more of your brain. This forces you to concentrate, which helps to explain why increasing reading speed to 400–500 words per minute usually leads to improved comprehension.

4. The first thing you learned in giving the reading rate exercise was that all students do not read at the same rate. Although reading rate is sometimes related to intelligence, you probably noticed that some of your brightest students are slow readers. It is helpful for students to look at some of the causes of slow reading because many students can improve once they see what they are doing wrong.

   One word of caution: Students who have difficulty reading do not usually benefit from speed-reading. Those who have difficulty understanding will not be helped by being asked to misunderstand faster. A student should develop adequate vocabulary and comprehension skills before attempting to speed up the process.

   Hand out "The Causes of Slow Reading," Reproduction Page 59, and go over it with your students. Point out that they can overcome these problems once they have recognized them.

5. Once students have found their own reading rate and examined the causes of slow reading, they will want to know how they can learn to read faster. In

order to teach students to speed up their reading you will need a set of timed reading materials such as James Brown, *Efficient Reading,* and Edward Spargo and Glenn R. Williston, *Timed Readings.* The important features to look for in speed reading materials are interest, flexibility, and independence. Correction keys and progress charts are necessary for students to be able to use the materials and work at their own pace.

There is no real secret to speed-reading. In order to read faster you must push yourself, pace yourself, and, above all, avoid looking back. This will mean a loss of comprehension, initially, but, in the long run, both comprehension and rate will improve.

To begin, tell the students you want them to go back to first grade. They are going to point to the words or underline with their finger as they read. The purpose of this is to help them focus on the words as they begin to speed up. This finger underlining method is employed by many commercial speed-reading courses, and it is effective in helping students to overcome slow reading habits.

Using practice material they have already read, have students underline the first paragraph as they read it. Now pick up the pace. Using a pencil or stick, and tapping once each second (one thousand one . . .), have students try to read one line for each tap. Read two or three paragraphs this way. Then begin tapping a bit faster and faster, until you are tapping at half-second intervals (one thou-) by the end of the reading. Students will complain that they didn't understand a thing, but this is why they are reading a familiar article.

Next, have students read a new article from their practice materials. This time you will not tap, but students should underline with a finger, pushing themselves to read as fast as they can without losing the general thread of the reading. After this second reading they are ready to slow down and read one article for comprehension. They will probably discover that both their rate and comprehension have increased since their first reading. Continue going back and forth between reading for rate and reading for comprehension.

At the end of about ten class days of speed-reading practice give a "final exam" consisting of a typical selection from the practice material. Ask students to read as fast as they can while still reading for understanding. Most of your students will have doubled their reading rate and improved their comprehension. Once they have completed this unit, they should be given a timed reading about once a week to stay in practice. This could be a chapter from your textbook or articles relevant to your content.

6. The purpose of this activity is to help students improve their reading rate through everyday reading of paperback books. It is true that without training students will not increase their reading rate by simply reading more. But given the motivation to improve and a few simple techniques, students can use ordinary paperback books to double their reading rate.

Ask students to bring a paperback book to class. Any good novel will do, though it is best not to use anything too difficult or unusual in style.

Tell students about the many machines that have been invented to teach people to speed-read: *tachistoscopes* which flash words or phrases on a screen in a fraction of a second, *controlled readers* which unroll a story on the screen through a little window, and *reading pacers* which move a bar down a page at a specified rate, covering what you have read. Although these machines may help, they have several disadvantages: 1) they are cumbersome, so that you cannot carry them around with you; 2) they are not flexible, since they force you to read everything at the same rate; 3) they are expensive.

Tell your students that you can offer them a speed-reading machine that has solved all of those problems. It is inexpensive, lightweight, portable, and can be carried around in a pocket. It is flexible, in that it can speed up or slow down according to the type of material they are reading. It can also remember their place in the book and keep track of their reading times. It is called the Amazing Reading Machine.

What is it? Take out a 3" × 5" card and show them how it can act as the Amazing Reading Machine. First, they can use it as a reading pacer to cover what they have read. This will keep them from looking back, while reminding them to read faster. Second, it acts as a bookmark, keeping their place. And third, using the methods described in "How to Increase Your Reading Speed," Reproduction Page 60, it can be used to keep track of their progress as they move through the book.

Here is how the card should be set up:

	Your Name
Title, Author	
Number of Pages	Words Per Page
First Timing, WPM	Best Timing, WPM
Timings:	
1. Pages/Minutes	6.
2.	7.
3.	8.
4.	9.
5.	10.

Have the students do at least ten timings per book. If they do more they can put them on the back. They only need to compute their words per minute for the first timing and their best timing. Have students hand in this card when they report on their book.

7. As students practice speed-reading they often complain that they are losing comprehension, even when their comprehension test scores go up. The suggestions contained in "Speed With Comprehension," Reproduction Page 61, will help students focus on understanding as the main goal of reading, and show them how they can improve both speed and comprehension.

Topic 4: Flexibility

1. If someone were to ask you "How fast do you read?" you would know that he or she didn't really know much about reading. The strategic reader doesn't

read everything at the same rate, but has several different rates to call on as the task demands. Reading everything too rapidly would be just as inefficient as reading too slowly. The strategic reader develops *flexibility,* rather than just speed. As people read they are constantly shifting from one speed to another, depending on their purpose. If they just need to get the gist of something, they can read it much more rapidly than if they have to read carefully to remember. The difficulty or familiarity of the material will affect how fast or slowly we read. Students can be helped by teaching them "The Four Gears of Reading," Reproduction Page 62.

2. The flexible reader is able to shift from one rate to another within a single reading such as a chapter of a textbook or an article. To show students this, have them look at a chapter from a textbook and tell you which gear they would use for each of the following:

   • Surveying the chapter—Your purpose is to look over the entire chapter to get the general idea. (Reference Rate)

   • Chapter introduction—Your purpose is to get a general idea of what the chapter is about. (Rapid Reading)

   • The whole chapter—Your purpose is to understand the main ideas. (Moder-ate Reading Rate)

   • The first two paragraphs of a section—Your purpose is to get a good under-standing of what the section will be about. (Study Rate)

   • Paragraphs that give examples of main ideas—Your purpose is to get the general idea of the examples. (Rapid Reading)

   • A list of important points—Your purpose is to understand and remember these points. (Study Rate)

   • A specific name or fact—Your purpose is to find the answer to a question. (Scanning)

   • An insert or special section giving the background on a famous person— Your purpose is to have a general idea about this person, but you will not be tested on it. (Moderate Rate)

   • A chapter summary—Your purpose is to review the important points of the chapter. (Study Rate)

   • The whole chapter—Your purpose is to review the chapter for a test. (Rapid Reading)

   Students' answers may vary on this exercise, and they should be en-couraged to discuss the reasons for their choices. Students could also suggest other reading situations and how they would respond.

3. Skimming and scanning are useful rates for rapidly previewing material to get the main ideas or locate specific information. In order to help students see the advantages of skimming and scanning, have them do the following exercises:

   • Take an article from a newspaper and prepare five questions about the content. Tell the students the questions in advance. Then give them one minute to "read" the article for the answers.

- Prepare questions for a second article, but this time do not give them to the students in advance. Again give them one minute to "read" the article; then pass out the questions.

- Prepare ten or fifteen questions that require students to locate information on a newspaper page. Have a contest to see who can locate the information the fastest. When they find the information, students should raise their hands.

- Give students two minutes to preview a chapter in your textbook. Have them write an outline of the chapter from that survey.

- Tell students they will have twenty minutes to read a chapter completely. After five minutes, have them write down the main ideas of the chapter, and ask them for information they could only gain from skimming the chapter, including the summary.

4. The purpose of this activity is to help students see how study reading differs from other reading rates. Although students can learn to read at speeds of 400–500 words per minute with good comprehension, this will not substitute for slow careful reading when complete understanding and remembering of study material is required. A student cannot learn physics by skimming a science book. A true understanding of history cannot be achieved by rapid reading. It takes time to think about the ideas presented, weigh the arguments, and draw conclusions. If, as we said earlier, a person can think at about 1200 words per minute, and all of that thinking is focused on the ideas contained in the reading, then 230 words per minute may be too fast. It is a paradox that many of the undesirable factors that cause slow reading may be desirable when careful study reading is required.

For this activity have students read "Reading Paradoxes," Reproduction Page 63, and then discuss how they read when they have to know the material thoroughly. You could have them read a chapter for detailed comprehension, give a test, and then discuss how they went about studying the material. This activity could be done in small groups, or students could write about their study reading before they discuss.

Topic 5: Reflecting

1. Study reading requires students to reflect on their reading. This skill has been dealt with extensively in other chapters in this book (Chapters 6 and 9). It is important for students to see the relationship between setting purpose before reading, choosing appropriate reading strategies, and reflecting on the success of those strategies after reading.

Assign a typical chapter from a textbook, and promise them a detailed test when they have finished. Have students pair off and decide upon their purpose for reading. Then have them determine which strategies will be most effective for achieving their purposes. Then have them read the chapter.

When they have finished reading ask the groups to answer the questions in "How Did You Read This?" (Reproduction Page 64).

ASSESSING ACHIEVEMENT OF OBJECTIVES

The following suggestions may be used for evaluation or as learning activities:

1. Repeat the exercise "How Do I Read?" Specifically, note how your reading rate and flexibility have changed.

2. List ten different purposes for reading. Then tell what strategies you would use to achieve those purposes.

3. What is your current reading rate for reading exercises? What was your beginning rate? Has your comprehension gone up or down? Do you read faster or slower in your paperback book?

4. Name the four reading gears and give three uses for each. Tell how you use each of these reading speeds in your daily reading.

5. Tell how speed-reading and study reading differ. When is it important to reflect on your reading?

RESOURCES FOR TEACHING

Below is a selected list of resources for teaching the concepts and topics for this chapter. Addresses of publishers can be found in the alphabetical list in Appendix A.

Brown, James I. *Efficient Reading, Revised Form A and B.* Lexington, Mass.: D.C. Heath, 1976. College-level articles and challenging comprehension exercises make this ideal practice material for the college-bound student.

Carver, Ronald P. "Speed Readers Don't Read; They Skim," *Psychology Today* (October 1972), pp. 84–105. A discussion of the claims of commercial speed-reading courses.

Pauk, Walter. *How to Study in College.* Boston: Houghton Mifflin, 1984, "Improving Your Reading Speed," pp. 305–317. This offers sound advice on improving reading rate.

Rial, Arlyne F. *Speed Reading Made Easy.* Garden City, N.Y.: Dolphin Books, 1977. This offers a description of the reading methods used in commercial speed-reading courses.

Spargo, Edward, and Williston, Glenn R. *Timed Readings: Levels 1–8.* Providence, R.I.: Jamestown Publishers, 1975. Fifty 400-word passages with questions at each level for building reading speed.

12

Application to Content Areas

Beyond the elementary level students frequently experience education as fragmentation. At this point, they often have a different teacher for each subject and go to separately organized departments for their courses. Since the content and language are so different from science to accounting, English to industrial arts, the students do not perceive any connection. They experience each course in isolation so that education seems disjointed. What can unify these diverse elements so that students will perceive that learning how to learn in one course is relevant to their learning in another course, even if these courses differ in content?

In every course in each department the student uses the same instrument for learning—the human brain. Therefore, if I help a student know how to process information so that he can remember it in biology, variations of these same procedures are relevant for remembering in algebra or in social studies. Thus, for the students, improving learning process can be a unifying factor in education at the middle-school and secondary levels. The wisdom of this approach is captured in that old adage, "Give me a fish and I eat for a day. Teach me to fish and I eat for a lifetime."

This chapter, then, will focus on your role as a content-area teacher and the strategies and materials used by teachers. The latter are alphabetized by department.

ROLE OF THE CONTENT-AREA TEACHER

Why are you, the content-area teacher, the logical person to teach the skills needed by students for coping with the materials in your course? The teacher of science, foreign language, mathematics—the teacher in any content field—is in a unique position to help students because he or she is:

- Most concerned about creating student interest in that particular content.
- Most familiar with the technical vocabulary of that field.

- Most knowledgeable about the concepts crucial to understanding the subject.

- Most adept at analyzing the thought processes required for understanding.

- Most able to motivate student interest in study skills in a real situation.

- Most capable of reinforcing skill development through direct application within the class.

Whenever students enter the next higher level of education, they face the challenge of dealing with increasingly sophisticated materials and teachers' higher expectations. Meeting this challenge requires continuing refinement of learning-process skills through the help of each content-area teacher. How does each teacher become involved in helping students with the learning process so that these students are enabled to become independent learners? Interdepartmental sharing of the responsibility for teaching and reinforcing study skills is a logical approach. This cooperation results in less time used by each teacher for instruction, but more help for each student in his or her total program as teachers reinforce study skills taught in other departments.

STUDY SKILLS ACROSS THE CURRICULUM

What is a logical division of study-skill responsibility? In cooperative planning, each department may choose to give instruction on particular study skills. However, all teachers reinforce what is appropriate for their courses. At our school, materials from this book and other sources are shared so that each teacher has a file folder of materials on each study skill. *All* teachers know what each department is using for skill development so that they can reinforce each other.

Initially, the following division of responsibility for instruction was mutually agreed upon at the ninth-grade level. (Activities and materials from this book are used for teaching the skills.)

Responsibility for Instruction

How to organize time ⎫
                      ⎬ Mathematics
How to learn technical vocabulary ⎭

How to study a chapter ⎫
                       ⎬ Social Studies
How to concentrate ⎭

How to remember ⎫
                ⎬ English
How to analyze questions and write essay tests ⎭

How to take objective tests ⎫
                            ⎬ Science
How to listen and take notes ⎭

Within each department, other skills may also be developed that are particularly appropriate for that content area: how to write a laboratory report in science, how to practice for progress in music, how to get the most out of a demonstration in industrial arts, how to listen and follow directions in business education, how to organize a notebook in mathematics.

Focus of the Month

Throughout the country educators are concerned about the high dropout rate of high-school students, particularly minority students. What is becoming clear is that many of these students have a different cultural perspective on time. As a result, "date due" on assignments may not concern students. Many other students struggle with the problem of procrastination—intending to do their homework but somehow becoming distracted by other involvements.

   Implementing a schoolwide study skills program can give students the needed support for making a major behavioral change such as setting priorities for the use of their time. Since all teachers are involved, students become motivated to change. In conjunction with an author of this book, the total staff at Santa Barbara Junior High School in California developed the following program, "Focus of the Month," to help their students with time management:

PREP-TIME	• The mathematics teachers explain the program with the help of the handout "WHY BOTHER WITH A TIME SCHEDULE?" (Reproduction Page 11). When students take this home, parents see the purpose of the program.
	• The English teachers administer "HOW DO YOU ORGANIZE YOUR TIME?" (Reproduction Page 14), to diagnose students' current use of time.
	• The social studies teachers give assignment sheets with the following columns to all students: *Date, Assignment, Due Date, Study Time, Checkmark When Done,* and *Reward* or *Grade.* Students are encouraged to reward themselves when they finish an assignment. (The last four columns are very narrow.)
WEEK ONE	• The mathematics teachers give each student a file folder with two time schedules stapled together ("COPING WITH STRESS—SCHEDULING," Reproduction Page 12). On Chart 1 students record required classes and activities: music lessons, meetings, jobs, etc.
	• On Chart 2 each student draws a line diagonally across those times already scheduled. This leaves blank spaces for students' "free time."
	• Now students are ready to determine prime time to do homework or study for tests. On Chart 1 each student writes "Study" or "Review" in the time spaces he plans to use for that purpose. This is the "experimental schedule"; however, students need to compare daily the planned schedule with what really happens.

- Each day as students enter math class, they pick up their file folders with the time charts. On Chart 2 students record how they used their free time the previous day, i.e., baby-sitting, TV-viewing, talking on the telephone.

- Students then briefly compare the two charts and evaluate their time-plan for that day.

- Each day the teacher encourages the students in their efforts to get organized.

- After managing time for one week, students develop a schedule based on actual experience. The teacher interacts with the students as they plan their time for the following week.

WEEK TWO

- The students take their new schedules to social studies class where the teacher checks informally on their time management for the second week and hands out "TWELVE TIPS FOR STUDYING AND MANAGING YOUR TIME," Reproduction Page 16.

- Students then experiment with any of the suggestions to see what works for them.

- Students take home all handouts for parents to examine.

- On Friday the students share their tips and, if necessary, revise schedules for the third week.

WEEK THREE

- Students take schedules to science class where the teacher shares ideas of college students in the handout "TEN WAYS OF STUDY THAT WORK," Reproduction Page 69. The class begins to see what students at all levels experience as being helpful for learning. Science teachers encourage experimentation.

WEEK FOUR

- By the fourth week students realize that their achievement is affected by how they use their time. They are in control.

- The students take their time schedules to English class.

- The English teachers readminister "HOW DO YOU ORGANIZE YOUR TIME?," Reproduction Page 14. By comparing how they responded to the questions the first week, the students can now see improvements in their study habits and time use.

- The students place these pre- and postevaluations with their time schedules in the folder which is given to the guidance counselor. This becomes a resource for further helping each student.

REINFORCEMENT TIPS FOR ALL TEACHERS

1. Request students to write down any *assignment* you give and *when* they will do it. Using these special assignment sheets throughout the year will keep a continuing focus on setting priorities for use of time.

2. Be sure students know the *purpose* of an assignment, *what* to do, and *how* to do it.

3. Have students *begin* the assignment in class, if possible, and *estimate* time needed for finishing.

4. Take a few minutes for lively *reviewing* several times each week. Without review, students cannot remember. Experts estimate that 40 percent is forgotten by the second day and 60 percent by the fourth day.

5. Have students *map* (Chapter 7) chapter headings which are magnets for learning information in an organized way. This is the secret of retrieval and aids review.

6. *Positive expectations* inspire students to make needed changes. Anticipate that assignments will be done more regularly by your students. Cheer them on in every class!

Strategies and Materials

When a teacher assists students in developing effective study skills, the students perceive this teacher to be a caring person. Students expect teachers to focus on content, and therefore they are pleasantly surprised when a teacher wants to help them learn more efficiently as well.

Underlying the strategies and materials in this section is the philosophy that students' assessments of their own learning procedures are valuable. After students receive instruction and experiment with strategies for learning, they delight in sharing their insights. To expedite this process, for example, the last question on a chemistry test may be, "How did you study for this test?" At the end of a semester the teacher might ask, "What tips would you give other students for learning in chemistry?" The purpose of the questions is to keep the students evaluating what is helpful for learning so that their suggestions may be shared.

In this section we also include some teacher-made materials developed to meet the needs of students. These materials are in a continuing state of revision as students and teachers evaluate what enhances thinking and learning. Any of the strategies, procedures, or materials can be adapted to fit a variety of situations.

BUSINESS EDUCATION

Business teachers experiment with the activities and materials for teaching specific study skills that have already been presented in this book. They also assume responsibility for two skills necessary for success in business—the ability to listen attentively and the ability to follow directions meticulously. Since students often have problems with these skills, but seldom realize it, the following activities are used to heighten their awareness of the need to concentrate and think as they hear or read instructions. Then students themselves can help solve the problem.

Listening and Following Directions

These directions will be read once. After you have done what is asked, compare your drawing with that of another student.

- Draw a large circle.
- Draw a square within the circle with all four corners touching the circle.
- Divide the square into four equal squares.
- Draw a small circle around the central point touched by all four squares.
- Put a small x inside each small square without touching the sides of the squares.
- Draw a circle around each x without touching the sides of the squares.
- Fold the paper once lengthwise.

_____

Giving clear directions can be a real challenge. Ask a student to direct the class in drawing the diagram illustrated by Figure 12-1. Beginning with the top square, he or she is to note the relationship of each successive square with the preceding one. Directions for lines within the squares may be given last. After students quickly compare their diagrams, the presenter draws the figure on the board. Students may create similar direction experiences.

Figure 12-1. Diagram of squares.

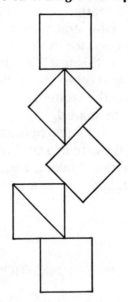

_____

Challenge your students to ignore what is nonsense but to follow specific directions in this activity. After reading the following four sentences of directions, ask the students to create as many sentence directions as possible in two minutes. These may be used at a later time to remind students to listen and to think.

1. Write your middle name even if the weather prediction is rain tonight.

2. If 12 × 2 equals 28, make a circle; if not, make a triangle.

3. Write the name of our school incorrectly.

4. If today is not Tuesday, draw a rectangle; if it is, write the word *car*.

To further develop the skills of listening and following directions, explain assignments once only. Questions of clarification may be honored, but do not indulge in sheer repetition. (Exceptions are made for students with special needs.)

When *all* staff members at our school cooperated in this effort, students started to take pride in their ability to listen and follow directions. Business persons voiced their support in classes they visited.

ENGLISH

The richness of literature is that it offers food for thought on many levels. Reproduction Page 65, "Profundity Scale for the Evaluation of Literature," is a kind of taxonomy of questions meant to draw out these various levels of meaning. Through our own and each student's awareness and application of these levels, more of the richness contained in short stories, essays, poems, and novels may be ours.

Experiences with literature beckon us to participate more fully in the human experience and, consequently, to journey into self-discovery. Thus, we are touched not only intellectually, but also emotionally. The "Taxonomy of Cognitive and Affective Dimensions of Reading Comprehension" recognizes that fact. Its four components—literal comprehension, inferential comprehension, evaluation, and appreciation—encompass simple to complex mental challenges and the personal dimension of appreciation. Applying this taxonomy and acquainting students with it assures a more student-centered, animated classroom atmosphere as well as diversity in classroom questions and activities that nurture students' intellectual development and their emotional growth.

Taxonomy of Cognitive and Affective Dimensions
of Reading Comprehension

Thomas C. Barrett[1]

1.0 *Literal Comprehension.* Literal comprehension focuses on ideas and information that are explicitly stated in the selection. Purposes for reading and teacher's questions designed to elicit responses at this level may range from simple to complex. A simple task in literal comprehension may be the recognition or recall of a single fact or incident. A more complex task might be the recognition or recall of a series of facts or the sequencing of incidents in a reading selection. Purpose and questions at this level may have the following characteristics:

---

1. Reprinted by permission of the author.

1.1 *Recognition* requires the student to locate or identify ideas or information *explicitly* stated in the reading selection itself or in exercises that use the explicit ideas and information presented in the reading selection. Recognition tasks are:

1.11 *Recognition of Details.* The student is required to locate or identify facts such as the names of characters, the time of the story, or the place of the story.

1.12 *Recognition of Main Ideas.* The student is asked to locate or identify an explicit statement in or from a selection that is a main idea of a paragraph or a larger portion of the selection.

1.13 *Recognition of a Sequence.* The student is required to locate or identify likenesses and differences in characters, times, and places that are explicitly stated in the selection.

1.14 *Recognition of Comparisons.* The student is requested to locate or identify likenesses and differences in characters, times, and places that are explicitly stated in the selection.

1.15 *Recognition of Cause-and-Effect Relationships.* The student in this instance may be required to locate or identify the explicitly stated reasons for certain happenings or actions in the selection.

1.16 *Recognition of Character Traits.* The student is required to identify or locate explicit statements about a character that help to point up the type of person he is.

1.17 *Recognition of the Author's Organization.*

1.2 *Recall* requires the student to produce from memory ideas and information explicitly stated in the reading selection. Recall tasks are:

1.21 *Recall of Details.* The student is asked to produce from memory facts such as the names of characters, the time of the story, or the place of the story.

1.22 *Recall of Main Ideas.* The student is required to state a main idea of a paragraph or a larger portion of the selection from memory, when the main idea is explicitly stated in the selection.

1.23 *Recall of a Sequence.* The student is asked to provide from memory the order of incidents or actions explicitly stated in the selection.

1.24 *Recall of Comparisons.* The student is required to call up from memory the likenesses and differences in characters, times, and places that are explicitly stated in the selection.

1.25 *Recall of Cause-and-Effect Relationships.* The student is requested to produce from memory explicitly stated reasons for certain happenings or actions in the selections.

1.26 *Recall of Character Traits.* The student is asked to call up from memory explicit statements about characters that illustrate the type of persons they are.

1.27 *Recall of the Author's Organization.*

2.0 *Inferential Comprehension.* Inferential comprehension is demonstrated by the student when he uses *the ideas and information explicitly stated in the selection, his intuition, and his personal experience as a basis for conjectures and hypotheses.* Inferences drawn by the student may be either convergent or divergent in nature, and the student may or may not be asked to verbalize the rationale underlying his inferences. In general, then, inferential comprehension is stimulated by purposes for reading and teachers' questions that demand thinking and imagination that go beyond the printed page.

2.1 *Inferring Supporting Details.* In this instance, the student is asked to conjecture about additional facts the author might have included in the selection that would have made the selection more informative, interesting, or appealing.

2.2 *Inferring the Main Idea.* The student is required to provide the main idea, general significance, theme, or moral that is not explicitly stated in the selection.

2.3 *Inferring Sequences.* The student, in this case, may be requested to conjecture as to what action or incident might have taken place between two explicitly stated actions or incidents, or he may be asked to hypothesize about what would happen next if the selection had not ended as it did but had been extended.

2.4 *Inferring Comparisons.* The student is required to infer likenesses and differences in characters, times, or places. Such inferential comparisons revolve around ideas such as: "here and there," "then and now," "he and he," "he and she," and "she and she."

2.5 *Inferring Cause-and-Effect Relationships.* The student is required to hypothesize about the motivations of characters and their interactions with time and place. He may also be required to conjecture as to what caused the author to include certain ideas, words, characterizations, and actions in his writing.

2.6 *Inferring Character Traits.* In this case, the student is asked to hypothesize about the nature of characters on the basis of explicit clues presented in the selection.

2.7 *Inferring the Author's Organization.*

2.8 *Predicting Outcomes.* The student is requested to read an initial portion of the selection, and on the basis of this reading, he is required to conjecture about the outcome of the selection.

2.9 *Interpreting Figurative Language.* The student, in this instance, is asked to infer literal meanings from the author's figurative use of language.

3.0 *Evaluation.* Purposes for reading and teacher's questions, in this instance, require responses by the student that indicate that he has made an evaluative judgment by comparing ideas presented in the selection with external criteria provided by the teacher, other authorities, or other written sources, or with internal criteria provided by the reader's experiences, knowledge, or values. In essence evaluation deals with judgment and focuses on qualities of accuracy, acceptability, desirability, worth, or probability of occurrence. Evaluative thinking may be demonstrated by asking the student to make the following judgments:

3.1 *Judgments of Reality or Fantasy.* "Could this really happen?" Such a question calls for a judgment by the reader based on his experience.

3.2 *Judgments of Fact or Opinion.* "Does the author provide adequate support for his conclusions?" "Is the author attempting to sway your thinking?" Questions of this type require the student to analyze and evaluate the writing on the basis of the knowledge he has on the subject as well as to analyze and evaluate the intent of the author.

3.3 *Judgments of Adequacy and Validity.* "Is the information presented here in keeping with what you have read on the subject in other sources?" Questions of this nature call for the reader to compare written sources of information, with an eye toward agreement and disagreement or completeness and incompleteness.

3.4 *Judgments of Appropriateness.* "What part of the story best describes the main character?" Such a question requires the reader to make a judgment about the relative adequacy of different parts of the selection to answer the question.

3.5 *Judgments of Worth, Desirability, and Acceptability.* "Was the character right or wrong in what he did?" "Was his behavior good or bad?" "What is your opinion of what Jack did at the baseball game?" Questions of this nature call for judgments or opinions based on the reader's moral code, value system, and personal criteria that have been internalized through experience.

4.0 *Appreciation.* Appreciation involves all the previously cited cognitive dimensions of reading, for it deals with the psychological and aesthetic impact of the selection on the reader. Appreciation calls for the student to be emotionally and aesthetically sensitive to the work and to have a reaction to the worth of its psychological and artistic elements. Appreciation includes both the knowledge of and the emotional response to literary techniques, forms, styles, and structures.

4.1 *Emotional Response to the Content.* The student is required to verbalize his feelings about the selection in terms of interest, excitement, boredom, fear, hate, amusement, etc. It is concerned with the emotional impact of the total work on the reader.

4.2 *Identification with Characters or Incidents.* Teacher's questions of this nature will elicit responses from the reader which demonstrate his sensitivity to, sympathy for, and empathy with characters and happenings portrayed by the author.

4.3 *Reactions to the Author's Use of Language.* In this instance the student is required to respond to the author's craftsmanship in terms of the semantic dimensions of the selection, namely, connotations and denotations of words.

4.4 *Imagery.* In this instance, the reader is required to verbalize his feelings with regard to the author's artistic ability to paint word pictures that cause the reader to visualize, smell, taste, hear, or feel.

Can exams serve as learning experiences for students in addition to being tools for evaluation? Unequivocally, yes!

Linking knowledge of various questioning taxonomies with a willingness to experiment, we teachers can create tests that allow our students to perceive new relationships among ideas and to gain new insights. Students will increasingly experience this kind of opportunity as we unleash our own imaginations in designing exam questions like the following.

Exam Questions Based on Keepers of the House[2]

1. Is Abigail justified in doing what she has just done to Robert? Explain your opinions with care.

---

2. Shirley Ann Grau, *Keepers of the House* (New York: Alfred A. Knopf and Random House, 1976). Susan Marie Erickson, teacher of English, creative writing, and independent studies in literature at LaFollette High School, Madison, Wis. Shared with Bragstad, January 1980.

2. If Grau had chosen to end the novel with the tea party, how would the meaning of the book change?

3. Does Grau succeed in making John a real person, or is he just a "bad guy"? Explain.

4. Is Abigail capable of killing? Explain, presenting evidence for your opinion.

5. If she had killed—she did put a couple of people in the emergency ward—how would she have dealt with if afterwards? (After all, her children are hidden, her grandfather and Margaret dead, and her love for John gone.)

6. What is your interpretation of Abigail's mysterious drive through the "twilight zone"?

7. If you were a Southerner, would you approve of this book? (If you like, you may distinguish among points of view of classes or races.)

8. Why does Grau include each of the following in the mob scene? What does each contribute to her picture of the South?

   a. the actions and words of Oliver Brandon

   b. the fact that one of the arsonists was only fifteen

   c. Abigail calls the arsonists mostly "good" people

9. In Abigail's last face-to-face meeting with John, he asks her a series of questions that she ignores or answers untruthfully. (Note: some of the answers are lies because they are incomplete.)

The question	The answer she gives	The answer she does not give
A. Where does Robert live?		
B. Why did William marry Margaret?		
C. Why did Robert come back?		
D. What did Robert and Abigail talk about?		
E. Why did Abigail take the children and run?		

FOREIGN LANGUAGE

Explain to the foreign-language students that they are already miracle workers. Despite a very serious handicap, each person in the class performed an astounding feat! What was done? The human brain is not fully developed until eighteen years of age; yet each person in the class learned to speak a foreign language before two years of age. Some may have learned Japanese; others, German. Everyone had the same handicap of a very underdeveloped brain, but everyone succeeded!

To stimulate thought about language learning, ask the students to list what helped them learn to speak their native languages when they were little children. Their responses may be shared and compared with the following summary.

How Did You Learn to Speak Your Native Language?
(Summary of student insights)

1. You were motivated. You felt the need to communicate and to be understood.

2. You wanted to understand others, so you listened very carefully to their speech.

3. You were surrounded by a loving, personal atmosphere of encouragement.

4. No one doubted your potential. Because your family was so certain that you would speak fluently in a matter of time, they were not disturbed when you spoke only individual words. They were so delighted that your first words were probably recorded in your baby book.

5. You had many models. Everyone around you was talking and often talked to you. Gradually you were absorbing the intonations and patterns of expression through listening and practice.

6. Your mistakes were tolerated—even enjoyed. In fact, many parents tape a child's unique mispronunciations for family fun years later. All the mispronunciations were looked upon as a temporary anomaly. No one was "uptight"; in fact, your errors simply provided the opportunity to clarify understandings so that you improved.

7. You kept practicing every day—including Saturday and Sunday. Friends and relatives expected to hear your progress whenever they came to visit.

8. Continuing positive responses from adults and your own satisfaction from learning kept you involved until you were a real "talker." You liked getting action in response to your requests.

Looking at the combined list of helpful factors, ask the students to make a corresponding list of what helps a student in learning to speak a foreign language. Now they can use a brain with thirteen billion brain cells—almost fully developed. What techniques would help them now?

_____

Distribute copies of Reproduction Page 66, "What Is Your Approach to Studying a Foreign Language?" Ask students to evaluate their current approaches. Later they may want to revise this instrument by adding some of their insights. Reproduction Page 1 also is helpful.

GUIDANCE AND COUNSELING

When a student is about to fail a course, he or she may make an emergency appointment with the guidance counselor. Before any extended discussion with the student, a guidance counselor may find it helpful to know about the student's study habits. The following brief checklist may aid you. It has been used in the following way: when 48 students in a class of 500 failed biology the first quarter, informal interviews were held with small groups of students to discover their modes of operation. Each student responded to the checklist and the items were discussed.

The investigation revealed that students did not study regularly outside of class, did not review, did not make specific preparations for examinations, did not study what they got wrong on a quiz or a test. However, with just a few exceptions, they did attend class, they did write down all assignments, they did know what would be covered in examinations. As long as they were doing some things right, these students did not seem to realize that they were causing their own failure by disregarding other important study procedures.

After the evaluation they knew what to change. The following quarter, 90 percent of these students passed. The other 10 percent (five students) had a serious attendance problem that was not solved. The investigation helped the teachers know what to emphasize in a preventive program. Inefficient study habits do have consequences. In cooperation with the teacher, guidance counselors often help students make necessary changes.

The following questionnaire helps students assess their needs.

What Needs to be Changed in My Study Habits?	Almost never	Less than half the time	More than half the time	Almost always
1. Do you study outside of class each day?				
2. Do you keep up to date in your assignments?				
3. Do you survey a chapter—check the headings, introduction, and summary—before reading it in detail?				
4. As you read an assignment, do you have in mind questions that you are actually trying to answer?				

(Continued)

What Needs to be Changed in My Study Habits?	Almost never	Less than half the time	More than half the time	Almost always
5. Do you try to get the meaning of important, new terms as you read the chapter?				
6. Do you recite to yourself at the end of each section in the chapter?				
7. Do you review regularly what you have covered in each course?				
8. Do you keep a well-organized notebook with sections for assignments, vocabulary, lecture notes?				
9. Do you write down all assignments for each class in a special section of the notebook?				
10. Do you know what will be covered in each test?				
11. Do you make specific preparations for tests?				
12. Do you study what you get wrong on a quiz or a test?				

For evaluation of a student's study skills, guidance counselors also may use "How Am I Doing?" Reproduction Page 1 (Chapter 1).

INDUSTRIAL ARTS

In order to help students assume responsibility for knowing necessary information, prepare study guides for the chapters to be studied in the textbook. The study guides may become more difficult as the semester progresses. As a result, the teacher actually sees his or her students improve in comprehending what they read. Here is the approach:

1. The teacher gives a demonstration that is closely observed by the students, who may take notes on the steps in the procedure.

2. The students go over the study guide with the teacher. This serves as a survey of the chapter so that the students know what they will learn. Technical vocabulary is taught through context clues, roots of words, demonstrations, and existing knowledge and experience of the students.

3. Students read and mentally recite at the end of each section in the chapter for the balance of the period or at home.

4. Students write responses to the study guide at home or at the beginning of the period the next day. Class time to work on the study guide is limited, though, to spur students to know the material well before coming to class.

5. No student begins his or her project until a perfect study guide is completed.

6. Responding to Reproduction Page 67, "Self-Evaluation Sheet for a Shop Project," provides the final answer to the question, "Are you ready to work in the shop?"

As a result of using this approach, an industrial-arts teacher reports that he has had fewer questions asked after shop work begins because the students are more knowledgeable, less "hassle" because the students are more purposeful, more rapid completion of the projects, and fewer injuries. The extra effort to make students accountable before beginning the project saves a great deal of teacher energy later, when students actually work in the shop. The teacher also observes real improvement in reading throughout the course of each semester.[3]

The following material is given to industrial-arts students to prepare them for learning from a demonstration.

Getting the Most Out of a Demonstration[4]

The demonstration is an important teaching and learning tool in industrial education.

Before the demonstration:

• Be ready to learn.

• Place yourself where you can see and hear.

---

3. Thomas Viken, industrial-arts teacher at LaFollette High School, Madison, Wis. Remarks to Bragstad, May 1977.
4. West High School Faculty, Georgia Cook, Reading Consultant, "A Study Skills Guide for West High Students" (Madison, Wis.: Madison Metropolitan School District, 1978).

- Don't expect to be bored, entertained, spoon-fed.
- Mentally review previous information on the demonstration.
- Know what the teacher expects you to learn.

During the demonstration:

- Watch and listen attentively. You will have to perform the steps being demonstrated at a later time.
- Watch for the important points of information.
- Ask questions if you don't understand the technical vocabulary or the process.
- Be alert to safety.
- Watch for major steps and their proper order.
- Observe changes in the material.
- Note specific tools and equipment and how they are used.
- Listen to the instructor's review.

After the demonstration:

- Mentally review the steps of the demonstration. Writing them out is the best way to review.
- Ask another student for additional help if you need it.
- Look up what you don't understand.
- Tie in new material learned with prior experiences.
- Make sure that you understand before you go further.

MATHEMATICS

In the fall when freshmen are asked to take notes in mathematics class, they often complain that they "can't listen and write at the same time." In the following needs assessment administered at the end of the semester, the teacher discovered that her insistence on students' taking notes paid dividends; in fact, students reported that notes on explanations are invaluable aids for learning. Not only does the teacher stay in touch with her students through this type of informal survey, but also the whole class discovers what is helpful.

Asking your students the following three questions can help you discover more about your students' learning in mathematics:

- What has helped you learn in this class?
- What has motivated you to do your homework?
- What changes should be made? Any suggestions for further help?

Categorizing Word Problems

One of the biggest challenges for students in algebra is solving word problems. When word problems are categorized into ten different types, the student is able to develop a framework of attributes for problems of each type. As a new problem is presented, the student can then analyze the type of this problem, and relate that determination to what he or she already knows about the process for that type of problem. In short, the student has an organized system of stored information for reference. Understanding and learning the process for different types of word problems provides a shortcut later for solving those word problems.

Giving students a handout containing an example of each of the following categories is helpful for algebra: number problems, age problems, value problems, geometry problems, distance problems, double-rate problems, digit problems, work problems, ratio problems, and solution problems.[5]

You may wish to make a transparency of the following information geared specifically to mathematics. Then students can compare methods for test-taking.

Test-Taking in Mathematics[6]

Before you start:

- Be prepared by studying before the test.

- Take notes when the teacher outlines the test.

- Know the teacher and what to expect from him or her.

- Pay attention to any additional test instructions from the teacher.

- Plan your time by looking over the entire test before beginning work on it, if you are permitted to do so.

- READ DIRECTIONS!

- Use a pencil, not a pen.

During the test:

- Write neatly and organize your thoughts. Partial credit may be given for an incomplete answer.

- Mark diagrams with given information, or make your own diagrams, charts, or drawings.

- Use some problems to help you answer others.

- Skip over problems that give you difficulty rather than waste time. Go back to them later.

- Reread each problem.

- Attempt a response for every problem; you have nothing to lose.

- Ask questions if you have trouble; your teacher might answer them.

- Check answers for reasonableness; for example, 4½ nickels? Bill weighs 850 lb.? The length of the rectangle is −24 cm.?

---

5. Wayne Halverson, mathematics teacher at LaFollette High School, Madison, Wis. Remarks to Bragstad, October 1974.
6. West High School Faculty, Georgia Cook, Reading Consultant, "A Study Skills Guide for West High Students."

After you finish:

- Check as much of the test as you can—especially the first few problems because you are more likely to make mistakes before you are "warmed up."

- Use all the time available; on a separate paper, rework problems of which you are unsure.

- Make sure that you haven't skipped any pages or sections or problems.

Using the Reproduction Pages on remembering (17–20; Chapter 4), have students experiment with these suggested approaches for three weeks. At the end of that time, ask students to respond to the following questionnaire:

> The differences in students' grades are frequently the result of differences in study habits. We want to share what is effective so that everyone can achieve.

> After three weeks of experimentation on remembering, what have you tried that has helped you remember what you needed to know?

When teachers and students cooperate in experimenting with effective strategies for learning how to learn, positive changes are reported: improved grades and increased knowledge of how to study are two of the most significant changes. For example, in an exploratory study at our high school involving twenty-five students in an experimental group and twenty-five students in the control group having the same teacher in geometry, the experimental group tried various strategies for learning over a period of three weeks. They not only became more knowledgeable about the learning process and study techniques but also improved their grades.

> The average number of study approaches listed by the experimental group nearly tripled, but increased only slightly for the control group.
>
> In comparing the quarter grades of the experimental group in geometry with their grades the previous quarter, it was discovered that twelve students raised their grades, nine students remained the same, and two students received lower grades. In the control group, two students raised their grades, sixteen students received the same grade, five students received lower grades, and two students dropped out of the course.
>
> Twenty-three of twenty-five students in the experimental group volunteered positive reactions on the postquestionnaire to the work on study skills; all the students strongly urged that this project should be conducted in every geometry class at the beginning of the school year.
>
> Although students differ in the way they intellectually approach learning in geometry, certain strategies were found to be effective by many of the students experimenting with the learning process in the following areas:
>
> - *What techniques help you learn vocabulary?* (1) Using the "divided-page" method, in which the term is written on one side and the meaning on the other half of the sheet; (2) reviewing every day by reciting to myself, since frequent review results in long-term memory; (3) noticing bold-print terms and their significance in meaning for the assignment; (4) taking notes on new concepts in class; (5) sitting in a quiet room and thinking out the meaning of the concepts, then drawing diagrams to check understanding.

- *How do you become skilled in the thinking process necessary for doing geometry?* (1) Making sure that I know whatever thinking is required, then simply making up problems similar to that one (to practice the thinking process) and doing those until I am positive that I know the thought process; (2) thinking everything out logically and continuing to read problems to drill thought processes into my brain; (3) after reasoning problems out, using figures or drawings to clarify the process; (4) thinking through a problem before writing anything down, since doing the problems is a test of my understanding of the processes involved; (5) being aware of thinking in all my classes so I see relationships in kinds of thinking done with different materials.

- *What helps you to remember?* (1) Understanding what I learn, so logic is clear; (2) using what has been learned; (3) reviewing frequently; (4) seeing relationships of one idea to another so I have a visual structure in my mind; (5) knowing what I am doing and why.

- *If you have difficulty in reading or in understanding geometry, what helps?* (1) Breaking down the reading material until I understand each part better; (2) studying examples or diagrams more carefully; (3) going back to where I understand, starting over again, reading carefully, and reasoning it out; (4) making sure I understand the vocabulary, since so much is built on this; (5) consulting with a friend or the teacher.

- *How do you prepare for tests?* (1) Doing work daily, no cramming but frequent review; (2) getting everything organized—vocabulary sheets, class notes, daily work, and quizzes—before reviewing each separately, and then putting it all together; (3) testing myself on material over and over; (4) checking with friends on important parts; (5) studying ahead of time to avoid test panic.

Indeed, these concrete responses obviously indicate that students have become very interested in the thinking process itself. Some were looking for additional information on the brain. Others were curious about abstract thought and its relationship to intelligence. All had become *aware of* alternative strategies for learning.[7]

MUSIC

Before human beings could read or write, they made music! In its sound and movement music communicates from age to age.

The performing musician must have such a grasp of "the thought, the picture, the feeling, the sound" of the music to be performed that he feels a need to communicate, to share the synthesis of sound, movement, thought, and feeling with others—until they too experience "becoming" through music.[8]

For the musician a composer suggests dynamics through specialized vocabulary terms like *brilliante, adagio, dolce*. These dynamics contribute to the richness of the musical experience. As students learn the meanings of these interpretation and direction words, they feel less uncertain and more capable of entering into the musical experience envisioned by the composer. The meaning of this specialized vocabulary must be stored in the long-term memory so that it is available for immediate recall as one sings or plays the music.

7. Bernice Bragstad, "Teaching Students How to Learn," *Journal of Reading* 19, no. 3 (1975): 226–230.
8. Rodney Witte, director of choirs, LaFollette High School, Madison, Wis. Remarks to Bragstad, February 1980.

The format of the "Musician's Vocabulary" presented in this section was designed for developing long-term memory through frequent reciting and review. All terms are listed alphabetically. The students do not study all the terms at once. Instead, as the terms appear in the music being rehearsed, they record the abbreviations; then by covering the definitions or the terms, the students can quickly quiz themselves in odd moments that ordinarily are wasted. Later, students can test themselves by looking at the definitions only and writing the abbreviations in the right-hand column.

As the terms are learned, the students may make a categorized list of all terms related to particular dynamics, such as increasing volume or quickening tempo. Making associations with other terms of differing degree in the same category refines the definition and strengthens long-term memory.

The following sample shows how a band director adapted the "divided-page" approach after geometry students highly recommended this method as the best way to learn technical vocabulary:

Musician's Vocabulary[9]

Say it	Abbrev.	Define it	Write it
Ac'ce'le'*ran*'do		Gradually faster	
A'*da*'gi'o		Very slowly, leisurely	
Adli'bi'tum		At the pleasure of the performer	
A'gi'*ta*'to		Restless, with agitation	
Al'le'*gret*'to		Moderately fast, slower than Allegro	
Al'*leg*'ro		Lively, brisk, rapid	
An'*dan*'te		Moderately slow	

You may find the following handout a boon; it captures the flavor of a good rehearsal.

In Class—Rehearse for Results

The rehearsal is a growth experience—not a recreational sing or jam session. Make the right things happen through active involvement. Approach the music with a positive attitude. If a piece lacks appeal to you on the first reading, work to find the music in it. Be excited about the potential of new musical adventures; there's very little growth in repetition of old habits. Here are some points to ponder when rehearsing for results:[10]

1. Have some idea what the music is going to sound like before you play or sing; learn to listen for everything, not just yourself.

2. The conductor must have your eyes before the music begins, especially if you begin with "rests."

---

9. James L. Knutson, "Musician's Vocabulary," band director at LaFollette High School, Madison, Wis. Shared with Bragstad, May 1976.
10. Frederick Fennell, "Points for Performance" (Omaha, Neb.: Used courtesy of Progress Publications, Inc.)

3. Prepare! Be ready! Listen!

4. Play or sing with intensity. Use breath support. Keep your stomach in it.

5. Learn to look at the conductor at least once every bar in music of a slow pulse, frequently in music of a rapid pulse. Listen!

6. Music is also a waiting game. Wait for "one!"

7. Vibrate! Music is controlled and ordered vibration. You must make it a vibrant sound; support your sound constantly.

8. Pulse is music's life blood as well as yours. Learn to feel it, for it is always present.

9. Learn to listen and look for the phrase. Listen for phrase endings.

10. Help stamp out mechanical error—listen!

11. Don't repeat your mistakes; they become a disease!

12. The group that plays together stays together.

13. Get it the first time—get it right—listen!

14. You can read a piece of music for the first time only once; make that one memorable.

15. Constantly widen your range of dynamics.

16. At a pianissimo release, let the sounds evaporate.

17. When the dynamic is fortissimo, hear only yourself; when the dynamic is pianissimo, hear only your neighbors.

18. Uncontrolled silence is the energy of music. Listen!

19. The group that breathes together, plays or sings together.

20. Music is not an art for the chicken-hearted. Seek what is right, but don't be afraid to be wrong.

21. The music turns you on, but only you can wind yourself up for it.

22. Give all your energies to performance.

23. Seek the style of the music; this you can only do by listening to and for everything.

24. Good performances are planned that way.

_____

When a group of students excel in a musical performance, we need to know what dynamics make this moving experience possible. These were the questions posed and a few of the responses from members of a choir who learn the words and music of approximately seventy selections each year:[11]

1. What motivates you to learn the words and music of so many selections?

   • "Feelings of group responsibility with everyone working hard."

_____

11. Survey by Bragstad in choir directed by Rodney Witte, LaFollette High School, Madison, Wis., November 1980.

- "Living up to the high expectations of the director."
- "Memorizing the music quickly so that we have more time to work on the quality of sound."
- "Feeling the response of the audience when we sing."
- "More freedom in expressing the music when we know it well."

2. What teacher qualities help you achieve at this high level?

- "Having the director believe in what we can do so that we expect perfection from ourselves."
- "Impatience in wanting quality but patience in helping us learn."
- "Really caring about everyone—not just a number in the grade book."
- "Identifying the problems in our singing but helping us until they are solved."
- "Knowledge, enthusiasm, sense of humor, and love of music."

3. Specifically what techniques helped you memorize the music?

- "Reviewing every night until I move beyond memorizing to knowing and living the music."
- "Being interested in what I'm singing—the meaning of the song."
- "Remembering major points of rehearsals and incorporating those into my practice."
- "Associating words with the feeling the song is expressing so that the mood of the music helps in remembering the words."
- "Sectional practices where we help each other."

Administering a similar survey to your students can spark discussion and students' awareness that what works in one class may also work in another. Share all the comments from your survey; this helps the students see why they are having a meaningful learning experience in music. (Over 90 percent of the students in our study mentioned continuous review and practice.) Discuss with students which memory techniques or approaches would be helpful in other courses.

PHYSICAL EDUCATION

As the five sophomore athletes walked into the elective Reading Improvement class in September, they appeared to be on a special mission. A moment later, they informed the reading teacher, "Mr. Maas advised us to take this course. When the time comes that we are on the varsity football squad, we may not have as much time to study. Mr. Maas said we should improve our reading and study skills this year." Who is Mr. Maas? He is the varsity football coach who talks to every freshman boy participating in football who is below the fortieth percentile in reading. Talking to all these boys individually takes time. The varsity football coach works only with juniors and seniors in football, so the freshman boys feel honored to have any attention from him. Parents report a corresponding increase in motivation to learn and to improve in reading.

Physical-education teachers and coaches must acknowledge all the "clout" they have with students. Students' academic problems have been solved because of the interest, the words of encouragement, the follow-up by these important staff members. The sophomore boys report their reading scores to Mr. Maas at the end of the year.

The coaches want to be sure that students are equipped for further education and are able to accept any college scholarships that they may be offered. They encourage students to take advantage of the opportunity to take Efficient Reading, an elective course for upperclassmen. The course focuses on vocabulary development, comprehension, study skills, reading rate, and extensive reading of books.

To be certain that all students have an opportunity to do extensive reading during the summer, the physical-education teachers invite students to fill out city library card applications. The teacher is listed as a personal reference. The students receive their library cards in the mail. Then they are ready to check out books recommended on the "Students' Favorite Book List" provided by the English teachers for summer reading.

During the Reading Break described in the next chapter, the physical-education teachers do not permit the students to get dressed for class until after the fifteen minutes of reading. Where do they read with their students? Sitting on the floor, leaning against the wall in the field house, on the bleachers in the gymnasium, in the spectators' section around the swimming pool, on the pads in the wrestling and weight-lifting room. All these teachers and coaches model lifelong learning through reading for fifteen minutes every day with their students.

For a check of both students' attitudes and procedures, you may wish to develop a survey instrument similar to the following:

Self-Evaluation Checklist for Physical Education

As you evaluate your attitude, your preparation, your performance, you will gain insight on ways that you can improve. Assuming responsibility for your own progress is a sign of maturity. The items on this checklist have been suggested by students. After reading each item, rate yourself from 1 to 5 in the space before the numeral.

1	2	3	4	5
Excellent	Good	Fair	Poor	Unsatisfactory

Our goal? Naturally, everyone wants to be "Number One"!

_____ 1. Do you come to class ready to learn and to participate?

_____ 2. Do you focus complete attention on explanations or directions given by your teacher?

_____ 3. As you listen carefully, do you visualize what is being explained?

_____ 4. Do you know what your teacher expects you to learn?

_____ 5. Do you place yourself in a position where you can observe the teacher?

_____ 6. Do you ask questions when you don't understand?

_____ 7. Do you study the motor-skill guide for the activity in which you are involved?

_____ 8. Do you mentally simulate the activity while reading the motor-skill guide?

_____ 9. Do you discuss what you read with other students?

_____10. Do you review what you learn each week?

_____11. Do you predict questions that may be asked on an examination?

_____12. Do you make specific preparations for an examination?

_____13. Do you study what you get wrong on a test?

_____14. As you participate in activities, do you mentally note how you can improve?

_____15. Do you strive to do the best that you are capable of doing?

Please list ways that you can improve in attitude, preparation, or performance.

SCIENCE

The following information sheet given to each student in biology is to be signed by parents and returned:

Reading and Learning Process Emphasized in Biology

Study skills

1. Understanding how the brain functions in learning

2. Developing purposes for reading or learning

   • What you are to do or learn (content)

   • Why you are to do it (motivation)

   • How you are to do it (skills)

3. Using a textbook effectively

   • Table of contents

   • Use of right approach in studying a chapter

   • Use of graphic aids (charts, diagrams, illustrations)

4. Taking lecture notes

5. Taking examinations

6. Reading and following directions

7. Locating information in the Science Resource Center

8. Experimenting with "Ten Ways of Study That Work" (Reproduction Page 69)

Reading skills

1. Developing vocabulary (context clues, roots, and affixes)

2. Finding the main concepts

3. Determining and remembering supporting details

4. Understanding organization or major patterns of writing in science

- Enumeration

- Classification

- Generalization

- Problem solution

- Comparison or contrast

- Sequence

5. Drawing conclusions

The Learning Center

About two hundred upperclassmen recommended by the faculty are on the tutoring staff of the Learning Center. Any student can get immediate help in any subject by going to the Learning Center whenever he or she begins to have difficulty. Each period an English teacher is in the Writing Workshop to assist students with any writing assignments. The Learning Center and the Writing Workshop have been designed to help students learn more, enjoy it more, and improve their grades!

To the parents: For six years faculty members at LaFollette have been developing this program on reading-learning process coordinated across departmental lines. The science teachers reinforce study skills taught by history teachers, and vice versa. We are all working together. All teachers know what is being emphasized in each class the freshmen have. With the help of upperclassmen in the Learning Center, each freshman has the opportunity to get additional help on a one-to-one basis. We hope to tell you more about it on "Go to School" night.

Signature of parent _____

Students feel more secure when they know a teacher's expectations.

Laboratory and Classroom Expectations[12]

1. You will be expected to purchase a separate spiral-bound notebook to be used just for Biology I, and a pocket folder for course handouts. Both are available in the school store. Your name, Biology I, and the hour you have class should be printed neatly on the inside of the front cover of your notebook and folder.

2. You will be expected to attend class every day with your notebook, pocket folder, and a pencil.

3. Notebook Organization: Since it is impossible for you to remember all of the details of what is said in class each day, a notebook can be a valuable aid to you. If, however, notes are taken in the front of the notebook one day, and in the back the next, your notes will be worthless. You must keep up your notebook in an orderly fashion so that you can easily find the information at a later date. Notebooks should be organized as follows:

• Assignments: Write *Assignments* at the top of the first page of your notebook, and save the first five pages just for the purpose of writing down the assignments your teacher explains and writes on the board.

• Vocabulary: Write *Vocabulary* at the top of the sixth page of your notebook, and save five pages for this section. Most scientific terms contain similar roots and prefixes. For example, what do all of these terms have in common?

thermometer	thermal pollution
thermos bottle	thermostat
diathermy	exothermic
thermistor	

Answer: They all have to do with heat, since they all contain the root *therm*—which means heat in Latin. Even though you may not know what most of these words mean, you could know something about them from the root *therm*. Your teacher will talk about roots and prefixes throughout the course, and by keeping them in one section of your notebook, you will find understanding new scientific terms a much easier task. Use the "divided-page" approach you learned in math with the term only in the left-hand column and the definition in the right-hand column. Recite to yourself as you cover one side.

• Class Notes and Lab Reports: The remainder of your notebook is reserved for sequential entry of your daily activities in class. Every day you should prepare for the start of the class period by opening your notebook to the page where you left off the day before and put the date in the left-hand column. If you have a lecture that day, you take notes on that page; if you see a film, you take notes there; if you have a lab activity, you organize your lab report there. Lab reports should be organized as follows:

1. Date and title

2. Purpose

3. Condensed procedure

4. Data and graph (if required)

---

12. Steven P. Lanphear and Paul du Vair, former biology teachers at LaFollette High School, "Lab and Classroom Expectations." Shared with Bragstad, May 1977.

5. Answers to questions

6. Summary (What did you learn?)

In the back of your notebook, reserve a twelve-page study-skills section.

Taking Lecture Notes[13]

Most students know they should take notes in class, if only to impress the instructor, but many don't know how to go about it. They take either too many or too few notes, and they may not record what is important. Taking lecture notes is an art that must be developed by practice. It requires effort and an alert mind. As soon as possible after class, you need to edit and sometimes to rewrite sections of your notes. Good lecture and classroom notes can be the key to remarkable improvement.

1. *Surveying.* As soon as you get to class, open your notebook to the page where you finished writing the previous day. Record the date in the left-hand column on the next page. Naturally you cannot survey a lecture in advance unless the instructor does it for you. Many teachers do give a preview of what they will be saying. When one does, be alert and make notes very rapidly on the points he or she is going to cover. Thus you will know what to expect and you will have a better idea of what is important.

2. *Questioning.* A questioning attitude will help you focus your mind on what is happening in the class. What is being said about the topic? What is the purpose of the lab? The more you involve yourself, the more you will gain from the class.

3. *Listening.* In class you listen, and you listen hard. Since there is no opportunity to hear the lecture a second time, each moment you must absorb and evaluate everything you hear. You must listen to the total lecture to determine what is important and what is not important.

4. *Organizing.* Somehow or other you must understand and note the organization of what the teacher is saying. This is the same as noting the headings in a book, only in a lecture you must often figure out for yourself what the headings are. Some teachers use the blackboard to write down the topics they are talking about. If so, fine. It will provide the skeleton for your notes. If not, you must somehow determine the outline for yourself. Sometimes this is almost impossible and you will have to write down all that seems to be important and then organize it after class. Remember to have a 2½" margin on the left-hand side of each page for organizing and listing the main concepts.

   Even the most disorganized teacher usually gives you many clues to his organization if you recognize and make use of them. Clues may be as follows:

   • The main point is this . . .

   • Note this . . .

   • Remember this . . .

   • This is what I'm leading up to . . .

   • This is the core of the chapter . . .

---

13. Ibid.

Another clue may be the mere repetition of a statement. If the teacher takes the trouble to say something twice, he must think that it is important. Sometimes the teacher may say the same thing in two or three different ways, which is a kind of repetition, and this may be your clue.

When a teacher suddenly slows down and says something as though he especially wants you to get it, the statement is probably important. If his voice changes in tone or volume, this gives the statement emphasis that signals an important point.

Finally, here are some "Do's and Don't's of Organization":

Do . . .

• Try to understand the teacher's style of lecturing.

• Search for clues to the organization.

• Leave space between the teacher's main points.

• Notice when the teacher gives you a precise statement and take it down word for word.

• Boil down what is said into the major concepts and record in the left-hand margin after the lecture.

Don't . . .

• Don't spend so much time trying to take neat, well-written notes that you lose the point of the lecture.

• Don't make the error of taking too few notes in class or you may never regain what you have lost.

• Don't hesitate to compare your notes with those of a classmate or to ask the teacher for help.

5. *Reviewing and revising.* Your lecture notes, unlike your textbook, may be incomplete when the lecture is finished. It is, therefore, necessary to review them carefully. Your first review should be right after the lecture or within a few hours. At that time much of what the teacher said is still fresh in your mind, and you can fill in essentials that you did not include in your notes. You can even correct errors that crept in by writing something down hurriedly or before you understood it. Record major concepts in the left-hand margin. If you wait too long to revise your notes, you may say, as many students have, "My lecture notes just don't make sense." After revision, review your notes frequently. You build on this information as you continue to learn in the course.

Self-evaluation helps students become independent learners. After students have used Reproduction Page 68, "Self-Evaluation Sheet for Reading Laboratory Procedures," ask for their reactions to the instrument. When they are involved in discussion of the process, they participate more fully in the evaluation.

SOCIAL STUDIES

"Ten Ways of Study That Work," Reproduction Page 69, is a concrete guideline for students to be efficient as they learn. It may be handed out in every freshman social-studies class each fall, as we do at our school, or it may certainly be used by any individual teacher as a ready guide to help students. We suggest reinforcing the content with occasional "checks" to see if students are actually keeping a class notebook with assignments listed, etc. Students seem to appreciate the fact that their social-studies teacher is so interested in helping them "get it together" for study success.

Having students respond to Reproduction Page 70, "Getting to Know Each Other," can help you know students personally. The students share responses in small groups so that they become acquainted in a different way. Our action research indicates that students discuss more freely in class when they are comfortable with each other.

At the end of the first quarter, social-studies teachers administered the "How Am I Doing?" questionnaire on Reproduction Page 1 to freshmen. On the Answer Key the freshmen circled the questions that were incorrect according to study experts. Then they circled those question numbers on the chart "What Are My Strengths and Weaknesses?" If a student had the most wrong on concentration, he or she reviewed those questions to see what changes he or she needed to make. Then each teacher asked students to respond to the following questionnaire to be kept by the teacher:

Name _____ Home Room _____

Social-Studies Teacher _____ Period _____

Grades for first quarter:

English	_____	Science	_____
Social Studies	_____	Mathematics	_____

Study-Skills Areas of Need:

1.

2.

Actions I plan to take for improvement this quarter:

1.

2.

3.

The students wrote the above information on the back of the questionnaire "How Am I Doing?" before taking the questionnaire home to be read and signed by their parents. The principal had informed the parents that they would be receiving the results of the study-skills evaluation. Their enthusiastic response encouraged the teachers.

Teachers compliment the students on any improvement and help them monitor their grades as well as their methods of study throughout the quarter.

Finding different ways of reinforcing study skills is always a challenge! In the sophomore year audiovisual materials on study skills from the Center for the Humanities (Resources for Teaching, Chapters 8 and 9) effectively reinforce previous instruction. However, regardless of what materials are used, student involvement is the key. As students experiment with any suggestions, they discover what is effective for them; thus, each student consciously develops his or her own learning style.

RESOURCES FOR TEACHING

Below is a selected list of materials and resources for teaching reading and study strategies in various content areas. A review of the "Resources for Teaching" section in other chapters may lead to the identification of additional materials that can be used for this same purpose. Addresses of publishers can be found in the alphabetical list in Appendix A.

Books, Pamphlets, and Articles

Christ, Frank L., ed. *SR/SE Resource Book.* Chicago: Science Research Associates, 1969. A general study-skills book that addresses time management, memory, SQ3R, marking a book, concentration, note-taking, and test-taking, plus other dimensions.

Herber, H. L. *Teaching Reading in Content Areas.* Englewood Cliffs, N.J.: Prentice-Hall, 1970. Emphasizes methods and materials for helping students acquire the skills they need for adequate study of all their subjects. According to the author, the focus is on showing the learner "how to do what is required of him and do it in such a way that he develops an understanding of the process."

Hoitsma, Virginia L. et al. *Understanding Psychology.* New York: CRM/Random House, 1977. Presents learning and cognitive processes, the workings of the mind and body, human development and human relations.

Pauk, Walter L. *How to Study in College.* 3rd ed. Boston: Houghton Mifflin, 1984. Provides practical study techniques for taking notes, remembering, reviewing for exams, and other areas of need. Much information based on years of experience with helping students. Excellent resource book for college-bound students and for teachers of study skills in any content area.

Robinson, H. Alan. *Teaching Reading and Study Strategies: The Content Areas.* Boston: Allyn and Bacon, 1978. Emphasizes the specific teaching and learning of significant reading and study strategies applied to the patterns of writing used in various content areas. The purpose is to help students become independent learners.

Shepherd, David L. *Comprehensive High School Reading Methods.* Columbus, Ohio: Charles E. Merrill, 1973. Provides a detailed description of the relationship between reading and learning in the content-area class. Along with activities for vocabulary development in all content areas, methods for helping students relate new terms to known experiences are included. A variety of reading-study techniques are described.

Smith, C.; Smith, S.; and Mikulecky, L. *Teaching Reading in Secondary School Content Subjects: A Bookthinking Process.* New York: Holt, Rinehart & Winston, 1978. The focus of this book is to teach students to read and to learn from subject-specific texts. Bookthinking is the ability to extract information and interact reasonably with a written message. Procedures are given for helping students process information in various content areas.

Smith, Donald E. P. *Learning to Learn.* New York: Harcourt, Brace, Jovanovich, 1961. Focuses on SQ3R, test-taking, how to read, learning styles for subject areas, and timed readings. Interesting material for college-prep reading course.

Spargo, Edward. *The Now Student.* Rev. ed. Providence, R.I.: Jamestown, 1977. Intended for junior-college freshmen; especially readable text. Contains articles on memory, concentration, listening, note-taking, test-taking, rate, among others. Cloze test and suggested activities follow each chapter.

Thomas, Ellen Lamar. *Reading Aids for Every Class: 400 Activities for Instruction and Enrichment*. Boston: Allyn and Bacon, 1980. A windfall of ready-to-use ideas on study skills, such as adjusting reading rate, organizing time, streamlining study, learning vocabulary, finding the main ideas in paragraphs, attacking words. Master Copy Pages that can be duplicated in any quantity make this book especially helpful for teachers in all subject areas.

Thomas, Ellen Lamar, and Robinson, H. Alan. *Improving Reading in Every Class: A Sourcebook for Teachers*. Boston: Allyn and Bacon, 1972. Provides a wide variety of helps for content-area teachers; motivating activities, teaching procedures, practice exercises, and many enrichment activities.

13

Total School Programs and Results

Recent research indicates that "positive reading habits and attitudes seem to deteriorate with each successive year students spend in school."[1] What are the consequences? When students are not in the habit of reading and do not enjoy reading, a study-reading assignment is a grim task—an obedience exercise to be endured. Because of students' negative attitudes toward reading and the probability that many students will not or cannot read assignments, teachers may resort to lecturing instead of asking students to learn through reading. As a result, students have less chance to practice reading—less chance to improve. How can we help our students learn to enjoy reading and to read more effectively when they study?

In this chapter two programs, the Reading Break and the Learning Center, effective adjuncts to the total school study-skills program, are presented. Then the tangible and intangible results of these programs are reported.

THE READING BREAK

As educators we have faith in what teachers can do for students, but we often underestimate what students can do for themselves—if they acquire the reading habit. The "complex interaction" of many thought processes necessary for reading effectively and fluently must be developed by the students themselves through the experience of reading, and reading, and reading some more. Without practice, improvement is limited and is likely to be temporary in nature.

---

1. G. Bullen, *The Development and Validation of a Reading Attitude Measure for Elementary School Children.* (Washington, D.C.: Office of Education Project No. 1 A045, 1972. ERIC Document Reproduction Service No. ED 109 211); see also L. Mikulecky, *The Developing, Field Testing, and Initial Norming of a Secondary/Adult Level Reading Attitude Measure That Is Behaviorally Oriented and Based on Krathwohl's Taxonomy of the Affective Domain.* Unpublished doctoral dissertation, University of Wisconsin-Madison, 1976.

After a basketball team won the state tournament, the coach reflected that "after the first three weeks of the season, only 10 percent of the time was used for instruction, 90 percent for practice."[2] He helped the faculty to recognize the crucial importance of practice for improvement in reading. Students' inability to read effectively and to enjoy reading may be the result of little practice rather than lack of instruction. What interferes with this practice of reading?

We must recognize that, outside of school, reading or studying of any kind has strong competition today. Middle-school and secondary students have many options available for the use of their time. Frequently they feel pressured and torn emotionally as they choose among all the alternatives.

What dominates students' time today? What competes with time for studying or reading outside of school? Talking on the telephonre and socializing. Increased participation in sports and other activities. Driving around in their cars. One reality: the number of students working has increased dramatically. Concerned about students' lack of time for study, a gifted teacher surveyed her honors English class of seniors; as anticipated, she discovered that 90 percent of her students were employed 20 to 40 hours per week. Many students leave school early in the afternoon to begin working. This is a developing phenomenon, originating in the last decade, that not only consumes the time that students need for reading and studying but also results in their taking fewer and less demanding courses. Without practice, students' reading capability will deteriorate.

Meanwhile, many younger students are in danger of becoming "vidiots" through watching television for inordinate amounts of time. A survey of 467 freshmen at our school revealed the following information on television viewing habits:

4 to 5 hours daily	11 percent
3 to 4 hours daily	20
2 to 3 hours daily	25
Less than 2 hours	44

These freshmen claimed that they spent even more time watching television during their middle-school years. Spending many hours viewing television as a passive spectator, lounging, half-involved, does not prepare one for the intense focusing, the persistent effort, the mental action or even struggle needed to transform print into meaning when one is studying. Consequently, it is not surprising that freshmen wanted help with concentration and study-reading of a chapter (Chapter 12—Social Studies). Neither is it surprising that 300 freshmen listed television viewing as their biggest waste of time.

The evidence suggests that the first initiative in solving this problem of practice in reading for effectiveness and enjoyment must be accomplished with models on school time. Do students have adult models for reading? Many busy Americans claim to have no time to read books, but do they read magazines? A random survey of over 5,000 American adults revealed only 26 percent to be reading magazines.[3] Only 38

---

2. Peter Olson, basketball coach, LaFollette High School, Madison, Wis. Remarks to Bragstad, April 1977.
3. A. Sharon, "What Do Adults Read?" *Reading Research Quarterly* 9 (1973–1974): 148–169.

percent of our students had ever seen a teacher reading a book; only 55 percent could remember seeing any adult reading a book. If we want students to read effectively and to be lifelong learners, not only do they need school time to experience the joy and satisfaction of growth through reading, but also to experience the inspiration of adult models who communicate their enthusiasm for staying intellectually alive through reading. Teachers can be these inspiring models. Students do enjoy reading with teachers.

To dramatize the high value placed on extensive reading, faculty and administrators, the student council, and the parent-student-teacher advisory committees at each grade level all gave strong support to implementing a new program, the Reading Break, at our high school. Since the third day of school in August, 1978, the whole school has "shut down" every day from 10:05 to 10:20 A.M. so that 2,400 students and staff members are able to read simultaneously for 15 minutes. To prepare for this Reading Break, the students have the first two days of school to check out books from the school library. Since the students choose what they would enjoy reading, they use all their reading skills interactively to get the meaning just as an athlete "puts it all together" in playing the game. Consequently, reading scores improve so that a reading assignment is less threatening.

Perhaps you may gain some insights for initiating your own program by examining the following guidelines, which have been effective for us:

1. It was negotiated to lengthen the school day by ten minutes and to shorten the homeroom period by five minutes to accommodate this program with fifteen minutes to read. In exchange for the fifteen minutes, teachers may leave school fifteen minutes early.

2. The Reading Book is scheduled at the beginning of the third hour for the total school.

   Schedule:

Homeroom	8:05– 8:10	
Period 1	8:15– 9:05	
Period 2	9:10–10:00	
Period 3	10:05–11:10	Reading Break 10:05–10:20
Period 4	11:15–12:35	(Three lunch schedules)
Period 5	12:40– 1:30	
Period 6	1:35– 2:25	
Period 7	2:30– 3:20	

3. Students select their own materials to bring for reading during the morning break. Homework is discouraged for teachers as well as students. No writing is permitted.

4. All administrators, teachers, aides, and secretaries read with the students. Students need adult models.

5. Strong administrative leadership and total faculty commitment gives power to the program. This cooperation is vital to success.

6. All students having no third-period class are assigned a place to read with a teacher having the third hour free.

7. The Reading Break means a quiet time for reading and relaxing. Even visitors are given material to read during this period.

8. Publicity and posters by the library staff, publication of book lists in various categories, and interclass competition in gathering paperbacks for classroom libraries get additional materials in circulation.

9. The student council sponsors several Book Fairs giving students a 20 percent discount. Teachers help students choose the books to be sold and also volunteer their time every period of the two days so that several teachers are always at the Book Fair.

10. Frequently a "celebrity" is invited to read silently with students. Celebrities have been school board members, politicians, university professors, the governor's wife, the state superintendent of public instruction, the mayor, parents, students and teachers from other schools, and career representatives such as the manager of a garage. Each visitor talks to students in the class after the reading period.

11. If a student quite regularly does not bring materials to read, the teacher has the student respond to this brief questionnaire:

Name _____   Grade _____

Reading Break

Location _____   Teacher _____

Pleast list any books that you have ever enjoyed:

_____

Please list any topics that interest you:

_____

The librarian then gathers books accordingly from which the student may choose.

Who provides the initiative for implementing a Reading Break? In one high school a social-studies teacher was the initiator; in another school an English teacher and a guidance counselor. Anyone who cares can mobilize staff interest, cooperation, and commitment to this program.

If students are given a chance to enjoy reading and to develop the habit of reading, they will more readily read their daily assignments as well as other materials. When business-education teachers discuss novels with their students, when the athletic director reads *To Kill a Mockingbird* in the calculus class he also teaches, when the principal obviously enjoys reading *Roots* in the presence of students, when students bring "must" books for teachers to read, the learning atmosphere of the school is affected. Teachers, administrators, and students have an opportunity to build a more personal, supporting relationship in which love of learning is even more likely to flourish.

THE LEARNING CENTER

Frequently, we underestimate what the concern of one teacher can generate in program development within a school. A science teacher felt frustrated because of his inability to give more special help to his students. As he shared this concern with other teachers, he discovered that, because of schedule conflicts and lack of time, few high-school teachers were able to help all the students who needed further explanation or reading assistance in their respective courses. The staff members shared a common frustration in meeting the needs of their students.

The solution? Every teacher could think of capable students who could help others if a program were organized with a staff of student tutors.

This was the beginning of a Learning Center that currently has a staff of about 200 student tutors recommended by teachers. Although other procedures may be effective in a different situation, here are some of the procedures that helped us implement the tutoring program:

- Science teachers and the reading consultant convinced the principal of the need for a Learning Center with an aide to coordinate the program.

- Representative teachers and student-council members set up guidelines for the program.

- All teachers were asked to recommend student tutors who fulfilled the following criteria: expertise in the subject matter, ability to relate effectively, ability to communicate clearly with other students.

- Each student recommended to be on the Learning Center staff as a tutor received an individual congratulatory note in recognition of being selected by a faculty member. The following note is typical of what the students received in their homerooms:

  > Congratulations, David!
  > Mr. Bruce Swanson has recommended you to be on the Learning Center staff as a tutor in chemistry. You are invited to come to a meeting on Thursday at 8:20 A.M. in C17. The principal and department chairpersons will be there to welcome you.

- At the preliminary meeting of all recommended tutors, several department chairpersons and the principal congratulated the students on the honor of being selected as tutors and emphasized the importance of their service. The reading consultant explained the criteria used by teachers for choosing student tutors. Only one criterion remained by which students were to evaluate themselves before consenting to be on the staff: "Do you have a heart big enough to care about other students who are having difficulty achieving in the subject in which you have expertise? Frequently, short-term help is needed—perhaps a few periods. If you want to help, we would like to have you fill out the card that you were given at the door." (Almost 95 percent of the students offer their help each year.)

Here is a sample of the card filled out by the tutors:

Volunteer Tutoring Program   Hours Free _____

Name _____   Telephone No. _____

Grade _____   Homeroom _____

Recommended Subjects: Teachers Making Recommendation:

_____   _____

_____   _____

- Later the aide who coordinates the Learning Center makes additional cards for students who volunteer to tutor in several subjects. Then the cards are filed in a recipe box under course titles like Economics, General Math, English, and Accounting. If a physics student having McIntosh as a teacher wants help, the aide checks the card file in an attempt to pair that student with a tutor who has had McIntosh for physics. Teachers appreciate this careful matching so that their students get effective help.

- Teachers assist in training tutors in their respective content areas.

- In May student tutors receive a special award on Honors Day and may accumulate service credit for being accepted into National Honor Society. Parents are notified of the award and invited to attend Honors Day.

Students' growth in caring about others is evident as they willingly assume more responsibility for helping those in need. In addition to the work in the Learning Center during the school year, over 100 LaFollette High School students tutor elementary and middle-school children twice weekly during the summer, one to one, at each child's home. Seniors who graduate in June still volunteer to tutor during the summer.

The high-school reading consultant initiated the program and, with the help of reading resource teachers in the participating schools, has coordinated it for five summers. The children are selected by their teachers who also give suggestions and materials to the tutors. The tutoring is done at a time that is convenient for the child, the parents, and the tutor. Each tutor keeps a "Diary of Happenings." The high-school students receive no pay and no academic credit. The program is built on the cooperative effort of students, children, parents, teachers, and administrators. The dominant spirit is expressed by a tutor who stated, "It is a lot of hard work, but I'm ready to do it again next summer."

THE RESULTS

When administrators, teachers and students work together to improve reading-learning process and when they read together every day for enjoyment, what are the results? Heightened interest in reading, a positive learning atmosphere, and improved reading scores can be documented.

HEIGHTENED INTEREST IN READING

What tangible evidence reveals that students read more extensively and grow in enjoyment of reading when they read daily with staff members? Library circulation has increased sharply. Prior to the program, students checked out about 800 fiction books and 380 nonfiction books during the first five weeks of school (August–September); after two years of the Reading Break, students checked out 1,847 fiction and 821 nonfiction books during a comparable time period.

This checkout of books was in addition to all the paperbacks purchased at the September Book Fair. At the outset of the Reading Break (1978), students, receiving 20 percent discount, purchased $1,083 in paperbacks at the first two-day Book Fair; three years later, September Book Fair sales totaled almost $2,326. Because of increased interest in books, the student council now sponsors three Book Fairs each year as a service to the student body. The increased purchase of books, whether classics or auto-maintenance manuals, and the increased library circulation provide tangible evidence that students increasingly value reading as a means of recreation as well as a means of learning. Also, teachers notice less resistance to reading assignments when students are in the habit of reading.

When students voted on whether to continue the Reading Break at the end of the first year, 85 percent voted to continue reading every day.[4] Further, they made two major requests: more time to read and more materials. When all students read daily, schools must have a greater supply of magazines and books available—the only increased cost for this program.

POSITIVE LEARNING ATMOSPHERE

Although the learning atmosphere and the teacher-student relationship may be intangible, they are important for effective learning. Are they enhanced by students and staff members reading together? Business-education teachers think that a new student-teacher relationship develops around reading interest. After observing their business-education teacher deeply immersed in a mystery day after day during the Reading Break, eight students read the same book.[5] An industrial-arts teacher enjoys "keeping up" on solar energy and the new developments in his field in addition to reading about Canada.[6] The choral director read *Murmurs of Earth* when a student brought him this "must" book.[7] In his physical-education classes the basketball coach has read all of Hemingway's novels during the Reading Break.[8] Both teachers and students experience the relaxing effect of reading what they want to read in the middle of the morning.

One of the biggest tributes to the program was the voluntary return of a former LaFollette student—football player and editor of the school paper—who is a student

4. Business Department, LaFollette High School, Madison, Wis.
5. Jean Sholts, business-education teacher at LaFollette High School, Madison, Wis. Remarks to Bragstad, October 1979.
6. Michael Walker, industrial-arts teacher at LaFollette High School, Madison, Wis.
7. Rodney Witte, director of choirs at LaFollette High School, Madison, Wis. Remarks to Bragstad, February 1980.
8. Peter Olson, physical-education teacher and basketball coach at LaFollette High School, Madison, Wis. Remarks to Bragstad, February 1980.

at the University of Wisconsin-Madison. He urged students and faculty to "keep the Reading Break going," and made a videotape explaining to students why the program is crucial for those planning to go to college. "Get into the habit of reading daily," he urged.[9] His appreciation of the Reading Break has been strengthened by his college experience.

Do students with serious reading difficulty react positively to reading every day? Here are some of their reactions:

- "I can read faster now."

- "I have finished a whole book. Usually I quit before I'm through."

- "It's fun to read now. I enjoy it."

- "I have better grades now because I'm really into reading."

- "I've discovered that reading is a leisure-time thing to do. Never knew that."

- "I missed my bus stop because I was reading such a good mystery."

- "I didn't read before we had the Reading Break."

- "I'm becoming a 'reading monster.' I read 65 pages last night."

- "I've discovered that I can imagine."

Teachers are still a powerful influence in the lives of students. When teachers help students develop effective study skills, the students perceive that these teachers really care about them and their learning. When personal interests are shared in reading together, students feel closer to teachers; they become co-learners. Now—during the Reading Break every day—each high-school student has many models who enjoy reading to grow intellectually, from the football coach to the principal. Love of learning is contagious!

IMPROVED READING SCORES

As a result of the cooperative effort described in this book, students learn to read more effectively, which removes a major barrier to studying productively. Using varying levels of the same standardized test of reading achievement, the Madison, Wisconsin, Metropolitan School District tests all students citywide at various grade levels. In their final year of middle school, all eighth grade students are tested.[10] They are tested again in the spring of their junior year in high school.[11] Because of low family mobility, the student population in each class remains relatively stable during the three years covered by the testing period.

The chart below reveals the improved reading scores of seven successive classes (500-600 students per class) from the spring of eighth grade (using eighth-grade norms) to the spring of eleventh grade at LaFollette High School:

---

9. Jeffery G. Rasmussen, former student at LaFollette High School, Madison, Wis. Remarks to faculty and students, March 1980.
10. STEP Series II Form 3A (Menlo Park, Calif.: Addison-Wesley Publishing Co. Educational Testing Service, 1971).
11. STEP Series III Level J Form x (Menlo Park, Calif.: Addison-Wesley Publishing Co. Educational Testing Service, 1979).

Reading scores

Eighth-grade median percentile rank			Eleventh-grade median percentile rank	
1st class	1975–76	33rd percentile ⟶	1979	60th percentile
2nd class	1976–77	40th percentile ⟶	1980	70th percentile
3rd class	1977–78	48th percentile ⟶	1981	73rd percentile
4th class	1978–79	65th percentile ⟶	1982	76th percentile
5th class	1979–80	65th percentile ⟶	1983	76th percentile
6th class	1980–81	67th percentile ⟶	1984	76th percentile
7th class	1981–82	72nd percentile ⟶	1985	78th percentile

Over the past ten years, the improvement of students' reading scores from eighth grade to eleventh grade dispels the myth that if students cannot read effectively when they enter high school, it is too late. The opposite is true! With our assistance, students can learn more at a faster rate while they are in high school. In this case over 3500 students became more effective readers from eighth to eleventh grade as a result of (1) the teachers' concerted efforts to fuse reading-learning process with content, (2) the Reading Break, (3) the Learning Center, (4) strong administrative support of a total school reading-study skills program, and (5) the consistent leadership of a reading consultant.

We must remember that students have more learning power to use each year that they are in school. They bring more experience and more information to each page that they study. The more knowledge the students possess, the more readily can they absorb and retain new learning in relationship to what they already know. The brain does improve with use as the neural network becomes increasingly complex.

As teachers, we must continue to stimulate students' curiosity about their developing potential so that they are motivated to improve, motivated to use their increased brain power to study, to learn, and to grow. Our firm commitment to a reading study-skills program coupled with our positive expectations do make the difference.

Addresses of Producers
of Resources

Allyn and Bacon, Inc.
7 Wells Avenue
Newton, MA 02159

Annenberg Project—CPB Project
1213 Wilmette Avenue
Wilmette, IL 60091
1 800 532-7637

Avon Books
A Division of The Hearst Corp.
1790 Broadway
New York, NY 10019

Ballantine Books
201 East 50th Street
New York, NY 10022

Center for Humanities
Box 300
White Plains, NY 10603

Charles E. Merrill Publishing Company
1300 Alum Creek Drive
Columbus, OH 43216

CRM Books
A Division of Random House, Inc.
201 East 50th Street
New York, NY 10022

D. C. Heath and Company
125 Spring Street
Lexington, MA 02173

Dell Publishing Company, Inc.
1 Dag Hammarskjold Plaza
New York, NY 10017

Dolphin Books
Doubleday & Co., Inc.
501 Franklin Avenue
Garden City, NY 11530

E. P. Dutton & Company
2 Park Avenue South
New York, NY 10016

Educational Developmental Laboratories
Division of McGraw-Hill Book Company
1221 Avenue of the Americas
New York, NY 10020

Guidance Associates
757 Third Avenue
New York, NY 10017

Harcourt Brace Jovanovich
757 Third Avenue
New York, NY 10017

Harper & Row
10 East 53rd Street
New York, NY 10022

Helen Dwight Reid Education Foundation
4000 Albemarle Street N.W.
Washington, D.C. 20016

Holt, Rinehart & Winston
521 Fifth Avenue
New York, NY 10175

Houghton Mifflin Company
2 Park Street
Boston, MA 02108

Human Nature, Inc.
757 Third Avenue
New York, NY 10017

Human Resource Development Press
Box 863, Department M39
Amherst, MA 01002

Indiana University
Audio-Visual Center
Bloomington, IN 47401

International Reading Association
800 Barksdale Road
Newark, DE 19711

Jamestown Publishers, Inc.
P.O. Box 6743
Providence, RI 02940

Macmillan Publishing Company
866 Third Avenue
New York, NY 10022

McGraw-Hill Book Company
1221 Avenue of the Americas
New York, NY 10020

NAESP (National Association of Elementary
  School Principals)
1801 N. Moore Street
Arlington, VA 22209

National Council for the Social Studies
Suite 400
2030 M. Street N.W.
Washington, D.C. 20036

Ontario Institute for Studies in Education
252 Bloor Street W.
Toronto, Ontario
Canada 175S N6

Prentice-Hall
Englewood Cliffs, NJ 07632

Project Innovation
P.O. Box 566
Chula Vista, CA 92010

Random House, Inc.
Education Division
201 East 50th Street
New York, NY 10022

Scarecrow Press
52 Liberty Street
Box 656
Metuchen, NJ 08840

Scholastic Magazines, Inc.
50 West 44th Street
New York, NY 10036

Science Research Associates, Inc.
155 N. Wacker
Chicago, IL 60606

Scott, Foresman and Company
1900 East Lake Avenue
Glenview, IL 60025

Television Licensing Center
Division of Films Limited
1144 Wilmette Avenue
Wilmette, IL 60091

University Counseling Service
905 University Ave.
Madison, WI 53706

University of North Carolina Press
P.O. Box 2288
Chapel Hill, NC 27514

H. W. Wilson Company
950 University Avenue
Bronx, NY 10452

Selected Answers
to Reproduction Pages

1. MOTIVATING STUDENTS TO LEARN

Reproduction Page 3 (Topic 2: Activities 1–2)

1. 4 E	4. 4 I	7. 3 E	10. 4 E	13. 3 E
2. 3 E	5. 3 E	8. 3 E	11. 4 I	14. 3 E
3. 4 I	6. 4 I	9. 4 E	12. 3 E	15. 4 E

Reproduction Page 4 (Topic 2: Activity 3)

1. 4	4. 3	7. 3	10. 3	13. 3
2. 3	5. 3, 4	8. 3, 4	11. 4	14. 4
3. 3	6. 3, 4	9. 3	12. 3	15. 3

Reproduction Page 5 (Topic 2: Activity 4)

1. 3	4. 3	7. 4	10. 3	13. 3
2. 3	5. 3	8. 3	11. 3	14. 3
3. 3	6. 3	9. 3	12. 4	15. 3

Reproduction Page 6 (Topic 2: Activity 5)

1. 4	4. 4	7. 4	10. 4	13. 3
2. 3	5. 4	8. 4	11. 3, 4	14. 4
3. 4	6. 3	9. 3, 4	12. 4	15. 4

Reproduction Page 7 (Topic 2: Activity 8)

1. Yes	5. Yes	9. No	13. Yes	17. No
2. Yes	6. No	10. No	14. Yes	18. No
3. Yes	7. No	11. Yes	15. No	19. No
4. Yes	8. Yes	12. Yes	16. Yes	20. Yes

2. CONCENTRATION: LEARNING TO FOCUS

Reproduction Page 9 (Topic 2: Activity 2)

1. A	6. A	11. A	16. R	21. R	26. A
2. A	7. R	12. R	17. A	22. A	27. A
3. R	8. A	13. A	18. A	23. R	28. A
4. A	9. R	14. A	19. R	24. R	29. A
5. A	10. A	15. A	20. R	25. R	30. A

7. MAPPING: DISCERNING THE DESIGN

Reproduction Page 25 (Topic 1: Activity 1)

A		B		C	
4		1		4	
2	At first	5	Initially, *such* . . . instrument	3	For example
5	But then a second later	2	In addition	2	*This* insight
1	a *second* bullet, *again*	3	then, *this* potential	1	Consequently
3		4			

Reproduction Page 28 (Topic 2: Activity 2)

Central figure on map contains focus of chapter—bacteria. Four lines emanating from that figure indicate the four major concepts of study material: (1) discovery of bacteria, (2) structure, (3) nutrition, (4) reproduction.

First major concept, discovery, reveals that

- Leeuwenhoek discovered bacteria in 1695.
- Bacteria are 2–10 microns long and 0.2–2 microns wide.
- Bacteria may be shaped as spirals, rods, or balls.

Point out the liberty the mapmaker has taken in "drawing" information: the content dictates the form for second major concept, bacterial structure.

- Bacteria are 90 percent water.
- Bacteria are composed of vacuoles, granules, and ribosomes.
- Some bacteria develop endospores.

About bacterial nutrition, third major concept:

- Bacteria are either autotrophic (make their own food) or heterotrophic (get food outside themselves).
  - Autotrophic bacteria are either chromosynthetic or photosynthetic.
  - Heterotrophic bacteria are either parasitic or saprophytic.

Fourth major concept, reproduction, indicates that

- Bacterial reproduction is either asexual or sexual.
  - Asexual reproduction occurs by simple cell division.
  - Sexual reproduction occurs in any of three ways:
    - through the transforming principle,
    - through transduction, involving a donor and recipient,
    - through conjugation.

8. NOTE-TAKING: LISTENING, WRITING, LEARNING

Assessing Achievement of Objectives 7

Comparison:

1. The *purpose* is the same: to learn and remember the content and, ideally, to apply it to life.

2. Although the medium (lecture vs. print) is different, the *procedure* is similar:

   a. Get an overview—thesis and major concepts.

   b. Use structural clues (transitions, key words and phrases) to detect the major concepts and significant details.

   c. Recite to check comprehension.

   d. Reflect and review intermittently thereafter.

   e. Use the learnings to avoid losing them.

Contrast:

Listening to a lecture	Study-reading
1. oral—cannot "rehear" it; basically one chance to get content	1. written—can reread it; many chances to get content
2. must keep pace with the lecturer	2. self-paced—accelerate, pause to reflect and ponder at will

Listening to a lecture	*Study-reading*
3. structural clues "invisible"—must *listen* for transitions, key terms	3. structural clues "visible"—typographical clues to structure such as indentations, boldface type, headings, punctuation; transitional phrases, i.e., in addition, thus, as a result

9. TAKING TESTS: MEETING THE CHALLENGE

Reproduction Page 39 (Topic 2: Activity 3)

1. synthesis   5. analysis

2. memory   6. interpretation

3. evaluation   7. application

4. translation

11. STRATEGIC READING: RELATING RATE TO PURPOSE

Reproduction Page 58 (Topic 3: Activity 1)

1. c   2. a   3. a   4. b   5. b   6. b   7. c   8. c   9. c   10. b

Topic 3: Activity 1

Time–Rate Conversions

Reading Time	Words per Minute	Reading Time	Words per Minute	Reading Time	Words per Minute
:10	2400	1:50	220	3:30	115
:20	1200	2:00	200	3:40	110
:30	800	2:10	185	3:50	105
:40	600	2:20	170	4:00	100
:50	480	2:30	160	4:10	95
1:00	400	2:40	150	4:20	92
1:10	345	2:50	140	4:30	89
1:20	300	3:00	135	4:40	85
1:30	265	3:10	125	4:50	83
1:40	240	3:20	120	5:00	80

APPENDIX C

Reproduction Pages

The pages that follow have been provided to facilitate the reproducing of materials needed for activities suggested in the preceding pages. Each page is perforated to make removal from this book easier. Once removed, a page can be used in several ways:

1. *For projection with an opaque projector.* No further preparation is necessary if the page is to be used with an opaque projector. Simply insert it in the projector and the page can be viewed by the entire class.

2. *For projection with an overhead projector.* The Reproduction Page must be converted to a transparency for use on an overhead projector. Overlay the Reproduction Page with a blank transparency and run both of them through a copying machine.

3. *For duplication with a spirit duplicator.* A master can be made from the Reproduction Page by overlaying it with a special heat-sensitive spirit master and running both through a copying machine. The spirit master can then be used to reproduce 50 to 100 copies on paper.

Name _____ Class _____

HOW AM I DOING?
(Study Habits Questionnaire)

The purpose of this questionnaire is to help you get information about how you study right now. As you examine the results, you will discover your areas of strength and of weakness. The results will have meaning only if you are honest and respond as accurately as possible. If the statement is true about you, circle Y for yes. If the statement is false as it applies to you, circle N for no. Be sure to circle Y or N for each statement. Answer carefully so that you get accurate information.

1. I have trouble finishing tests on time.	Y N
2. I set aside a regular time for studying every day.	Y N
3. Before I read a chapter, I turn headings into questions so that I know what I'm going to learn.	Y N
4. I don't have much luck following a definite study schedule.	Y N
5. I give up if an assignment is difficult.	Y N
6. I have difficulty determining important points in lectures.	Y N
7. Before class starts, I review yesterday's lecture notes.	Y N
8. I waste time because I am not organized.	Y N
9. I focus entirely on my work when I study.	Y N
10. I feel uncomfortable reading a chapter unless I've read all the headings and the summary first.	Y N
11. I don't bother taking notes on lectures.	Y N
12. I get sleepy when I study.	Y N
13. I check my lecture notes to fill in any missed words soon after the lecture.	Y N
14. I seldom hear a lecture that is well organized.	Y N
15. I enjoy learning.	Y N
16. Before I begin an assignment, I estimate how long it will take me and then try to beat the clock.	Y N
17. Before answering an essay question, I organize what I am going to write.	Y N

18. I have difficulty concentrating when I study.   Y N

19. Using lecture notes and the textbook, I can usually predict 50–60 percent of the questions on a test.   Y N

20. I could get better grades.   Y N

21. I take time to study every day.   Y N

22. I try to record everything a teacher says in a lecture.   Y N

23. I set aside time every week to review for each course.   Y N

24. Every time I study for a course, I spend some time in review.   Y N

25. I'd rather get through fast than have a perfect paper.   Y N

26. I usually lose points on my exams because of careless mistakes.   Y N

27. I usually seek a quiet place to study.   Y N

28. Before I leave class, I make sure that I know what homework to do and how to do it.   Y N

29. I have a hard time getting interested in some of my courses.   Y N

30. Good grades are important to me.   Y N

31. I stop to recite what I remember after reading each section in a chapter.   Y N

32. I know what time of day I do my best studying.   Y N

33. I study only when I feel like it.   Y N

34. I seldom read the questions at the end of the chapter before I begin reading the chapter.   Y N

35. I often have trouble finding enough time to study.   Y N

36. I remember little of what I study.   Y N

37. I put off studying that I should be doing.   Y N

38. To remember better, I check main headings and the summary before I read a chapter or article.   Y N

39. Tests make me so nervous that I can't do my best.   Y N

40. I wait until the night before a test to review my lecture notes.   Y N

41. I listen carefully to a lecture but I do not take notes.   Y N

42. I take time to review the chapter soon after I read it.   Y N

Name _____   **Class** _____

43. I really "dig in" when I study.   Y   N

44. Before starting a test, I plan how much time to use on each section
of the test.   Y   N

45. I spend too much time on some subjects and not enough on
others.   Y   N

46. I skip over charts, graphs, and tables when I read a chapter.   Y   N

47. I find it difficult to know what is important in a chapter.   Y   N

48. If I have any time left, I check over my test to avoid errors.   Y   N

49. Because I want to remember, I listen carefully to any explanations
in class.   Y   N

50. Daydreaming interferes with my studying.   Y   N

Answer Key: How Am I Doing?

1. N	11. N	21. Y	31. Y	41. N
2. Y	12. N	22. N	32. Y	42. Y
3. Y	13. Y	23. Y	33. N	43. Y
4. N	14. N	24. Y	34. N	44. Y
5. N	15. Y	25. N	35. N	45. N
6. N	16. Y	26. N	36. N	46. N
7. Y	17. Y	27. Y	37. N	47. N
8. N	18. N	28. Y	38. Y	48. Y
9. Y	19. Y	29. N	39. N	49. Y
10. Y	20. Y	30. Y	40. N	50. N

What Are My Strengths and Weaknesses?

Concentration	9	12	16	18	27	33	50
Remembering	23	24	29	36	38	40	49
Organizing time	2	4	8	21	32	35	45
Studying a chapter	3	10	31	34	42	46	47
Listening and taking notes	6	7	11	13	14	22	41
Taking tests	1	17	19	26	39	44	48
Motivation	5	15	20	25	28	30	37	43

Name _____   Class _____

MASLOW'S HIERARCHY OF NEEDS

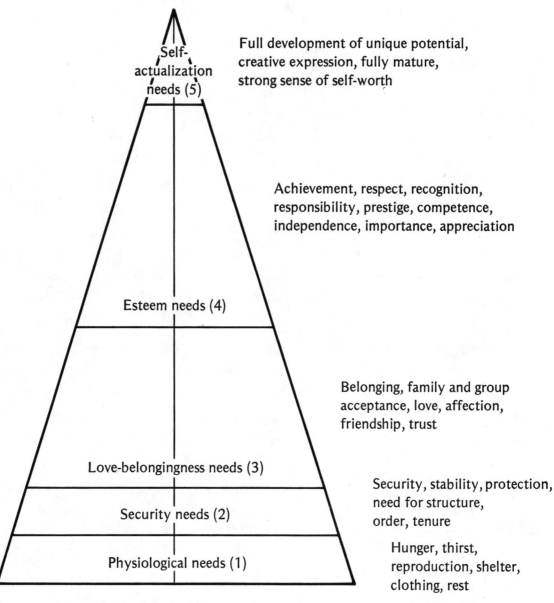

Self-actualization needs (5) — Full development of unique potential, creative expression, fully mature, strong sense of self-worth

Esteem needs (4) — Achievement, respect, recognition, responsibility, prestige, competence, independence, importance, appreciation

Love-belongingness needs (3) — Belonging, family and group acceptance, love, affection, friendship, trust

Security needs (2) — Security, stability, protection, need for structure, order, tenure

Physiological needs (1) — Hunger, thirst, reproduction, shelter, clothing, rest

The diagram depicts the five levels of human need as theorized by Abraham Maslow. Most individuals will exhibit needs from the higher levels of the hierarchy. This assumes that the basic needs—physiological and safety-security—have been satisfied. Maslow contended that as lower-order needs are satisfied, higher-order needs develop.

Abraham Maslow, "A Theory of Human Motivation" in *Motivation and Personality,* 2nd ed. Copyright © 1970 by Abraham H. Maslow. Reprinted by permission of Harper & Row, Publishers, Inc.

Name _____   Class _____

STUDENTS: WHAT MOTIVATES YOU TO LEARN?

Question: *Based on your experience in any courses you have taken, what has motivated you to learn, to work, to achieve?*

Decide whether the source of each response is internal or external. Then write I or E in front of each item. Using Maslow's hierarchy, Reproduction Page 2, write the number of the level of need that is the source of motivation for each response.

Maslow level	Internal or external	Students' positive experiences
_____	_____	1. "Getting good grades."
_____	_____	2. "Having a teacher who cares."
_____	_____	3. "My wanting to learn and to understand."
_____	_____	4. "Having success now when I never understood before."
_____	_____	5. "Teacher wanting to know each student."
_____	_____	6. "My own satisfaction from doing well."
_____	_____	7. "Teacher paying attention to me."
_____	_____	8. "Teacher never giving up on me."
_____	_____	9. "Getting on honor roll."
_____	_____	10. "Getting a good job in the future."
_____	_____	11. "Knowing how to do the work—understanding."
_____	_____	12. "Parents caring about me."
_____	_____	13. "Not wanting to disappoint the teacher."
_____	_____	14. "Having a bright, happy teacher who is interested in me."
_____	_____	15. "Teacher explaining well so I enjoy the subject."

Name _____   Class _____

TEACHERS: WHAT MOTIVATES YOU TO LEARN?

Question: *Based on your experiences in any courses you have taken, what has motivated you to learn, to work, to achieve?*

Maslow level	*Teachers' positive experiences*
_____	1. "Being given an award for good work."
_____	2. "Having a professor recognize me on campus when I wasn't in class."
_____	3. "Having professors believe that I had some basic worth."
_____	4. "Teachers offering their free time to help me."
_____	5. "Being given unusual responsibility in class."
_____	6. "Praise for a good long-term project."
_____	7. "Teacher helping a friend and me solve a personal problem."
_____	8. "Teacher being fair but strict so that we accomplished more."
_____	9. "Teacher sincerely interested in correcting my disruptive behavior."
_____	10. "Teacher taking time to communicate with my parents."
_____	11. "Having a well-organized professor with clear objectives."
_____	12. "A teacher who was human and treated students with respect."
_____	13. "Having friendly teachers and professors."
_____	14. "Doing well on tests."
_____	15. "Teacher sharing personal experiences of difficulty."

Name _____   Class _____

STUDENTS: WHAT INHIBITS YOUR MOTIVATION?

Question: *In your educational experience, what has inhibited or blocked your motivation to learn?*

Maslow level	*Students' negative experiences*
_____	1. "Teacher who is 'all business'—no personal interest in students."
_____	2. "Lack of trust in students."
_____	3. "Teacher who never smiles or jokes."
_____	4. "When a teacher only pretends to listen to me."
_____	5. "Picking out a certain group of students as pets."
_____	6. "A teacher who always 'cuts you down.'"
_____	7. "Going through assignments too fast for us to understand."
_____	8. "Teacher getting angry with one student, but punishing everyone."
_____	9. "Teachers who don't take any time to get to know me."
_____	10. "Teacher personally 'cutting down' a classmate."
_____	11. "Comparing me with another student in front of the class."
_____	12. "Teacher just assuming that everyone understands something hard."
_____	13. "Making errors in names even late in the semester."
_____	14. "Teacher ignoring all the quiet kids."
_____	15. "Teacher reprimanding students for giving 'stupid answers.'"

Name _____   Class _____

TEACHERS: WHAT INHIBITS YOUR MOTIVATION?

Question: *In your educational experience, what has inhibited or blocked your motivation to learn?*

Maslow level   *Teachers' negative experiences*

_____   1. "Teachers who did not know their subjects."

_____   2. "Course with straight book work and no personal relations."

_____   3. "Disorganized lectures."

_____   4. "Having to do work without any challenge."

_____   5. "Going over new material too quickly."

_____   6. "Machine-like teacher who couldn't show any excitement."

_____   7. "Teachers who grade on the curve regardless of all the bright kids."

_____   8. "Teacher asking questions but expecting his answers."

_____   9. "Themes with nothing but negative comments on them."

_____   10. "Teachers not taking time to answer students' questions."

_____   11. "Professor who didn't care whether or not we learned."

_____   12. "Teacher who gives grade with no tips for improving."

_____   13. "Being reprimanded in front of class when not necessary."

_____   14. "Being bored in class."

_____   15. "Being taught material I didn't understand with no help available."

Name _____ Class _____

ASSESSING MOTIVATION TO ACHIEVE

1. Respond Yes *or* No *on the blank in front of each item.*

2. *Compare your responses to the suggested answers.*

3. *In small groups, decide if the items actually measure "achievement motivation."*

4. *Suggest changes in the instrument and add any quality items that you think are appropriate.*

_____ 1. Are you dissatisfied until you really understand what you are learning?

_____ 2. If you can't understand something, do you ask the teacher to explain it to you?

_____ 3. Do you anticipate what questions will be asked on a test?

_____ 4. Would you rather be graded with a letter grade than Pass-Fail?

_____ 5. Do you like the challenge of having hard assignments?

_____ 6. Should you set only those goals that you can easily reach?

_____ 7. If you had a choice, would you prefer to take a course in which you would not receive a grade?

_____ 8. Do you make a real effort to get the best grades you can in every class?

_____ 9. If you were playing a game and you lost several times, would you quit?

_____ 10. Do you believe "As long as I make a real effort, I won't be concerned about the grade"?

_____ 11. If you are bored with an assignment, do you keep working anyway?

_____ 12. Are you usually on time in completing assignments?

_____ 13. Do you continue to try even if you don't do as well as others?

_____ 14. Does knowing that you are improving give you a sense of achievement?

_____ 15. Do you believe "Win or lose, who cares?"

_____ 16. Do you try to learn from any errors that you make on a test?

_____ 17. Must a student have high grades in order to have a sense of achievement?

_____ 18. Do you prefer to sit in the back of a classroom?

_____ 19. If you don't understand something, do you ignore it?

_____ 20. If you have been absent, do you make up the work without being reminded?

Name _____ Class _____

GETTING TO KNOW YOU

1. *If you received $500.00 that you had to spend immediately, what would you do with it?*

2. *If you could be on one TV show, which one would you choose, and why?*

3. *If you had all day Saturday to spend exactly as you wished, what would you do?*

4. *What one change would you like to make in this school?*

5. *What one thing have you changed your mind about recently? Briefly tell about it.*

6. *If you could be any age you wish, what age would you choose? Why?*

7. *If you could make one change in the world, what would it be?*

8. *If you could spend an hour with any person who has ever lived, whom would you choose? Explain.*

Name _____ Class _____

HOW WELL DO I CONCENTRATE?

The purpose of this survey is to help you examine how effectively you concentrate when you study. If you will honestly and carefully respond to each question, you will be able to learn how you can improve in the study habits that contribute to your concentration. Answer on the basis of what you are in the habit of doing or feeling.

R = *Rarely*

H = *Half the time*

A = *Almost always*

Based on your own experience, answer R, H, or A on the blank in front of each question.

_____ 1. Are you interested in learning in your courses?

_____ 2. Do you vary your activities when you study—read, write, recite, take a break—so that you are more likely to sustain your attention?

_____ 3. Do you let your thoughts wander so that daydreaming becomes a habit when there is work to do?

_____ 4. Do you challenge yourself to get through in a certain amount of time?

_____ 5. Do you quickly review relevant material from the past before you start the new assignment?

_____ 6. Do you start to work as soon as you sit down at your desk?

_____ 7. Does watching TV often cause you to postpone doing your homework?

_____ 8. Do you make your family aware of your need for a quiet time to study?

_____ 9. Do you spend a lot of time studying without much progress?

_____ 10. If you can't concentrate because of a personal conflict, do you make plans for resolving the conflict?

_____ 11. Do you study in a well-lighted, well-ventilated room?

_____ 12. Are you easily distracted from your work?

_____ 13. Do you study the same subject in the same place at the same time each day?

_____ 14. Do you choose to work in a place where there are very few distractions?

_____ 15. Do you have all the necessary equipment and materials within easy reach?

_____ 16. Do you wait for inspiration to strike before you begin your work?

_____ 17. Do you turn off the music if it is distracting?

_____ 18. Do you make a special effort to find an interest in the courses you take?

_____ 19. After the first week of a new semester, do you gradually lose interest in your classes?

_____ 20. When you study, do you often feel tired, bored, or sleepy?

_____ 21. Do you study only what you are "in the mood" to study?

_____ 22. Do you intend to work hard even though you don't like a subject?

_____ 23. Does it take a long time for you to "get into" studying?

_____ 24. Do you neglect your schoolwork in order to have a good time?

_____ 25. Do you spend too much time watching TV, talking to friends, listening to music instead of studying?

_____ 26. Do you prefer to study your assignments alone rather than with others?

_____ 27. Before studying, do you organize your work so that you use your time effectively?

_____ 28. Do you quickly bring your attention back to studying when your thoughts wander?

_____ 29. Do you seek help if you are frequently distracted by personal problems?

_____ 30. With understanding and effort, can students improve concentration?

Name _____   Class _____

CONCENTRATE? OF COURSE YOU CAN!

After being in high school for a few years, we juniors realize how many changes we experienced as freshmen. All of a sudden we were in classes with many students we didn't know. We had a different teacher for each class. We could participate in a great variety of activities. We had more free time about which we had to make decisions. We also had regular homework, which was required for credit in our classes. In addition, we had to become familiar with a new building and new expectations from those around us. Sometimes we felt muddled and confused, but we wanted to do well.

Effective concentration contributes to success, and lack of concentration contributes to failure. Concentration is important. Realizing that all the changes we were experiencing as freshmen did affect our concentration, we decided to give you some tips that we wish we had been given as freshmen.

What Interferes with Concentration?

1. *Noise, people talking, music, TV*. Having a quiet place to study is at the top of the list for upperclassmen. If your attention is divided or constantly interrupted, your mind will not be able to think effectively. Studying is thinking. Without these external interrupters, you can learn more and finish faster with improved concentration. Choose a quiet spot for study. If possible, choose the same place every day. Less distraction results in better concentration and improved learning.

2. *Daydreaming*. If your thoughts continually wander, stop and analyze yourself to determine the cause of the distraction. Whenever you find yourself daydreaming, make a mark on a piece of paper. Then work to reduce the marks per hour or per evening.

   Another suggestion: give yourself a few minutes to daydream every hour so that you can concentrate the rest of the time. Don't let extensive daydreaming become a habit just to avoid the work of studying. Dig in and you'll soon involve those brain cells. Just quickly guide your attention back to studying when you begin to daydream.

3. *Being hungry and tired*. If you are hungry or tired, how about eating a little food or taking a short nap? Being alert when you study is important so that you

become involved. Otherwise studying is just an obedience exercise. You can think and learn. Don't let hunger or fatigue be stumbling blocks for you.

4. *Personal problems.* Not thinking about personal problems is difficult. All students have problems of one kind or another—so do adults. Even if there is no immediate solution, having the support of others feels good. Talking privately to your guidance counselor, who has had a lot of experience with problems, may help you in coping with or solving your problem. Even deciding that you will talk to someone may help you postpone thinking about a problem until you have finished studying. That "someone" may be a teacher, a friend, or your parents. We all need someone to listen. There are people who would like to help you.

What Develops Concentration?

1. *Wanting to learn!* Every sophomore wants to learn what is in the Driver's Manual because getting a driver's license is important. The desire to drive is so great that each sophomore is totally involved in learning. That is concentration.

   Observe students in any class you take. You'll see some who are really paying attention and others whose attention is drifting from one thing to another.

   Do you want to learn? This is a decision that you will have to make for yourself. No one can learn for you. Your mind is always active and ready to receive new ideas. Wanting to help your mind grow is a good stimulus for concentration.

2. *Becoming interested!* The more you know about any subject, the more interested you become. You may not care about snakes, but if you really learned a lot about their habits and their problems, you might become fascinated. In high school try to find an interest in any course you take. Try to become an independent learner, instead of limping along with your teacher as your crutch. Don't expect your teacher to carry you. The teacher is there only as your assistant. You have the responsibility to learn. If you work, you'll very likely become interested. This helps concentration.

3. *Being organized.* We have a few tips for this. First, make a weekly study schedule that you can usually follow. Be flexible if change is needed, but also be purposeful. Having a regular time for studying makes it easier to begin.

Name _____ Class _____

Second, know exactly what your assignments are and get the materials you need. Keep a detailed record of your assignments: the date, what the assignment is, the pages of relevant material in the text, and (after numbering the pages in your notebook for that course) the number of your notebook pages on the topic. One line in your notebook will look like this:

Date	Assignment	Pg-book	Pg-notebook
9/15	Factoring Prob. 1–15 Review.	35–40	15–16

Teachers and students claim that this continuing record is a reminder of makeup work after being absent. You'll also have a review record for a test.

Third, start studying the minute you sit down at your desk. If you always do this, you may find yourself concentrating with less effort. Fourth, varying your activity by switching subjects gives you a change. Plan ahead for a break between subjects so you really work, or plan a little reward for yourself when you finish.

4. *Competing with yourself.* Don't worry about all the work you have, just concentrate on what you are doing right now. Set a time when you think you should finish your science or English; then see if you can beat the clock. Timing yourself prevents you from daydreaming and poking along. You'll concentrate better when you're competing against the clock—even if you lose.

5. *Being a question mark.* Asking questions is a sign of intelligence. Listen carefully in class, but if you don't understand an assignment, be sure to ask the teacher for further explanation. You can't remember when you don't understand. In doing homework, if you know what to do and how to do it, you'll have less difficulty really "digging in."

6. *Being realistic.* Expect to have some distractions. Unbroken concentration for long periods of time is not a common experience. When your thoughts wander, quickly refocus on your work. This simple reaction saves time and emotional energy. In the face of distractions, your growing power of concentration will give you a sense of achievement.

Name _____   Class _____

WHY BOTHER WITH A TIME SCHEDULE?

Each year in school assignments seem to become longer and more difficult. If you want to be a successful student, scheduling your time will be helpful. Here are some of the advantages of scheduling time that other high-school students have discovered:

1. Parents will "get off your back" when they see that you have planned your study time. As they observe you becoming responsible, they may gradually stop checking on what you are doing.

2. Writing down what you must do each day relieves your mind. Then when you study, you can focus and think more effectively. Get into the habit of having a daily "to-do list" to free your mind.

3. You are less likely to procrastinate, that is, to put off your work, if you have a set time to begin.

4. When you set a certain amount of time to do each assignment, your concentration improves so that you work better. This saves time. You may even beat the clock as you become more efficient.

5. With a schedule, you are less likely to let a ten-minute break extend into the rest of the evening. Gradually, you learn to discipline yourself to get the work finished so that you can really relax.

6. You experience a feeling of satisfaction when you are in control of your life, knowing *what* you want to do *when*. You feel better about yourself.

7. Organizing your time helps you to come to class prepared; you learn more because the class presentation or activity has more meaning. As a result, your grades improve.

8. When you assume control of your time, you feel relaxed and ready to have fun when you have some free time because your work is up-to-date. You get rid of that feeling of anxiety or pressure.

9. Scheduling your use of time is the intelligent way to operate if you want to learn, to achieve, and to have more time for fun with your friends.

Name _____ Class _____

COPING WITH STRESS—SCHEDULING

We have all experienced the pressure of too many things to do without enough time to do them. When we live with this pressure, we experience stress. It's unpleasant and disabling.

But stress diminishes through scheduling. Therefore, write down what you must do this coming week. Then tackle these items one at a time. Check them off as you finish. Revise only when necessary. You'll feel better once you can "see" the course of your week.

A.M.	Monday	Tuesday	Wednesday	Thursday	Friday	Saturday	Sunday
P.M.							

Name _____   Class _____

WHERE HAS THE WEEK GONE?

What have you done with your life for the past 7 days?

Item	Number of hours
Sleep	_____
Meals	_____
Job	_____
Transportation	_____
Class Time	_____
Additional	_____
Total Hours =	_____

Now subtract Total Hours from 168, the number of hours in 7 days. What is the result? _____ This is the amount of "free time" you had! Based on this knowledge, what changes would you make in your life—join the Ecology Club? more free reading? volunteer work?

List at least one below.

Do you have a problem getting things done comfortably and on time?

How could a schedule of some sort help you?

Name _____   Class _____

HOW DO YOU ORGANIZE YOUR TIME?

To gain perspective on your current use of time, please answer yes *or* no *to the following questions:*

Before Unit   *After Unit*

_____   1. Do you set aside time for studying each course that you're taking?   _____

_____   2. Do you study only when you are "in the mood"?   _____

_____   3. Whenever you study, do you spend some time reviewing?   _____

_____   4. Do you schedule time for starting early on a long-term project?   _____

_____   5. Do you have a regular time each day for studying particular subjects?   _____

_____   6. When you study, do you take a break every thirty to forty minutes?   _____

_____   7. Do you study only when you have nothing else to do?   _____

_____   8. Do you take time soon after class for revising lecture notes?   _____

_____   9. To help estimate time needed for a reading assignment in a particular course, do you know how many textbook pages you can read in ten minutes?   _____

_____   10. Before you study, do you estimate the amount of time needed for doing the assignment?   _____

_____   11. Do you know what is the best time of the day for you to study?   _____

_____   12. Do you prepare a weekly schedule to help you become efficient?   _____

Before Unit   *After Unit*

_____   13. To save time in doing assignments, do you question the teacher in class if you aren't sure of how to do the work?   _____

_____   14. Do you take time to write down all your assignments?   _____

_____   15. Do you review regularly even if there is no immediate test?   _____

_____   16. Do you always know the purpose of your assignment so that you are more interested and can work faster?   _____

_____   17. Do you set aside time for fun and recreation?   _____

Name _____ Class _____

TO DO LIST

A (most important)	B	C (least important—can wait)

Monday	Tuesday	Wednesday	Thursday	Friday

Name _____   Class _____

TWELVE TIPS FOR STUDYING AND MANAGING YOUR TIME

1. Plan a definite time for studying each day. This will discourage procrastination and prevent that pile-up of work.

2. Shorten your study time by knowing the purpose of each assignment, what to do, and how to do it before you leave class. Keep a record of all assignments in a special section of your notebook.

3. Predicting the amount of time needed for each assignment causes you to work harder so that you save time. By timing your assignments, you are more likely to concentrate and less likely to become bored.

4. Time yourself to see how long it takes you to read five pages of your textbook or a paperback. This will help you estimate the time needed to complete a reading assignment. Because a textbook is loaded with information, you may have to read some sections more than once. Even teachers have to reread material. Allow time for reflecting on what you read, too.

5. Pay attention to charts and diagrams. They can be shortcuts to understanding.

6. When a reading assignment is made, you can expect to have a discussion of the material or a quiz in class. Take a little time to review just before class so that you are ready to participate.

7. Every time you study spend ten minutes in review of previous assignments. These "refresher shots" are the secret for long-term memory. This habit of frequent review also results in less time needed for studying for a major test.

8. Use daytime for study if possible. At night you are likely to be less efficient.

9. After studying about forty minutes, take a five-minute break. This refreshes your mind so that you can concentrate better and finish faster.

10. Setting a "stopping time" at night will encourage hard work in anticipation of being through by ten o'clock or whatever time you set. Sometimes you may even beat the clock. The increased impetus helps you concentrate.

11. Don't cram for hours the night before a test. Instead, distribute your study in half-hour segments over a period of days.

12. Since learning is cumulative, new ideas must be incorporated with previous learning from lectures, readings, and lab experiments. You have to continuously make the connections and associations in your own mind. Putting it all together is easier if you schedule time daily to read, to think, to reflect, to review. Improved learning is the natural result of this approach to using your time.

Name _____   Class _____

A MEMORY HABITS CHECKLIST

Write yes *or* no *to each of the following questions:*

Before   *After*

  When studying do you:

_____   1. Try to get *interested* in the subject?   _____

_____   2. *Intend* to remember the content?   _____

_____   3. Give the subject your undivided *attention*?   _____

_____   4. Try to keep an *open mind* to new ideas?   _____

_____   5. Feel *confident* that you can remember if you want to?   _____

_____   6. Search for the *organization of ideas* (using headings, summary)?   _____

_____   7. Take care to *accurately understand and learn* the material in the first place?   _____

_____   8. *Recite* from memory or quiz yourself immediately after reading each major section in a chapter?   _____

_____   9. *Review* your class notes and readings once a week or more?   _____

_____   10. Use several methods to *reinforce* learning and remembering, i.e., note-taking, discussing with friends, reciting aloud?   _____

_____   11. Try to *relate* what you learn to what you already know and to your own life?   _____

_____   12. Study subjects that are *different,* rather than similar, one after the other (for example, study history, then math rather than political science) to avoid interference and forgetting?   _____

Before   *After*

_____   13. Study in **twenty- to forty-minute study sessions,** with short   _____
                        breaks in between, to keep comprehension and memory
                        at peak levels?

_____   14. Capitalize on special **memory systems** (mnemonics) to   _____
                        learn long lists of items?

Name _____   Class _____

MEMORY TIPS

Jot your personal comments on the suggestions under the headings in the left-hand column.

• ***What's your attitude?***

What is your very favorite thing in life—a person? baseball? music? reading? How tough is remembering new information about that particular thing? That answer reveals your "memory potential." Are you impressed? You should be! (One student knows the batting averages of all the best players in the baseball leagues.)

"But," you say, "math is no fun." Keep telling yourself that, and it never will be fun. Your prejudices affect your learning, so give some *extra time* to the subjects you dislike. Research indicates that the more you know about any subject, the more interested you become. Positive achievement is likely to follow.

Don't be victimized by your own biases. You more readily forget what you don't agree with, so reap remembering dividends by keeping an open mind!

• ***Do you intend to remember?***

Or do you just want to get the assignment out of the way? Without a conscious decision to remember, you probably won't, and no one remembers what she or he has never really learned in the first place.

Have high expectations of yourself! Focus on how good you'll feel after reading, when you know the material instead of just the three songs that played on the radio while you "studied."

Also, studying subjects that are different, rather than similar, one after another (for example, history, then math rather than political science) guards against interference and forgetting.

• *Do you personalize the material?*

Have you ever forgotten a friend's comments on why you're special? Or a compliment paid you by someone you truly admire? Probably not. This shows the power of your memory if you are personally involved. As much as you can, follow this same principle in studying. For example, while reading, ask yourself, "How am I affected by this?"

• *Do you "chunk" the learning?*

Right now, list three major ideas from the last reading assignment you completed. If you can't do it, then you're choosing to operate at a handicap. When you've finished studying a chapter and can recall seven or so major points, you've got those "key thoughts" that trigger your recall of the related significant details. A prime contributor to comprehension and memory, then, is to categorize ideas.

• *Do you "handle" the material?*

The more means you use to learn new material, the greater the likelihood you'll remember it. *Draw* pictures to illustrate points. *Talk* over assignments with friends. *Recite* information to yourself. *Write* notes on important points. Each one of these aids will increase your chance of recalling information the next time you need it. "Handling" the new ideas results in their moving from short-term to long-term memory.

Remember—if you don't use it, you will lose it!

• *Do you recite and review regularly?*

Without any special study approach, you will forget *80 percent* of what you learn within *two weeks!* Reverse that trend by reciting (speaking aloud) immediately after studying. Thereafter, review the content about once a week. When you feel that you've mastered the content, review it again—*overlearn* it—just to be sure.

• *Do you employ mnemonics?*

Don't forget—to memorize long lists of items, use the peg-word system, narrative chaining, or other memory systems. Your imagination is a powerful tool for memory, too!

Name _____   Class _____

TRY TO REMEMBER

Name _____   Class _____

ORGANIZING CONFUSION

psychology

FREEDOM

celery

daffodils

painting

Self

family

motivation

of

canvas

responsibility

milk

artist

humanity

oranges

brush

cotton

polyester

in

tulips

Name _____   Class _____

LEDGUSLLAITEIVE YSHOOZ

At a recent gathering at the Capitol here in Madison, a number of ledgusllaiteive yshooz were dhyscust. All dealt with tuhrizuhm in Wisconsin. Klyph Kharlsuhn who onze a small phische-pharm nier Wabeno, lead the phyte for tacks braxe for state bisnusmuhn whooze prauphutz halve bin sclascht beakuz uv the enuhrjee chrysusse. Other similarly kuhnsyrnde sytazunze joined hymn in demanding immediate rheleaph for psuch pursonze.

"Things are knough kwyte tuph for all of us in hour lyne of endhevuhr," he complained, "scynsce phyool is knough at such a preemieyuhm. The kroudze gust ahrnt kumeeng leyc they yuste twoo, and that pspelz lawsuhz, yew gno. And thatze kweye awhl theize phoxe are heer."

Comprehension test

1. The above selection dealt primarily with
   - (a) the ecological ramifications of certain legislative decisions.
   - (b) the economic plight of a particular group of Wisconsin business people.
   - (c) the judicial directions being taken by the State Bar Association.
   - (d) the philosophical issues inherent in several new state laws.
   - (e) the recreational needs of citizens in various communities.

2. The major spokesman for the group reported on was
   - (a) the manager of a Northern Wisconsin resort hotel.
   - (b) the owner of an amusement park near Appleton.
   - (c) the owner of a seafood-raising establishment in Wisconsin.
   - (d) a restaurateur from near Green Bay.
   - (e) a stockholder representing a major oil company.

3. The group's specific goal was to obtain for themselves
   - (a) eased license fees.
   - (b) a lengthened season.

Courtesy of Professor Ken Dulin, University of Wisconsin-Madison.

  (c) lowered taxes.

  (d) raised revenues.

  (e) shortened business hours.

4. The word "prauphutz" in the first paragraph was used to mean

  (a) those who can forecast the future.

  (b) those who can control the future.

  (c) money remaining after operating costs are paid.

  (d) money available before operating costs are paid.

  (e) women professors.

Name _____   Class _____

CONTEXT CLUES TO NONSENSE WORDS

1. Because he had never been around large groups of people before, having spent the early part of his life in the seclusion of a small island in the Pacific, he was now somewhat of a chellad.
A chellad is

   _____ (a) a bitter, suspicious, untrusting man.
   _____ (b) an eager, jovial companion.
   _____ (c) an evil, greedy, grasping man.
   _____ (d) a shy, retiring, bashful person.
   _____ (e) none of the above.

2. Though he usually dashed through the tasks at hand, today he simply plugged bordilly along.
To behave bordilly is to be

   _____ (a) aggressive and demanding.
   _____ (b) eager to act and to be responded to.
   _____ (c) impulsive and quick to act.
   _____ (d) quick to move into action.
   _____ (e) none of the above.

3. Because he'd a full night's sleep now, eaten a good breakfast, and washed, shaved, and changed his clothes, he was able to participate much more plassily than he had last night.
To do something plassily is to do it

   _____ (a) cautiously.
   _____ (b) comfortably and efficiently.
   _____ (c) dangerously and recklessly.
   _____ (d) slowly and painfully.
   _____ (e) none of the above.

Courtesy of Professor Ken Dulin, University of Wisconsin-Madison.

4. The crowd became quieter and quieter, all motion gradually ceased, and the facial expressions of those present lost their fire and feeling; in short, the group had become elegonic.
   To be elegonic is to be

   _____ (a) calm, placid, and settled.

   _____ (b) divided in purpose or intent.

   _____ (c) nervous, highly emotional, and fidgety.

   _____ (d) unified in goals and objectives.

   _____ (e) none of the above.

5. Running, skipping, jumping, grenching—these are the activities most likely performed by the typical seven-year-old. It won't be until he reaches nine, ten, or eleven that group activities will take their place.
   To grench is probably to

   _____ (a) behave in unison with others.

   _____ (b) move carefully and methodically.

   _____ (c) move slowly and methodically.

   _____ (d) operate with care and extreme caution.

   _____ (e) none of the above.

6. Instead of using one of his light, delicate tools, for this job he chose a bessen.
   A bessen must be

   _____ (a) a fragile, fine-tooled craftsman instrument.

   _____ (b) a large, powerful tool especially suited to heavy work.

   _____ (c) a piece of protective clothing worn by certain workmen.

   _____ (d) a type of material often used for carving.

   _____ (e) none of the above.

7. Because they had been extravagant during the early part of the month, and had only a limited income, they now had to delit if they were to get by until next payday.
   To delit is to

   _____ (a) conserve one's immediate resources.

   _____ (b) make a wise investment.

   _____ (c) spend money impulsively.

   _____ (d) squander money on useless luxuries.

   _____ (e) none of the above.

Name _____   Class _____

IMPROVING GRADES WITH SQ3R: A STUDY APPROACH THAT WORKS

You own an instrument more amazing than any computer. You have a brain with thirteen billion brain cells! Do you know how to use this instrument for learning? First, you "turn it on" by wanting to learn. Second, you become a detective searching for meaning by using the following approach in reading your textbook.

1. **Survey.** Search for clues to the organization of the information in the chapter. Detailed information can be remembered only if it is learned in relationship to more important ideas. Where are the clues to this important structure, the organization of ideas?

   • Think about the *title*. What do you already know about this subject? What do you anticipate learning in a chapter with this title?

   • Read the *first paragraph*. Here you may find the author's plan of organization. The introduction may state the topics included as well as the author's purpose for writing the chapter.

   • Hit the *headings* in the chapter. These are the main topics or concepts that have been developed by the author. How many major divisions do you find? Take a few minutes to make a map or chart of those headings. Give your brain cells that idea structure of the whole chapter that you need for understanding and remembering.

   • Read the *last paragraph* or the *summary*. Here you may find a review of the main concepts or final conclusions.

2. **Question.** Questions create curiosity, improve concentration, give purpose to your search, make important ideas more visible—all aiding comprehension.

   • Turn main headings and subheadings into questions.

   • Jot down questions that occurred to you while you were surveying the chapter.

   • Compare your questions with those at the end of the chapter.

3. **Read.** Now read the first section only (the material under the first heading) to search actively for the answer to your questions. You are a detective with

Francis P. Robinson, Adaptation of "Steps in the 'SQ3R' Method" in *Effective Study*, 4th ed. (New York: Harper & Row, Publishers, Inc. Copyright 1941, 1946; copyright 1961, 1970 by Francis P. Robinson.) By permission of the publisher.

purpose, grabbing ideas faster because you've surveyed the chapter. Instead of floundering, you know where you are going.

4. **Recite.** At the end of *each section,* look away from the book for a few seconds, recite, and think about what you've just learned. This makes a deeper imprint on your brain. Don't hesitate to recite out loud. Hearing yourself paraphrase the ideas will help put the information into long-term memory. Then check your recall against the book. Reciting is a crucial step for remembering! Without reciting, you may forget half of what you read after one day.

5. **Review.** After you've read the material, section by section—questioning, reading, reciting—you're ready to look at the total chapter so that you can see all the parts in relationship to each other. This *total review* is the final step for organizing the information to understand and remember it. We cannot remember what we do not understand. At this point, some students draw a *flow chart* or *map* of the ideas for future review.

    If you recite and review each week, you will understand and remember better. Reviewing whenever you study results in less time needed for test preparation later. Expect your grades to improve with regular review!

Name _____   Class _____

HELP! THIS ARTICLE HAS NO HEADINGS

An ancient Chinese proverb states: "I hear and I forget. I see and I remember. I do and I understand." Here are the "why" and "how to do" steps that enhance understanding and remembering what you read.

Why survey an article without headings? Surveying gives you a mental map of where you are going, what logical divisions of thought are explored, and how the ideas are related. You may also become aware of the author's purpose and conclusions. With this perspective of the whole, all parts are more understandable and more readily remembered. Surveying to get an overview before reading results in *less* time needed for reading with a *greater* return.

How do I survey an article without headings?

1. Examine the first two paragraphs by searching for an explanation of the subject, the author's purpose, and any clues to how the ideas are organized. Sometimes the author will list the major concepts so that you know what is coming. If the initial paragraph is written just to get your interest, read it rapidly and begin your search in the second paragraph.

2. Skip to the final paragraphs in search of a summary of the author's thoughts. In one paragraph the main concepts may be restated for final emphasis, or a short paragraph may be devoted to each major concept. Keep an eye out for structure words like the following: *to sum up, therefore, in conclusion, in brief, thus, in summation.*

3. Read the first sentence or two in each paragraph. Note any organization or structure clues like the following transitions: *in the first place, to begin with, furthermore, in addition, finally, at last.* Other transitions indicate "Watch out—we're changing gears." These include the following: *on the other hand, in contrast, however, nevertheless, conversely.* These are indicators of the logical interrelationships of ideas within the body of the article. Terminology used in the summary may also be a clue to major ideas. For example, the author may speak of "three areas of consideration," so watch for that word *area* in reading first sentences. If you see "another aspect," this may be the terminology used to indicate important concepts. Gradually, you become sensitive to the language used by the author to highlight the major divisions of thought in an article. Get that mental map of idea organization!

4. Examine any graphic aids—charts, diagrams, maps, tables, timelines. These can be shortcuts for presenting information or for clarifying abstract concepts. Visual aids contribute to understanding.

Name _____   Class _____

SENTENCE SCRAMBLE

2 At first I thought it was an insect.

3 Blackberry jam lost its appeal as I scurried from the woods.

1 As I stood uncertainly, a second bullet whined, and again the rifle cracked.

4 One day I ventured into the woods to pick blackberries when I suddenly heard a whir overhead.

5 But then, a second later, I heard the crack of a .22 rifle.

_____

5 Initially, they are amazed to know that they possess such a beautiful instrument for learning.

3 They then become curious about how the brain could be used to fulfill this potential for learning.

1 What happens when students discover the wonder of the brain?

2 In addition, they are impressed that they must have a great deal of unused potential.

4 Some students even wonder why teachers spend so much time telling them *what* to learn and so little time teaching them *how* to learn—how to use such a complex instrument.

_____

4 Students gain new perspectives as they discuss the relationship of maturity (willingness to accept responsibility) to motivation.

3 For example, they soon determine that the more one is inner-motivated, the more likely one is to fulfill one's unique potential, the ultimate need of a human being.

2 This insight gives students a perspective of life as a continuing process of growth beyond the time of formal education.

1 Consequently, the top level of Maslow's hierarchy, self-actualization, begins to have meaning.

Name _____ Class _____

TRANSITIONS MAKE THE CONNECTION

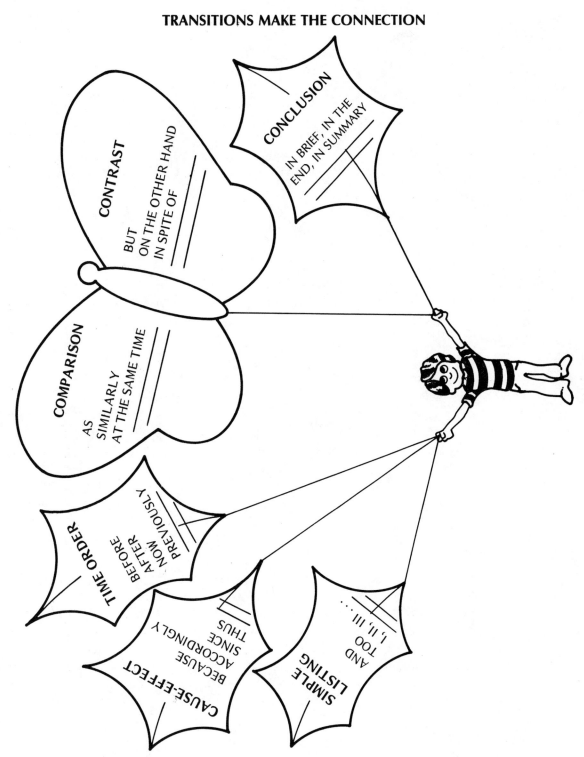

257

Name _____   Class _____

TRANSITIONS MAKE THE CONNECTION—ADDITIONS

Simple Listing

and
too
I, II, III . . .
finally
furthermore
first, second . . .
1, 2, 3 . . .

Cause-Effect

because
accordingly
since
thus
for this reason
consequently
hence
resulting
therefore
as a result
so
then

Time Order

before
after
now
previously
last
next
then
when
immediately
formerly
later
subsequently
meanwhile
presently
initially
ultimately

Comparison

as
similarly
at the same time
like
as well as
likewise
in comparison
both
all
by the same token
furthermore

———— Contrast ————

but
on the other hand
in spite of
conversely
despite
however
nonetheless
nevertheless
on the contrary
instead
rather

notwithstanding
though
yet
regardless
whereas
although
in contrast
unlike
for all that
even though

Conclusions

in brief
in the end
in summary
to reiterate
in conclusion
to sum up
finally
therefore
thus
as already stated

Name _____   Class _____

A CHAPTER MAP

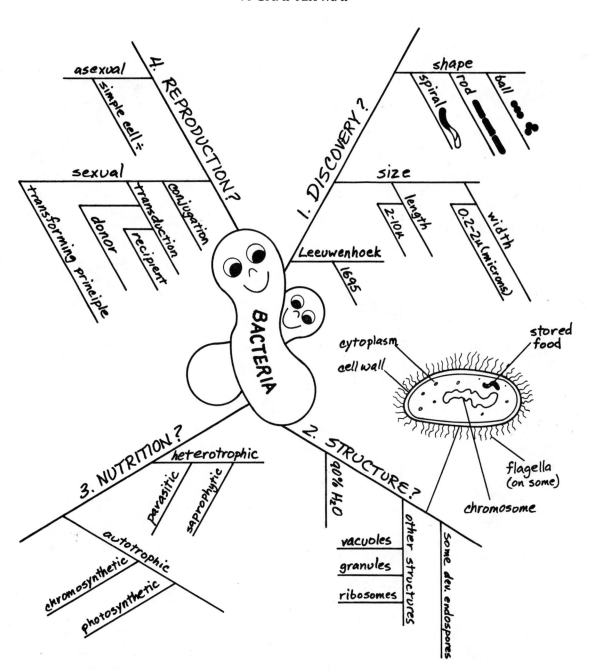

Adapted from pp. 198–213 of *Biological Sciences: An Inquiry into Life*, 2nd edition, by the Biological Sciences Curriculum Study, New York: Harcourt Brace Jovanovich, 1968. Map by Al Schwahn, science teacher at LaFollette High School, Madison, Wis.

Name _____   Class _____

HOW A MAP IS BORN

Step 1: Find the *topic* or the *thesis statement* (the subject and the author's attitude toward that subject) of the reading. To do this, read the title of the chapter, for example, "Bacteria." Illustrate that subject with an appropriate drawing.

Did you know that novelty facilitates both learning and memory? Therefore, be creative when you draw somewhere on your notebook page the "picture" that houses the topic or thesis. If you feel inept at art, use a triangle, hexagon, etc., for the central figure—just something a little out of the ordinary. Next, print the topic or thesis in capital letters. This crisp image is most readily learned and recalled.

Then pause. Reflect on all your previous learning and experiences related to this topic. This action will help you zero in on the topic.

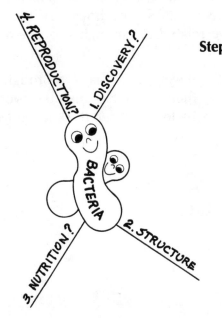

Step 2: Now *hypothesize* what the *major concepts* of the reading might be before actually checking the headings. In this chapter there are four: (1) discovery, (2) bacterial structure, (3) nutrition, (4) reproduction. If no headings are present, survey by reading the introduction, the first sentence of each paragraph, and the conclusion. Then decide what topic each paragraph focuses on. Synthesize and label paragraphs on similar aspects of the subject, thus arriving at the major concepts. This step is challenging.

Limit the number of major concepts to seven, even fewer if you can. Print these in capital letters and connect them to the topic or thesis, adding a question mark to each one.

Adapted from M. Buckley Hanf, "Mapping: A Technique for Translating Reading into Thinking," *Journal of Reading* 14 (January 1971): 225–230.

Map itself is adapted from pp. 198–213 of *Biological Science: An Inquiry into Life,* 2nd edition, by the Biological Sciences Curriculum Study, Harcourt Brace Jovanovich, Inc., 1968. Map by Al Schwahn, science teacher at LaFollette High School, Madison, Wis.

These are the principal questions you will need to answer as you read.

Now sit back and look at your map. What you see is the *essence of the entire chapter or article*. These are the powerful ideas that will later trigger your memory of the important supportive details.

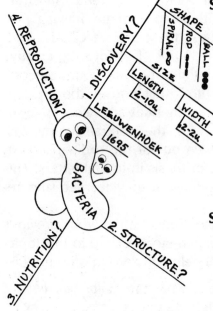

Step 3: Careful *reading for answers* to the questions—that's the next step. After reading under the first heading, *from memory* try to recall and write the significant support. (Notice that mapping has the unique feature of providing a chance to reveal relationships with drawn lines. Deciding how ideas relate to each other enhances your comprehension and memory of the content.)

Then, check yourself against the book. If you can't recall, quickly reread.

Step 4: After reading the chapter, focus on each major concept on your map and *recite from memory* the supportive details. See how easy this is when you've related the thoughts to one another.

Step 5: Intermittently *review* this map—thoroughly the next day, then for a few minutes every week or so thereafter—to keep the knowledge alive!

Name _____   Class _____

LUMBERJILLS
by Linda Myer

1.   Legend says that the flapjacks were bigger than platters, the griddle so vast that four men greased it by skating across on hogs strapped to snowshoes. The cook is usually described as a burly man with thick moustache and forearms like tree limbs. Reality paints a different picture. Sometimes the figure flipping the pancakes was a woman. Though women are not a part of logging-camp folklore, they went "a-logging" all the same.

2.   Before 1890, Wisconsin lumberjacks hacked away at the edge of a wooded wilderness. Logging camps were all-male societies in which bigness and toughness were supreme values. It is said that because "only the toughest could survive," the camps "produced . . . veritable hellions—rough, tough, lusty and thirsty . . . whose only pleasures were booze, bawds, and battle." They had no homes, only rough-hewn, lice-infested bunkhouses, and were as transient as the rushing rivers on which they drove the logs to market in spring.

3.   As the lumber industry pushed westward, leaving behind great swaths of cleared land, an army of settlers came to farm the cutover. They brought with them to the frontier all the accoutrements of civilization—plows, dishes, churches, saloons, and schools. Some of these settlers obtained jobs in logging camps to earn cash for their farms. As a quieter, more stable class of men began to replace the Paul Bunyans, the character of the camps began to change; they became more settled and homey.

4.   The arrival of women in the camps accelerated this "civilizing" process. Transient lumberjacks . . . came into contact with women who wanted to marry and settle down. Even rough-mannered loggers spoke more politely and engaged in fewer fights in the presence of women and children. Most of the loggers were protective of the children and enjoyed making toys for them and teaching them woods lore.

5.   Most women joined logging camps to make money, often so they and their husbands could more quickly acquire enough cash to buy a farm. Some couples, already settled on farms, needed cash for tools, taxes, supplies, or emergencies. Esther Gibbs, of Spooner, became a camp cook to earn money for her two-year-old son's operation.

Linda Myer, *Wisconsin Trails* 20 (Winter 1979): 31–33. Reprinted by permission.

6. Money, however, was not the only reason women worked in the camps. Some wanted to keep their families together. Mary Padjen, whose husband was hired as camp cook, took a job as part-time kitchen helper, or "cookee," because she was reluctant about being left alone with a young baby.

7. Married women were hired as cooks and cookees, never for woods jobs. Unmarried women were allowed only as members of the cook's family or as assistants to a female cook.

8. What was camp life like for these women? The cookshack, a long rectangular building, was the center of their universe, the place where they worked and lived. Early cookshacks were made of logs. After 1920, they were nothing but cheap boards covered with tar paper. To reduce heat loss, there were few windows. The floor was made of rough planks. Cracks provided drainage when the floor was scrubbed, a convenient but very drafty arrangement. Aina Nyman, who was a cook in a camp near Ironwood, Michigan, remembers that her hundred-pound sacks of flour used to freeze to the walls.

9. Quarters for the cook and her family were usually just bunks in the kitchen. A blanket draped in front of the bunks provided the only privacy. In a few camps, small bedrooms were built onto the cookshack wall—a real luxury. Nails on the wall served as closets; blankets were thrown over the clothes to protect them from flour dust and grease smells.

10. Sylvia Niemi, who worked as cookee for her mother, once found a more private place, but her stay was brief. A married couple had built a cabin near the cookshack, but they left camp unexpectedly, abandoning the cabin. "So," recalls Sylvia, "I fixed it all up. I brought all my clothes in there and slept one night. I was scared stiff! Then I went outside and saw a big bear. I hauled all my clothes back into the cookshack!"

11. Dining tables filled one end of the cookshack. At the other end was the kitchen. It was unlike any household kitchen. Everything was on a giant scale and arranged for efficiency. Typically, the two wood-burning cookstoves were eight feet wide and had thirty-pail caldrons attached by pipes to the fireboxes to supply plenty of hot water. There were racks above the stoves for drying pans and dishes. Flanking the stoves were work tables for rolling out pie, bread, and cookie dough. Above them were cooling racks for baked goods.

12. The person overseeing the whole production, the cook, was the single most important person in camp, including the foreman. George Corrigan, an ex-foreman, explained, "If you didn't have a good cook, you didn't have anybody." Wages for lumberjacks were small, but decent meals could compensate for a lot.

Linda Myer, *Wisconsin Trails* 20 (Winter 1979): 31–33. Reprinted by permission.

Name _____   Class _____

13.   Where food was concerned, quantity was as important as quality. Esther Gibbs, a cook near Hayward, regularly served a "family" of sixty. One day's meat might be half a hog, a quarter of beef, or a hundred pounds of weiners. Sometimes she would stretch out the meat with a keg of pork sausage. Reported Esther: "Twenty-five pounds of lard, 25 pounds of navy beans, a bushel of potatoes, 50 pounds of flour, 15 to 20 pies, a bushel of cookies and doughnuts, 6 to 8 gallons of vegetables, 25 pounds of tea, 10 pounds of oleo, 25 pounds of white sugar, 25 pounds of brown sugar. . . . These were the staples day in and day out. There were raisins, rice, macaroni, dried apples used here and there too."

14.   Preparation of these enormous meals was usually executed by one cook. In camps with fewer than thirty men, she did the cleanup and service, too, though in larger camps cookees were hired for such tasks. Supplies came in only once a week, ingredients were sometimes unavailable, and refrigeration was impossible. In addition, it was the cook's job to keep daily food costs within a strict budget of about fifty cents per person. However, a cook who could serve tasty food promptly three times a day despite these limitations was in great demand and earned two or three times more than the average lumberjack. During the Depression, cooks' wages ranged from a low of thirty-five dollars a month to as high as one hundred dollars a month. Room and board were always included.

15.   The cook earned every cent. Typically, she arose at 3:00 A.M., lit the fires in the cookstoves, and mixed pancake batter in washtubs. She would fry hundreds of pancakes on long cast-iron griddles, stash them in the oven, and proceed to fry sausages, doughnuts, and potatoes. At 5:30 A.M., the men filed in. Tables were laden with serving bowls of each dish. The cookees scurried between tables and kitchen, refilling bowls and coffee cups. The men ate in silence and quickly left for the cuttings. The cookees cleared the tables, washed the dishes, and reset the tables. The cook, meanwhile, was hard at work on the next meal. Sylvia Niemi remembers her mother's labors: "Right after breakfast, she'd start making pies. She'd make ten, twenty pies a day. And biscuits and cake and bread. And she made cookies all the time. . . . She worked all day long." Such was the daily routine. The cook rarely hung up apron and spatula until nine or ten in the evening.

16.   Though this work load was no different for male cooks, many female cooks also had to find time to care for their children. Sometimes a woman went to her own or her parents' home to deliver, but occasionally babies were born right in the cookshack. Alex Kurki's mother told him that he was born "between dinner

---

Linda Myer, *Wisconsin Trails* 20 (Winter 1979): 31–33. Reprinted by permission.

and supper." The foreman would choose a substitute cook from among the other crew members or simply add cookees to the kitchen staff until the mother could return to work. Nonetheless, there were many months when a new mother had to fit feeding and diapering into her busy schedule. Children learned to amuse themselves and to do kitchen chores very early.

17.   Evening leisure time was fairly quiet. Esther Gibbs remarked, "At night, when those fellas came in, they were ready to fall in those ol' bunks." People talked, told stories, and sang. Often, the younger men chatted with the kitchen girls while helping them peel the next day's potatoes. The women also read, knit, crocheted, and embroidered in their spare time. The daughter of one cook remembered wearing slips that her mother made from flour sacks. They had four inches of crocheted lace at the top and bottom.

18.   Before the late twenties, transportation in the northwoods was slow and difficult, so people remained in camp most of the time. Although the loggers often went home or to town on Sundays, the cook and cookees could not leave because they had to feed all who remained in camp. Sunday was not a holiday for the kitchen crew, but it was an easier day because there were fewer to feed.

19.   With improvements in transportation came greater mobility. Passenger trains ran daily between Bessemer, Mellen, Ashland, and Duluth. It was possible to hop the train in the morning and go shopping, visit a friend, have a beer, and return by nightfall. Even in their few hours off, the kitchen staff could go somewhere and return in time to serve the next meal. When cars and trucks proliferated, in the mid-thirties, social life in the northwoods bloomed. "I didn't stay in camp very much in the evenings," said Sylvia Niemi, who was a sixteen-year-old cookee in 1936. "The young fellas there, they'd have a car. Well, we'd bunch up and go to dances. . . . We'd pick up my girlfriends on the way." There were dances several nights a week in neighboring towns like Ironwood, Bessemer, and Iron Belt. Battery radios were available, too, and Sylvia recalled listening to Major Bowes' Original Amateur Hour and Fibber McGee and Molly.

20.   Eventually, the camps were populated largely by people from the surrounding farms, people who had known each other for years and shared family and community ties. Logging camps were no longer isolated enclaves housing a "different breed" of men, but became instead an integral part of the northern farming communities. And while the camps were changing in character, they were also becoming fewer in number. By degrees, the large tracts of timber were decimated. The big camps themselves finally became part of northwoods folklore, along with river drives and two-man saws.

Linda Myer, *Wisconsin Trails* 20 (Winter 1979): 31–33. Reprinted by permission.

21.   As the heyday of the lumbering era came to an end in Wisconsin, the land began to cover its scars with second-growth timber. The burly lumberjacks became the subject of song and story. The women, few in number, were not heralded as folk heroes. Yet, in helping to tame the wilderness, they left their own indelible mark on the northwoods.

Linda Myer, *Wisconsin Trails* 20 (Winter 1979): 31–33. Reprinted by permission.

Name _____ Class _____

A mind map titled **LOGGING CAMP LIFE FOR ♀ / LUMBERJILLS**

① **CAMP HISTORY**
- PRE-1890: RAUCOUS, ALL-MALE
- POST-1890: B. FARM PEOPLE — COMMUNITY
- A. SETTLERS: STABLE, $ FOR FARMS
- WOMEN ARRIVE, "CIVILIZATION", RETAIN FAMILY, $

② **COOK**
- CHILD CARE — BIRTH IN COOKSHACK
- 1:30 MEN
- 18 HRS/DAY ALL WK.
- FOOD* — QUALITY, QUANTITY
- HIGHEST STATUS
- $35-100/MO. (2-3x LUMBERJACK)
- SINGLE — COOKEE TO ♀
- MARRIED — COOKEE, COOK

③ **COOKSHACK-HUB**
- COOK'S QUARTERS: NAILS, BUNKS
- KITCHEN: ICY FLOORS, HUGE, EFFICIENT

④ **LEISURE**
- TO LATE 1920's—HOMEY: TELL STORIES, SING, TALK
- 1930's—WORLDLY: RADIOS, CARS, TRUCKS, TRAINS

Map based on Linda Myers, "Lumberjills," *Wisconsin Trails* 20 (Winter 1979): 31–33.

Name _____ Class _____

UNLUCKY STRIKES

During the past forty years, cancer of the lung in the United States has shown the greatest increase of any cancer type. Compared to 3,000 deaths from lung cancer in 1930, the number of deaths is expected to rise to 84,000 in 1981. If the present trend continues, it is estimated that about one million persons who are now school children will die eventually of lung cancer.

in l.c. Such an alarming increase assumes the proportions of an epidemic. At least 70 percent of the total increase can be attributed to cigarette smoking. An additional factor is air pollution caused by industrial wastes, automobile exhausts and household sources.

The research

1. The first studies on the relationship of smoking to lung cancer were of patients with the disease who were asked about their smoking habits. Their answers were compared with those of noncancer patients. Almost all lung cancer patients replied that they had been long-term, heavy cigarette smokers.

2. The next studies were of large groups of men who were first identified by their smoking habits, then were followed for several years. Deaths from all causes increased among smokers according to the amount smoked. But the most striking proportional rise was in deaths from lung cancer.

3. While these clues were being obtained from population studies, scientists began to study the smoking and cancer relationship in the laboratory. Chemists isolated and identified at least a dozen carcinogenic chemicals of the hydrocarbon type in the tars from tobacco smoke. There is evidence that tobacco smoke contains yet further carcinogens.

How lungs are affected The membranes lining the lungs absorb cancer-producing chemicals from tobacco smoke. The protective mechanisms by which the lungs rid themselves of impurities are first paralyzed and then destroyed by tobacco smoke. Prolonged exposure of animals to tobacco smoke produces changes in cells that resemble early stages of cancer development. These changes are also seen in the lungs of heavy smokers who die of causes other than lung cancer.

Smoking also a factor in → Health hazards of smoking are not limited to lung cancer. Bronchitis, emphysema and other crippling lung diseases are produced in even larger numbers. Deaths from heart disease are accelerated and increased. While cigarette smoking is a major cause of lung cancer, other uses of tobacco are associated with cancers of the oral cavity among cigar smokers and cancers of the lip among pipe smokers.

From *The Now Student* by Edward Spargo, p. 91. Copyright © 1977 by Jamestown Publishers, Providence, R.I. Reprinted by permission. The markings have been added.

Name _____ Class _____

SAMPLE NOTES

	Biology November 21
	Unlucky Strikes
	Last 40 yrs. lung cancer (U.S.) < more than other cancers. 3000 (1930) → 84000 (1981) expected. At least 70% < in l.c. cuz of cig. smkg.
What does research indicate?	1st studies: interviewed l.c. patients about smkg. Almost all heavy smkrs. Next studies: followed many men smkrs for yrs. < smkg = more deaths, esp. l.c. Chemists: tars contain 12+ carcinogenic chem.
How does smkg. affect lungs?	Smks. lung membranes don't "filter" as well. L. cell changes at death.
What are other health hazards of smkg?	Smkg. → bronchitis emphysema heart disease oral cancers lip

Notes are based on a selection from *The Now Student* by Edward Spargo, p. 91. Copyright © 1977 by Jamestown Publishers, Providence, R.I.

Name _____   Class _____

WHAT'S YOUR NQ (NOTE-TAKING QUOTIENT)?

Check (√) the Yes *or* No *column for each item below.*

Before			*After*	
Yes	No	**Before the lecture do I**	Yes	No
_____	_____	1. read assigned work?	_____	_____
_____	_____	2. review yesterday's notes?	_____	_____
_____	_____	3. recall all my life experiences and learning that relate to the subject?	_____	_____
_____	_____	4. have a pen and spiral (looseleaf) notebook?	_____	_____
_____	_____	a. with a special section for each course?	_____	_____
_____	_____	b. with numbered notebook pages and the first few pages reserved for assignment information?	_____	_____
_____	_____	c. with a 2½-inch column on the left of each page for recall practice?	_____	_____
		During the lecture do I		
_____	_____	5. try hard to get interested in the subject so that I'm mentally alert?	_____	_____
_____	_____	6. ignore distractions?	_____	_____
_____	_____	7. listen for cues (transitions such as, "The first cause was," teacher's clues such as, "This is important") to the most significant content in the lecture?	_____	_____
_____	_____	8. **RECORD** LEGIBLY AND IN PEN?	_____	_____
_____	_____	9. RECORD ONLY THE CENTRAL THOUGHTS AND IMPORTANT DETAILS?	_____	_____

| *Before* | | | *After* | |
| Yes | No | | Yes | No |

_____ _____ 10. MATCH MY NOTE-TAKING STYLE TO THE LECTURE CONTENT (FOR EXAMPLE, USE CHARTS, LISTS, PARAGRAPHS, ETC., AS THE CONTENT DICTATES)? _____ _____

_____ _____ 11. ABBREVIATE? _____ _____

_____ _____ 12. remain flexible (If the teacher's disorganized, write what I can)? _____ _____

After the lecture do I

_____ _____ 13. FILL IN MISSED WORDS? _____ _____

_____ _____ 14. SUMMARIZE (noteSHRINK) THE LECTURE IN THE 2½-INCH COLUMN? _____ _____

_____ _____ 15. **RECITE** from memory (noteTALK), then check for accuracy? _____ _____

_____ _____ 16. **REFLECT** on the material (noteTHINK)? _____ _____

_____ _____ 17. **REVIEW** intermittently (noteREVIEW)? _____ _____

Overall, what is the quality of your note-taking on lectures? Mark an *X* at the appropriate spot on the continuum below.

Poor	**Fair**	**Good**	**Excellent**
"I'm limping along"	*"I manage but—"*	*"I'm quite satisfied"*	*"I'm an ace at it!"*

If simply wishing could make them come true, what two aspects of your note-taking would you wish to improve?

1.

2.

Name _____   Class _____

GAINING THE MOST FROM LECTURE NOTES

Taking notes is only half the story. Then follow up to truly conquer the content!

During the Lecture • **NoteTAKE**	Write legibly in the main column of your notebook the important facts and ideas in the lecture. (After the lecture, fill in any missed words or incomplete ideas.)
After the Lecture • **NoteSHRINK**	That same day noteSHRINK (summarize), in the quiz column, the central thoughts. The benefits? This process rivets your attention, sharpens thinking, improves memory, and gives you a head start on exam preparation. Since you are so absorbed in listening and taking notes during a lecture, your summarizing the material soon after may be your first chance to grasp the Gestalt (the whole) of what you've heard. How do you noteSHRINK? After making the notes, SHRINK the lecture to its essence: a. *Survey* your notes by reading the first sentence of every paragraph or block. b. For each paragraph, ask: "In a word or two, what is this *entire paragraph* about?" Underlining these topics helps. c. Examine all the topics and ask: "What are the biggest 'thought chunks' possible?" RECORD those major concepts in the quiz column. (Note that paragraphs 3–5 of the sample notes that follow all deal with relating to others: competition, impact on others, regaining autonomy.)

This material is extensively adapted from the Cornell method presented by Walter Pauk, *How to Study in College,* 2nd ed. (Boston: Houghton Mifflin Company, 1974), pp. 128–133.

Psychology
Sept. 30

The College Experience Ahead

Personal implications for growth

Intell., soc., emot. maturity is sporadic.
role change = potential for growth.
ex. start school, dating, marr.

College stresses intell; BUT soc, emot.
too. Accepting conseq. of choices→
growth.

Relating to others

Must manage own life, emot., + relate
to others. Competition interferes
c̄ friendship.

We have great impact on others;
thus create own envir., good or
bad.

Conformity - beware. Retain some
autonomy.

Notes taken on a speech presented by Dr. John W. Gardner at the Westchester Scholastic Achievement Dinner, Westchester, New York, on March 2, 1965.

Name _____   Class _____

• NoteTALK	This step cannot be overemphasized! Psychologists have proved scientifically that one learning and memory technique is more powerful than any other—*self-recitation!* 　　Quiz yourself. Cover the main column. Now look at your first summary in the quiz column and recall all the relevant information in your notes associated with that phrase or key word. Talk through these *aloud* and in *your own words*. Then consult your notes to check whether you have been accurate and complete. This recitation results in your mastering the material and fixing it in long-term memory.
• NoteTHINK	Let the material "seep" in. Sit back and simply allow the new learning to work in you. To what in your life experience does this new material speak? Are there links with other courses? For example, if you've just studied about early U.S. gold rushes and the mining towns that resulted, can you see contemporary counterparts in our society (the rush to be the first inhabitants on the moon? to possess the oil fields in Alaska or in the oceans? to build "Olympic cities" to accommodate the Olympic games, a brief event)? 　　Record your perceptions in a different color ink or in parentheses on your notes themselves. Or place them at the back of your notebook in a special section reserved solely for your great insights! Don't forget to review that section before test time, too. 　　Learning is more enjoyable when you personalize it.
• NoteREVIEW	No surprise—here it is again! For at least two reasons, a five- to ten-minute review of each subject every week or so is a sound investment. This continual reviewing (1) reinforces *retention* and (2) allows you to see the *continuity* and *interrelationships of ideas* presented over an extended period of time, so that they're readily available for test-taking, problem-solving, and living more creatively!

Name _____ Class _____

PRELECTURE PREP

Get set for peak-performance listening and learning! A little preparation helps.

		Personal Analysis
• **Get Set— The Mechanics**	• Ideally, use a ***looseleaf binder*** divided into sections according to subject. This allows you to consolidate handouts with your notes. If you buy instead a spiral notebook, be sure it has pockets for handouts.	
	• Designate one twelve-page section exclusively for ***study skills.***	
	• Use a ***pen*** for easy readability.	
	• Reserve the first several pages for ***assignments.*** The format? Head the pages with the following:	

Date	Topic or Assign.	Page Book	Number Notes	Completed

Under *page number* write the number of any pages in your notebook (number these pages yourself) and your textbook that deal with the assignment.

		Personal Analysis
	• Divide your paper into ***two columns*** by drawing a line 2½ inches from the left margin. This is done on every page.	

Quiz	*Record Column*

		Personal Analysis
• **Get Set— The Mind**	• **Read** any **assigned work before** going to class. You'll feel confident and oriented as a result. Not doing assigned work before classtime is like reporting to phys. ed. without gym clothes or to band rehearsal without an instrument.	
	• **Review yesterday's notes** a few minutes before class starts or earlier. This provides an excellent context for today's lecture so that you can jump immediately into the thought.	
	• **Reflect** for a few minutes on all your personal experiences and previous learning that relate to the subject. New learning "sticks" most readily when it fits into a meaningful context.	

REVIEW BOX

From memory, write all that you can recall from this handout. Then check your accuracy!

Name _____   Class _____

AT THE LECTURE

		Personal Analysis
• **Be a Keen Listener!**	• *Get interested!* This attitude rivets your attention and concentration and heightens your learning and remembering. Getting interested also helps you ignore distractions: noise or judging the lecturer's delivery (external distractions) and your own reruns of last night's movie (internal distraction).	
	• *Sort* the wheat from the chaff! You're most interested in the major concepts and significant details. What aids you in finding these? Listen for *cues*. The following are a few mental signals to listen for: Contrast: *on one hand, on the other hand* *but* *on the contrary* *in opposition to* Additional points: *and* *in addition* *another* *plus* *moreover* *as well as* Conclusion: *in summary* *as a result* *in the end* *finally*	

• **Be a Keen Listener!** (cont.)	Not only transition clues but also the **teacher's forthright statements** are signs to direct your thinking and note-taking: *"Thus, the important point is . . ."* *"Don't forget that . . ."* *"What is essential to understand is . . ."* *"I want you to remember that . . ."* *"The three conditions are . . ."*	
	• Place an (*) in the margin of your notebook as a red flag to indicate anything the teacher emphasizes.	
	• **Be mentally alive!** Use that "extra" mental space to anticipate what the speaker will say next or to summarize what has already been stated. Listen between the lines to the speaker's changing volume, voice quality, actions. What do they convey?	
• **Record**	• **Legibly** and in **pen,** record only the central thoughts and significant details. Remember notes are just that: you're not aiming for a complete transcript. Record in the main 6-inch column.	
	• Write the notes generally in **block, paragraph,** or **outline** form, whichever you can manage most quickly and accurately.	
	• **"Freestyle"** when the content dictates it. For example, a chart is best for contrasting two ideas: Listing, for a lab procedure: 1. 2. 3.	

Name _____   Class _____

		Personal Analysis
• **Record** (cont.)	*Skip a line* whenever the lecturer moves to a new facet of the topic. Transitions and direct teacher statements will usually alert you.	
	• *Abbreviate* to expedite recording. For example, psych = psychology indiv = individual resp = responsibility govt = government ex = example cuz o = because of Do be cautious, though, not to use so many abbreviations that the notes are meaningless when you study and review them later.	
	• *Be flexible.* If the teacher is disorganized, glean what you can. You'll have to sift through and reorganize your notes after the lecture.	

REVIEW BOX

Write all you can of the important points in this handout; then check back to see how successful you've been!

Name _____ Class _____

SYNOPSIS OF TAXONOMY OF QUESTIONS

Underlying Ideas

1. All thinking can be classified into seven kinds, which have been named memory, translation, interpretation, application, analysis, synthesis, and evaluation.

2. All categories of questions fit all subjects.

3. Every category of questions has both easy and difficult questions. Thus, everyone can experience questions on every level.

4. The definitions of the seven kinds of questions overlap somewhat so that equally knowledgeable experts often differ on the best classification of a certain question. This need not bother you.

5. By knowing the definitions of the kinds of questions, you can learn how to respond to these varying levels of questions.

6. The word *question* refers to any intellectual exercise calling for a response; this would include both problems and projects.

MEMORY

A memory question asks you to recall or recognize ideas presented to you previously in reading or listening. Memory questions can require you to recall a single fact or a much more involved idea.

Examples

1. *Conditions for this question:* The teacher has given the definitions of *solid, liquid,* and *gas.* Examples of each were displayed.

   Question: What is the definition of a solid, a liquid, and a gas?

Reprinted by permission of Norris M. Sanders, former professor, University of Wisconsin-Green Bay.

2. *Conditions for this question:* You have drilled on your multiplication tables.

Question: Solve these problems: 5   2   6
                                          ×4   ×6   ×7
                                          ――   ――   ――

TRANSLATION

In translation you are presented with an idea and then asked to restate exactly the same idea in a different way.

Examples

1. *Conditions for this question:* You have read a paragraph in the textbook.

   Question: Now tell me in your own words what you read.

2. *Conditions for this question:* The teacher demonstrates the operation of a siphon.

   Question: Draw a picture of a siphon you were shown.

INTERPRETATION

The question asks you to *compare* certain ideas or to *use* an idea that you studied previously to solve a problem that is new to you. The idea may be in the form of a skill, definition, law, rule, or generalization. You do not have to figure out which idea is to be used in interpretation because the question or the classroom context tells this. The question can be in short-answer or discussion form. Usually the answer is quite objective. In other words, there is usually a right answer, which the teacher expects you to reason out.

Example

Conditions for this question: After seeing a film on customs of marriage and bringing up a family in an African society, you are asked:

Question: In what ways are the marriage and family customs in the movie similar to those in our society, and in what ways are they different?

Name _____   Class _____

APPLICATION

Application questions are similar to interpretation questions in that you are to use ideas learned previously in problems new to you. However, application goes one step further. In an interpretation question you must show that you can use an idea when told specifically to do so. In an application question you must show that you can use an idea when *not told* to do so, but when the problem demands it. In other words, application calls for the transfer of learning to new situations.

Example

> *Conditions for this question:* In language-arts class the teacher has taught you how to use an index and table of contents. Later in a social-studies class the teacher asks this question:

> *Question:*   Find the page in our social-studies book that tells about Booker T. Washington. (The question would have been interpretation if asked this way: Use the index to find the page in your social-studies text that tells about Booker T. Washington.)

ANALYSIS

Analysis questions are always preceded by instruction in some logical process. Some of the most useful logical processes are classification, induction, deduction, cause and effect. An analysis question asks you to solve a problem with a conscious observance of the rules for good thinking of the type called for by the problem.

Example

> *Conditions for this question:* You have been given explanations of three rules for classification: (A) Vocabulary clear in meaning; (B) Sufficient classes to include all data, and (C) Classes discrete.

> *Question:*   What problems do you see in grouping mankind under the headings of white race, black race, and yellow race?

SYNTHESIS

The question asks you to create something. The product to be created may be a physical object, a communication, a plan of operation, or a set of abstract relations. In other kinds of thinking there may also be products, but the distinctive thing about synthesis is the great freedom you have in deciding what is to be created and how it is to be created. A synthesis question never has one correct response. There are always many good answers that you may work out.

Examples

1. *Conditions for this question:* Your class has read a story called "Indian Bill." One student said he didn't like the way the story turned out. The teacher then assigned this synthesis question:

   Question: Write a different ending to the story of "Indian Bill."

2. *Conditions for this question:* A box is to be inserted into the cornerstone of a new school. The students in your class are in charge of filling the box with things that show what it is like to go to school at the present time.

   Question: What do you think should go into the box?

EVALUATION

You are asked to make a value judgment of some product, communication, event, or situation. By a value judgment is meant a rating of something as being good or bad; in other cases the judgment is of right or wrong, or perhaps beautiful or ugly. Part of the answer always requires you to tell what considerations led you to that judgment. A value judgment is never provable. The best that can be done is to present good supporting evidence.

Examples

1. *Conditions for this question:* You have studied the colonial period of United States history.

   Question: Did the colonists do right in throwing the tea overboard at the Boston Tea Party? Tell why.

2. *Conditions for this question:* You have read a story about two brothers. One is a good athlete but a poor student. The other is a good student but clumsy and weak.

   Question: Which of these brothers would you rather be? Tell why.

Name _____   Class _____

WIFE WANTED

WIFE WANTED

Are you tired of hanging around bars looking for a mate?

I am!

Do you refuse to settle for someone who isn't just what you want even though he appears to be the only available one around? Good for you!

If you have the attributes listed below and you like what you read about me, I want to meet you. Write me giving me only your description, background and a mailing address or, if you want to take a chance answering an ad like this one, your name and telephone number as well.

DESIRED ATTRIBUTES

Age: 23 to 28 years

Education: Substantial scholastic achievement culminating in at least a four-year degree from a national university with major study preferably in accounting, the physical or medical sciences, law, history or library science

Occupation: Any career employment consistent with educational background and with annual earned income of at least $19,000

Religion: Agnostic or member of any major denomination

Physical Attributes: Not larger than 5 feet 5 inches tall and 115 pounds,

Analyze the levels of the following questions and write your answers in the blanks provided.

1. _____ Imagine that you are a twenty-five-year-old woman who has just finished reading this ad. Write a response to it.

2. _____ How old is the man who composed this want ad?

3. _____ What kind of father might this writer be? Defend your answer.

4. _____ Why is this man using a want ad to search for a wife? Explain in your own words.

5. _____ What problems might the writer incur as a result of running this want ad?

6. _____ Compare the author's personal description with the attributes he desires in a wife.

7. _____ Several weeks after reading the "Wife Wanted" article, your teacher asks, "If you directed the evening news show, what unique ideas would you use to increase your ratings with the public?"

Reprinted by permission from *The Capital Times*, Madison, Wis.

healthy, clear complexion and
definitely attractive

Personality and Habits: Nonsmoker, in-
frequent drinker, frugal, aggressive,
never married and no children, studi-
ous, a late sleeper who prefers a home
temperature of not more than 65 degrees F. and possessing a good sense
of humor

Ancestral Origin: Northern Europe,
Britain or Ireland

Political Affiliation: Moderate Dem-
ocrat or Independent

Recreational Interests: Skiing, tennis,
backpacking, music and traveling

Other: Preferably has worked or
studied in Europe and is a Sierra Club
member

MY DESCRIPTION

Age: 31 years

Education: Eight years at three national
universities financed by scholar-
ship grants culminating in three
degrees

Occupation: Private professional
employment

Religion: Agnostic

Physical Attributes: 5 feet 10 inches
tall, 160 pounds, healthy, clear complexion and some say definitely attractive

Personality and Habits: Same as above

Ancestral Origin: Same as above

Political Affiliation: Same as above

Recreational Interests: Same as above

Other: Professional employment and
travel in other countries and Sierra
Club membership

Paternal Interest: Willing to negotiate
after two years of marriage for not
more than two children

Name _____   Class _____

GETTING TEST-WISE: PROFILE OF TEST QUESTIONS

Level of question	Course															
Memory																
Translation																
Interpretation																
Application																
Analysis																
Synthesis																
Evaluation																

Course Profile

Course	Results of test-question analysis

Copyright © 1987 by Allyn and Bacon, Inc. Reproduction of this material is restricted to use with *A Guidebook for Teaching Study Skills and Motivation,* Second Edition by Bernice Jensen Bragstad and Sharyn Mueller Stumpf.

Name _____   Class _____

LEVELS OF QUESTIONING "ACTIVATOR"—THE WEB

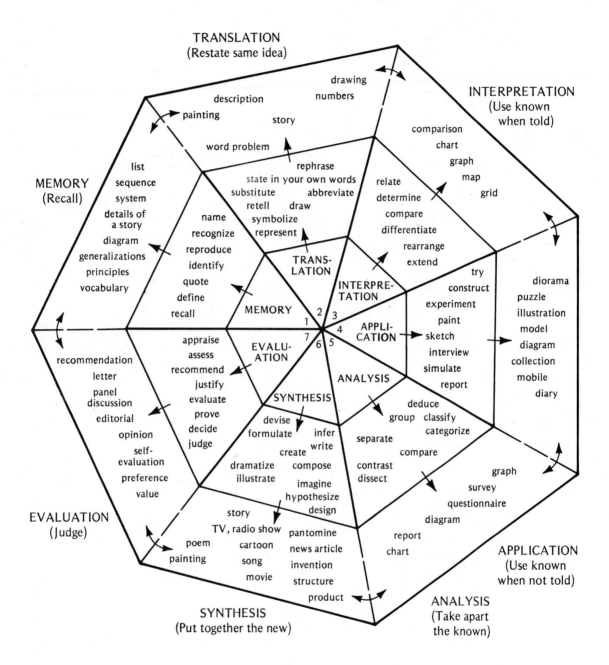

Adapted from Cheryl F. Biles and Pat Farrell Barnes, Educational Support Services, Irvine United School District, Irvine, Calif., 1976.

Name _____   Class _____

THINKING-SKILL GRID

Concept	Memory (recall)	Translation (Restate same idea)	Interpretation (use known when told)	Application (use known when *not* told)	Analysis (take apart)	Synthesis (put together)	Evaluation (judge)				
ex. Propaganda Techniques	Define the word "propaganda" as the book does.	In your own words, describe the bandwagon technique.	As you read a magazine ad, pick out 3 examples of propaganda and identify each.	Teacher in another class asks, "What criteria can we use to analyze campaign speeches?"	Analyze 3 current TV commercials for 3 types of propaganda.	Design a TV commercial that includes 3 propaganda techniques.	Assess which of these campaign posters is best. Justify your choice.				

Adapted from Cheryl F. Biles and Pat Farrell Barnes, Educational Support Services, Irvine Unified School District, Irvine, California, 1976.

Name _____   Class _____

BECOMING TEST-WISE: EXAM-ERROR CHECKLIST

Did you . . .	Course								
1. learn incorrectly the material?									
2. neglect to study the material?									
3. take inadequate notes?									
4. misread directions?									
5. misread the question itself?									
6. accidentally miss a question?									
7. consciously skip a question?									
8. run short of time?									
9. feel anxious about the exam?									
10. other?									

In addition, for essays did you . . .	Course								
1. forget to write a thesis?									
2. inadequately develop the body?									
3. forget to write a conclusion?									
4. omit needed transitions?									
5. ignore punctuation, grammar, legibility?									

Name _____ Class _____

TEST PREP

Here are some test-preparation hints to help you sidestep preexam panic.

The column to the far right is for your use in jotting brief comments on how adequately you meet each criterion. A simple note such as "Do more of this!" is sufficient.

		Personal Analysis
• *Keep Up*	Anxiety is diminished tremendously if you know that you've *taken notes* on or *mapped* all the material you've dealt with in class and in your textbooks. In addition, intermittently *reviewing* these materials gives you a giant step toward exam prep. Remember—organizing the ideas and reviewing frequently are the tickets to retrieval at test time and thereafter.	
• *Scout the Territory*	Objective tests contain true-false, multiple-choice, matching, and completion items; essay tests contain questions requiring longer, well-organized answers. If the teacher doesn't volunteer the general *content* and *format* of the exam, ask! You'll feel more mentally set to study and attack the test if you know what to expect. If you can, ask your teacher's former students whether he or she has any pet questions or quirks, i.e., does this teacher deduct 5 points if you write *true* or *false* instead of *T* or *F*, or does this teacher ask on every exam: "How many brain cells do you have?" Find out about *time*. Will you be allowed to remain after class if you don't finish the test?	

		Personal Analysis
• *Predict Questions*	Use the road signs—your quizzes and past tests as well as * sections in your notebook—to give you direction as you study, to help you sort out areas the teacher has emphasized. Then predict exam questions and prepare to answer them. Yes, this does take a certain amount of courage, and no, you can't be absolutely certain that your questions will be on the exam, but the fact that you have reviewed purposefully enough to come up with questions means that you've seriously considered the material. And think how delighted you'll feel if even a couple of those questions are on the exam, and you need only a minute to record your rehearsed answer.	
• *Think Big*	Focus on the *generalizations* and *major concepts*. Spread out your notes in order and survey the major points that way. Drawing a map of just these key points is an excellent review tactic, too. *Then* study the details, but always *in relationship* to the major concepts.	
• *Think Positively*	"Of course I can be a successful learner and test-taker!" Tell yourself that any time that doubts creep into your mind. Challenge yourself to do the best you can. How can you keep yourself mentally up for tests? Don't skimp on essentials—meals, rest, a little leisure time (a walk can be brief, but still refreshing). Retain some kind of normalcy even though you're studying intensely.	

Name _____   Class _____

BOOT CAMP FOR TEST-TAKERS: AT THE EXAM

		Personal Analysis
• **Settle In**	Arrive early enough to feel relaxed, yet alert when the test begins. If you can, avoid sitting near friends; they're usually a distraction. Depending on your psychological makeup, either do or don't review one last time some material that's difficult to remember. Some people prefer using the last minutes to review a complicated point so that they're ready to write it on the back of the exam as soon as it's passed out. Take a few slow, deep breaths, then . . .	
• **Survey!**	As soon as you've received your exam and written your name on it, survey the entire test in a minute or so to see what's ahead. The first time or two, forcing yourself to do this will be painful. Yes, people around you may be writing away while you're still surveying, but they may also discover, 5 minutes before time is up, the 25-point essay question on the back of page 3 that you've already answered!	
• **Pace Yourself**	After previewing, allot the time by quickly calculating how many minutes to spend on each section. This is based on the *point value* of each section. (If points are not indicated, ask your teacher. You have a right to know this information.) For example, during a 50-minute period,	

		Personal Analysis
• *Pace Yourself* (cont.)	*Time Allotment:* multiple choice = 30 points 14 minutes matching = 20 points 10 minutes two essays = 50 points 24 minutes _____ 48 (+2 minutes to proofread) Stick to your time schedule. Wearing your own watch facilitates this.	
• **Mark Up the Directions**	Have you ever been penalized on a test because you wrote the answer to only *one* essay question instead of *two*? Or because you chose the *best* answer in multiple choice items instead of *all* the correct answers? If so, you already know that accurately reading the directions is crucial. To encourage precision, underline the key facts in the directions, i.e., "In this essay section, of the 4 statements below, choose 2 on which to write." *Choose* and *2* are underlined because they state the boundaries within which you must operate.	
• *Pick Up Easy Points*	Psychologically, you'll be on top if you answer first all the easy test items. Then go back to pick up the more difficult ones. With this strategy you may also run across clues to the tough questions. (Put a check in the margin before difficult items so you can rapidly relocate them.) Unless there is a penalty for guessing, answer all test questions, even if you have to guess. Also, underline troublesome words if you're having a tough time figuring out a question and ask the teacher for clarification. A few more tips?	

Name _____   Class _____

		Personal Analysis
• **Pick Up Easy Points** (cont.)	Multiple choice items: • Cross out wrong options. • Read every option before answering. • Seriously consider an extremely long or short option since it is often correct. True-false questions: • Items containing qualifiers such as *all, always, never, none* are usually false. • Items containing qualifiers such as *some, sometimes, usually, often* are typically true. Completion items: • Do easy items first to eliminate them. • Use grammatical clues (i.e., the word *an* signals an answer beginning with a vowel sound). • Notice length of the blanks. *Caution: None of these tips is a substitute for your thorough knowledge of the subject matter on the test!*	
• **Trust the Teacher**	Don't be paranoid. Unless you know otherwise, assume the teacher is forthright in asking you test questions. Focus on what is actually stated rather than what you might infer. For example, "Thomas Edison invented the light bulb—true or false?" Although the light bulb is only one of Edison's innumerable inventions, the teacher probably wants a "true" for that answer.	

		Personal Analysis
• *Proof Your Answers*	Give yourself a break: in the last few minutes of the hour, skim your exam to be sure that you've followed directions and answered all questions. This is the time to catch mistakes if you've forgotten to answer an item or underlined answers when they should be circled. If you've written an essay, rapidly proofread, checking whether you've addressed the question and provided a thesis statement, adequate evidence that is clearly organized, and a conclusion. Also search for sentence fragments and run-on sentences, omitted words, punctuation errors, that require your last-minute attention. *Congratulations—mission accomplished!*	

Name _____   Class _____

ESSAY ESSENTIALS

Essay questions require unique treatment. In addition to applying the general test-taking hints, to be thoroughly equipped to attack that essay question or test, an invaluable aid is your knowing the meanings of key terms.*

Quickly skim the left-hand column and put an *X* in front of each word whose definition you don't think you know. Then read thoughtfully through this entire section, adding *X*s whenever definitions differ from what you anticipated. In the end, you'll need to review only the "marked" terms.

Compare: to cite both points of *similarity* and of *difference.*

Contrast: to stress *differences.*

Criticize: to point out both the *positive* and *negative* sides.

Define: to give a *clear, concise* meaning for a term.

Describe: to relate something in sequence or story form.

Diagram: to organize in some *pictorial* way—a flowchart, a chart, or some other graphic device—the parts and relationships of a set of facts or ideas.

Discuss: to examine and talk about an issue *from all sides;* must be carefully organized.

Enumerate: to write in list or outline form; numbering helps.

Evaluate: to make a value judgment, a statement of negative and/or positive worth; requires evidence for your opinion.

Explain: to clarify, to interpret, to analyze; emphasis on cause-effect relationships and sequence.

Illustrate: to show by means of a picture, a diagram, or some graphic aid; to relate specific examples.

Interpret: to explain, translate, or show a specific application of a given fact or principle.

Justify: to tell *why* a position or point of view is right; should stress the *positive.*

List: like enumerating, but requiring a formal numbering of sequence.

---

* Courtesy of Professor Ken Dulin, University of Wisconsin-Madison.

Outline: to organize a set of facts or ideas in terms of main points and subordinate points; a formal outline is suggested.

Prove: to give *evidence,* to present facts, to use logic as a basis for clear, forthright argumentation.

Relate: to show how two or more things are connected to one another through similar causation, similar results, or similar characteristics.

Review: to reexamine or summarize the key characteristics or major points of an overall body of facts, principles, or ideas.

State: to present a *brief, succinct* statement of a position, fact, or point of view.

Summarize: to give the *main points* relevant to an issue in condensed, abbreviated form, without details or examples.

Trace: to present in *sequence* a series of facts somehow related, in terms of time, order, or cause-effect.

To successfully write an essay test response, you must not only know the material but also think about and organize it effectively. The procedure that follows may aid you in becoming an "essay success"!

		Personal Analysis
• *Underline Key Terms*	As you read and underline the key terms that tell you what to do (criticize, trace, discuss), also underline key terms in the content of the question itself. Here is a sample essay question: "In our educational system, we need to *return to* the *basics* of reading, writing, and arithmetic. *Defend* or *refute* this statement." The topic is returning to basics; that is underlined to be certain that you don't wander from the subject. "Defend" and "refute" specify how to approach that subject.	
• *Jot Down Ideas*	As soon as you have read each essay question, immediately jot down relevant thoughts that occur to you. This safeguards you from forgetting as you quickly read	

Name _____   Class _____

		Personal Analysis
• *Jot Down Ideas* (cont.)	other essay questions to find the easiest one, which you'll want to tackle first. If the question is one of your predicted ones, you're ready to write!	
• *Take the Plunge*	Commit yourself immediately—there's no time to pussyfoot! "I firmly defend the need to return to the basics of reading, writing, and arithmetic, based on school and college entrance results and my own personal experience," is a lucid thesis statement that promptly informs the teacher where you stand. This direct approach also helps you keep sharply focused on the question. If the essay is to be brief, this thesis may stand alone as the introduction; however, if the essay is to be extended, this sentence can be included in a longer introductory paragraph.	
• *Fatten Up the Thesis*	Organization should flow logically from the thesis. Clearly state a *central thought* within each paragraph in the body. Use *transitional* words and phrases to keep your argument starkly clear, e.g., "In the first place, the results from reading tests administered to fourth and twelfth graders this year seem to indicate the need for more basic reading instruction." This sets clear direction for the facts that will make that topic sentence live and breathe. Beginning the next paragraph with a phrase such as "In the second place" or "In addition" helps the reader see you steadily accumulating evidence for your case.	

		Personal Analysis
• **Conclude**	No cliffhangers, please! After stating your case, *wrap it up* in a sentence or two with a statement of conviction: "Because of the declining scores from grade school to college entrance exams and because of the personal experiences I've cited, I staunchly affirm the need to return to the basics of reading, writing, and arithmetic."	
• **Persevere**	Despite every effort, if you still run short of time, never give up! Resort to *mapping* or *outlining* to confirm your knowledge of the subject. Teachers do usually give partial credit for such attempts. Quickly proofread for legibility, correct grammar, and accurate punctuation. *Hurrah! You've done it!*	

When your corrected exam is returned to you, don't forget to analyze any problem areas so that you can avoid them in the future.

Name _____ Class _____

SHARPEN YOUR ESSAY-WRITING SKILLS

Yes	No	
_____	_____	1. Does your essay speak to the question?
_____	_____	2. Is a clear *thesis statement* present (within an introductory paragraph, if the essay is to be an extended one)?
_____	_____	3. Are specific *facts* and *examples* developed in the body to substantiate the thesis?
_____	_____	4. Do *transitions* show thought relationships?
_____	_____	5. Is a clear, *concluding statement* (or paragraph for an extended essay) present and consistent with the thesis?
_____	_____	6. Is your *handwriting* legible?
_____	_____	7. Are your *grammar*, *punctuation*, and *spelling* accurate?

Other Comments:

Name _____ Class _____

STUDENT-TEACHER TIMELINE CHECKLIST*

_____ Introduction, hand out materials (include final grade sheet).

_____ Finalize Choices—set block of time for library work (Progress Report 1).

_____ Trial Bibliography and Survey of Material Due (Progress Reports 2 and 3).

_____ Trial outline work in class.

_____ Submit trial outline (Progress Report 4).

_____ Work in class on introduction and thesis statement, submit thesis statement (Progress Report 5).

_____ Submit introduction with thesis statement incorporated (Progress Report 6).

_____ Hand back introduction, begin work on body of paper and footnotes.

_____ In class, work on body and footnoting.

_____ Submit rough draft of body and footnote examples (Progress Report 7).

_____ Hand back body and footnote examples—student corrections.

_____ In class, work on conclusion of paper.

_____ Submit draft of conclusion (Progress Report 8).

_____ Hand back corrected conclusion.

_____ Submit entire bibliography (rough draft) (Progress Report 9).

_____ Work in class on final draft of paper.

_____ Submit final draft of paper with grade sheet as front page (Progress Report 10).

---

* Set due dates for each section of checklist. Student and teacher check off as they are completed.

Name _____   **Class** _____

OUTLINING

DEFINITION

An outline is an organized, systematized arrangement of important elements of a topic. The outline is a patterned summary. The topic is divided into several main parts. (It is wise to have at least three main topics and no more than five or six at the most.) Each main topic is divided into as many parts as needed, but there must always be two parts to the division. (This is true of any part of the outline.) The subdivisions may also be divided.

PURPOSE

An outline is used to

    a. prevent wandering off the subject

    b. give a quick overall view of the topic

    c. ensure proportionate space for each part

    d. aid in organizing and giving order to the paper

    e. enable one to spot missing or irrelevant matter

    f. guide one while writing the paper

SYSTEM

I. _____

    A. _____

    B. _____

        1. _____

        2. _____

Jeanette Carpenter, Stoughton High School, Stoughton, Wis.

a. _____

b. _____

   (1) _____

   (2) _____

     (a) _____

     (b) _____

      (1) _____

      (2) _____

II. _____

  A. _____

  B. _____

Name _____   Class _____

SURVEY OF MATERIALS

TRIAL BIBLIOGRAPHY

I. PURPOSE:

    A. To determine what materials to use for support data in your project

    B. To determine if there is enough material to do your paper

II. DIRECTIONS:

    A. Go to the areas of the library listed below. Check them for materials that could be useful and make a bibliography card for each source you find. Then have the blank by each area signed by your instructor or a media specialist.

    B. When your checklist is complete, hand it in, along with your trial bibliography.

        _____ 1. Card catalog

        _____ 2. Pamphlet file

        _____ 3. *Readers' Guide*

        _____ 4. Reference collection

        _____ 5. Microform indexes

        _____ 6. Special indexes

        _____ 7. Audio-visual collection

    C. Submit, in correct bibliographic form, the sources you found. You should be certain that there is enough material to accomplish your project. Do not continue researching your topic unless you found at least four sources.

Name _____   Class _____

RESEARCH PAPER—FINAL GRADE SHEET

	Poor	Good	Very Good	Excellent
1. Spelling, grammar, punctuation	1	2	3	4
2. Footnote and bibliography form	1	2	3	4
3. Organization of paper (Do topics build toward a logical conclusion?)	1	2	3	4
4. Originality (Is paper merely a collection of copied material or does it show individual work and thought?)	1	2	3	4
5. Does the paper have documented support where needed?	1	2	3	4
6. Does the paper accomplish the purpose explained in the introduction?	1	2	3	4
7. Is the presentation of material accurate?	1	2	3	4
8. Does the conclusion tie the paper together?	1	2	3	4
9. General appearance, proper manuscript form, neatness	1	2	3	4

10. General Comments:

11. *Final Grade* _____

Name _____   Class _____

PROGRESS REPORTS

Each report must be initialed by your instructor or, when appropriate, the media specialist. This sheet must be submitted with your final paper.

_____ 1. Topic Choice

_____ 2. Survey of Materials

_____ 3. Trial Bibliography

_____ 4. Outline

_____ 5. Thesis Statement

_____ 6. Introduction (Rough Draft)

_____ 7. Rough Draft of Body and Footnote Style

_____ 8. Rough Draft of Conclusion

_____ 9. Rough Draft of Bibliography

_____ 10. Submit Final Paper

Initials show that you have satisfactorily accomplished each step.

Name _____   Class _____

BEGINNING MEDIA ASSIGNMENT—USING THE *READERS' GUIDE*

BIOLOGY I—NUTRITION

Today you will be looking for an article about nutrition. There are a number of headings under which you may find an article on this subject:

diets	starvation
dietary supplements	food labeling
vitamins	anorexia
carbohydrates	bulimia
malnutrition	food fads
obesity	eating
snacks	eating habits
	eating, psychology of

MAGAZINE _____   DATE _____

PAGES _____   TITLE AND AUTHOR OF

ARTICLE _____

SUMMARY OF ARTICLE:

Tom Stokes, Biology Teacher, Stoughton High School, Stoughton, Wis.

Name _____   Class _____

THE RESEARCH PAPER—SOME WRITING TIPS

THE GOOD INTRODUCTION

Clearly states the purpose of the paper (What are you doing? Why?)

Limits the paper (Exactly what are you dealing with?)

States why the topic is important

Tries to create reader interest

THE BODY OF THE PAPER

Has major points and supporting subpoints

Contains original thought

Uses footnotes to document supporting points

Accomplishes purpose given in introduction

THE CONCLUSION

In the author's own words, gives a clear and final statement of the major points contained in the body

Demonstrates that the purpose of the study has been accomplished

GENERAL HINTS

Check your original outline, modify it where needed. *DO THIS BEFORE STARTING TO WRITE.*

Write your paper from the outline. Plug in footnotes where needed.

Carefully proofread your paper.

Produce a rough draft that can be examined and corrected.

Check footnote and bibliography form. Have you been consistent?

Give final draft a final proofreading before turning it in.

Name _____   Class _____

CHECKLIST FOR WRITING THE PAPER

CONTENT

1. Is the thesis stated in *one* sentence?

2. Is the thesis at the end of your first paragraph?

3. Is thesis proof clearly evident throughout the paper?

4. Does each paragraph have a topic sentence?

5. Have you tied paragraphs together with transitional words or sentences?

6. Do you prove your *best* point *last*?

7. Do your sentences show some variety?

8. Is the meaning of your sentences clear? Does your writing make sense? *HINT:* Have someone else read your paper to see if it is understandable and well written.

9. Can you say it more briefly and/or clearly?

10. Does the last paragraph contain a summary of your points of proof and a restatement of your thesis?

11. Overall, have you socked home your proof so your reader is convinced?

Jeanette Carpenter, Language Arts Instructor, Stoughton High School, Stoughton, Wis.

Name _____   Class _____

CHECKLIST FOR WRITING THE PAPER

MECHANICS

1. Are the margins correct?

2. Is your manuscript double-spaced and typed neatly?

3. Are pages correctly numbered?

4. Is the paper arranged in the correct order (Title Page, Body, Bibliography)?

5. Are the footnotes and bibliography in correct form?

6. Are footnotes correctly numbered?

7. Have you proofread *several* times? Check spelling, grammar, punctuation. *HINT:* Read from right to left to catch spelling errors.

Jeanette Carpenter, Language Arts Instructor, Stoughton High School, Stoughton, Wis.

Name _____   Class _____

HOW WILL YOU READ IT?

DIRECTIONS: Whenever you read anything you need to have a purpose. Decide what approach you would use for the following situations:

READING MATERIAL	YOUR PURPOSE	YOUR APPROACH
A History Chapter	To know this material for a detailed test	
A Mystery Novel	For entertainment	
The Daily Newspaper	For your own information	
Various Articles on Pollution	Your science teacher asks, "What are the causes of pollution?"	
A New Stereo Warranty	To understand the coverage of the warranty	
A Magazine Article	To learn about the record industry	
A Science Chapter	To know each of the nerves for a quiz	
A Biography	To know the background of Winston Churchill	
Hamlet	To translate Shakespeare's words into modern dialogue	
A Paperback Novel	To speed up your reading	

Name _____   Class _____

45. A SYMBOL OF THE FREE SPIRIT

We do not know the tribe of men that first used the horse. Scientists tell us our ancestors were eating horses long before they domesticated them. Historians claim that horses were harnessed before they were ridden.

The horse-drawn chariot dates back to 2,000 B.C. in actual records, and there is evidence it had been in use for a thousand years before that.

We also know the modern horse evolved from the dog-sized Eohippus. Its ancestors found their ecological niche on the open grasslands. There they developed the specializations that gave them the speed to outrun their predators and survive.

Fossil remains of the horse and all of his ancestors are common throughout much of North America. For many years, paleontologists believed that the horse first developed here, but later finds on the Euro-Asian continent have now raised questions about this theory. Whatever its origins, we do know that the horse either migrated to or from the Western Hemisphere and eventually became extinct in the New World.

Spanish conquistadors brought the horse back to the Western Hemisphere. In 1519 Cortés landed his troops and his herds of horses at the site of present-day Vera Cruz, Mexico. Coronado's expedition in 1540–41 took the horse to the plains of Kansas. Through the years, some of these Spanish horses escaped or were abandoned, and these became the nucleus of the first wild horse herds in North America.

Between 1519, when Cortés landed in Mexico, and 1803, when Lewis and Clark made their expedition into the West, was a period of 284 years. In the course of history, this is a considerable span of years—ample time to allow the great increase in the number of wild horses that had taken place by the time the pioneers began moving westward in the course of our national expansion.

Western grasslands provided an ideal habitat for the horse and a population explosion occurred. A few horses were captured by the Indians, but this had no significant impact on the wild horse population. By the time English-speaking settlers reached the West, the wild bands were firmly established, and it appeared they had always been a part of the western scene.

The image of the wild horse running free on the open plains has captured the mind and imagination of modern America, and has become a symbol of the free spirit.

103

Edward Spargo and Glenn R. Williston, *Timed Readings: Level 8,* Providence, R.I.: Jamestown Publishers, 1975, p. 103. Reprinted by permission.

RECALLING FACTS

1. Scientists know that the horse-drawn chariot dates back to
   □ a. A.D. 500.   □ b. 1,000 B.C.   □ c. 2,000 B.C.

2. The modern horse evolved from an animal about the size of
   □ a. a dog.   □ b. an elephant.   □ c. a zebra.

3. The horses' ancestors found their ecological niche
   □ a. on plains.   □ b. in forests.   □ c. near deserts.

4. For many years scientists thought that the horse evolved
   □ a. in Africa.   □ b. in North America.   □ c. in South America.

5. Cortéz brought herds of horses to Mexico during the early
   □ a. 1400s.   □ b. 1500s.   □ c. 1600s.

UNDERSTANDING IDEAS

6. The West provided an ideal habitat for horses because
   □ a. the weather was temperate.
   □ b. the area was mostly grasslands.
   □ c. larger predatory animals had not reached the West.

7. Horses defended themselves against attack by
   □ a. kicking their hoofs.
   □ b. using their sharp teeth.
   □ c. fleeing at great speed.

8. When Coronado explored the West,
   □ a. he found many herds of wild horses.
   □ b. he captured many wild horses to take home with him.
   □ c. he lost a number of horses that later became wild.

9. The author ends the article with a tone of
   □ a. sorrow.   □ b. sympathy.   □ c. nostalgia.

10. The author implies that American Indians
    □ a. nearly depleted the wild horse population.
    □ b. captured few wild horses for their own uses.
    □ c. brought most of their horses from Mexico.

Edward Spargo and Glenn R. Williston, *Timed Readings: Level 8,* Providence, R.I.: Jamestown Publishers, 1975, p. 104. Reprinted by permission.

Name _____   Class _____

THE CAUSES OF SLOW READING

Once you know the causes of slow reading, you can do something about improving your own reading rate.

Habit   Most people read everything the same way. Look at the material you are reading and decide what is the best rate

Lack of Purpose   If you know what you are looking for in your reading, you are more likely to read faster to find it.

Lack of Concentration   Reading quickly is difficult when your mind is wandering. Focus on what you want to get out of the material.

Looking Back   There is nothing wrong with looking back to pick up a point you missed, or correct a misunderstanding. But many people reread sentences, paragraphs, or even whole pages because they weren't paying attention the first time. When practicing speed-reading, force yourself to keep going and not look back. You will probably find that most regressions are unnecessary.

Talking to Yourself   Psychologists have proven that people hear the sounds of the words they read, and that is important for comprehension. But many readers say every word to themselves, which leads to unnecessarily slow reading. When reading easy, familiar material, very little subvocalization should be necessary. Only when the vocabulary or concepts are difficult should you read every word out loud to yourself.

Word-by-Word Reading   Reading one word at a time is not only slow but it is also inefficient. In order to comprehend, read in phrases or thought units. Your eyes can see about three words per fixation, and most phrases are three words long. Practice this by marking off phrases in a newspaper article, and then looking only at the whole units.

Lack of Motivation   Many people read slowly because they don't like to read, or are not interested in the subject. Given a gripping novel or an important news article, they will read it rapidly with good comprehension. Read everything as if it were interesting or important to you, and speed will come naturally.

Name _____ Class _____

HOW TO INCREASE READING SPEED

To increase your reading rate you will need a few simple techniques: a measure of how many words you have read, a method of timing yourself, and a way to figure out your words per minute. Complete the following steps:

GET A WORD COUNT

- Choose a typical page (not the first or last page of a chapter) and count the number of words in ten lines.

- Divide that number by ten to get the *average words per line* for that book.

- Count the number of lines on that page to get the *average lines per page.*

- Multiply the number of words per line by the number of lines per page to get the *average words per page.* For easy reference write this figure inside the front cover of the book.

  Example: Ten lines contain 110 words, or eleven words per line, times 30 lines per page equals 330 words per page.

- Repeat this step for every book you practice on, since books differ greatly in size of print and number of lines.

FIGURE YOUR WORDS PER MINUTE

- Set up some system of timing yourself: a timer, a clock with a second hand, or a watch.

- Read for five minutes at a normal rate, trying for good comprehension. Note when you begin and end.

- When you have finished reading, determine the number of words you have read by multiplying the number of pages you have read by the average number of words per page.

  Example: 330 words per page times 3½ pages equals 1155 words read.

- Divide the total number of words read by five minutes to get the average words per minute.

Example: 1155 divided by 5 equals 231 words per minute.

- Set up a practice sheet or keep a record on a 3″ × 5″ card which you can use as a pacer and a bookmark.

- For your next reading set a goal to increase the amount you read by half a page. Read rapidly, as fast as you can without losing the general idea of the story. Don't worry about small details, since rate improvement is your overall goal.

- It is not necessary to figure out your words per minute each time you read; simply record the number of pages you read each time.

- If you want to increase the amount of time you read to ten or fifteen minutes, just divide by that number.

- Set a goal that, sometime during the book, you will be reading twice as fast as when you began.

You can do it!

Name _____   Class _____

SPEED WITH COMPREHENSION

As you begin to read faster you may feel that you are losing comprehension. The following suggestions will help you to focus on the main goal of reading: understanding.

- *Preview the Material* A few seconds spent before reading can help you to know what you are going to be reading about. Take a look at the introduction, topic sentences, headings, and summaries to see how it is organized. Try to decide where you can speed up, and where you will have to read slowly and carefully.

- *Anticipate* Using your preview, try to guess what the author will say about the topic, and how he or she will support the arguments. As you read, try to anticipate what is coming next. Be an active reader.

- *Have a Purpose* Decide what you want to get out of the reading, how much you want to remember, whether you just want an overall idea, or if you need a thorough understanding of the material.

- *Search for the Meaning* As you read, look for the main idea for each paragraph. Once you have found it, you can read the rest of the paragraph rapidly because you know it will consist of supporting details and examples.

- *Recognize Signal Words* As you search for the main ideas, take advantage of the signals given by the author. If it says "fourth . . . ," you know there must have been a first, second, and third. If it says "However," you know you will get the opposite side. If it says "If . . . ," you know you will get "then."

- *Intend to Remember* When you start reading decide what you want to remember from this reading. Determine to stop at the end of a page or a section and summarize the main points that you think are important. This will motivate you to think about the material as you are reading it.

- *Set Goals* Each time you read set goals for yourself. Decide how much time it should take you to do a good job in light of the difficulty of the material, and try to meet or beat your goals. Set goals for comprehension as well, and check your understanding when you finish.

Name _____   Class _____

THE FOUR GEARS OF READING

First Gear

Study Rate: The first gear is slow, careful reading, where accuracy is important, and the intention is clear understanding and remembering. This can be used for:

- Difficult concepts or words
- New or unfamiliar material
- Remembering details
- Complete understanding
- Weighing all sides of an argument.

Second Gear

Moderate Reading Rate: The second gear of reading is what we think of as our normal reading rate when we are not trying to read fast, the material is not too difficult, and we want general understanding. We use this rate for:

- Most school assignments
- Novels, short stories
- Magazine articles
- Newspaper features, editorials

Third Gear

Rapid Reading: The third gear of reading is speed-reading or rapid reading, where complete comprehension is not demanded, but a general understanding is desired. Rapid reading can be used for:

- Light, easy fiction
- Newspapers, magazines
- Correspondence and memos
- Reviewing study material

Fourth Gear

Reference Rate: The fourth gear in reading involves skimming and scanning, which are not true reading but involve searching for information, which is important for research. We use SKIMMING for:

- Previewing material
- Getting an overview
- Searching through information
- Selecting information
- Sorting through correspondence

We use SCANNING for:

- Phone numbers
- Topics in an index
- Names, dates, or topics

Name _____   Class _____

READING PARADOXES

It is a paradox that many of the undesirable factors which cause slow reading may be desirable when careful study reading is required. Let's take a look at some of those paradoxes:

1. *Regressions*   Speed reading experts tell you not to look back or reread the material, because much rereading is simply a bad habit. If your purpose is full comprehension and you miss something, it is important that you reread it as many times as it takes. Do not just gloss over something when it doesn't make sense. Slow down and figure it out.

2. *Talking to Yourself*   When you are learning to speed-read you are told not to subvocalize because saying every word to yourself will slow you down. This is good advice when the material is easy and you can read in phrases. But when the material gets difficult, and full comprehension is desired, you suddenly should start talking to yourself. Maybe not out loud; that could get embarrassing, but silently you should hear the words in your brain.

   Writing is talk written down. When you hear the words, when you hear the phrasing and the intonations, often things that didn't make sense become clear. Poetry must be read out loud to be understood. Why not physics, mathematics, and philosophy?

3. *Read in Thought Groups*   In speed-reading you are taught to read groups of words, not one word at a time. This is good advice for slow readers because they often do not hear the grouping of words in natural language, which makes comprehension difficult. Speed-readers are taught to make fewer fixations by seeing groups of three or four words at a time.

   Study reading demands that every word be read carefully, so that the reader can see how the ideas fit together. Sometimes a single word or punctuation mark can be an important signal to meaning.

4. *Read for Key Ideas*   When your purpose is to get just the key points and main ideas, then it may be useful to locate quickly the topic sentences in paragraphs, and skim over the supporting details and examples. But when you are studying, a surface understanding will not be enough. It is essential to examine every supporting argument, see how the facts fit together, understand how the examples relate to the main ideas, and then decide if the argument is valid.

Name _____ Class _____

HOW DID YOU READ THIS?

- How fast did you read this?

- Were there some parts you read faster than others? Slower?

- Which parts of the chapter were the hardest? Easiest?

- Were the study aids helpful? (Headings? Pictures? Questions?)

- Was the vocabulary difficult? Were new words defined?

- How did the author organize the information? Was it clear?

- How does this material fit in with what you already know about this subject? How might it change your thinking?

- How does this chapter compare with other reading you have done?

- How accurate was the information? How up-to-date was it?

- Did you find any places where you wanted to question the author?

- Were there any places where you disagreed? Why?

- What notes could you have taken on this chapter? Did you take any notes?

- What questions would you expect to be on the exam?

- What facts will you be tested on?

- What thought questions might be asked?

- If you were writing this chapter, how would you have done it differently to make it clearer? To make it more interesting?

Name _____   Class _____

THE PROFUNDITY SCALE FOR THE EVALUATION OF LITERATURE

Physical Plane The reader is aware primarily only of the physical actions of the characters.

Mental Plane The reader is aware of the physical and intellectual actions of the characters.

Moral Plane The reader is aware of the physical and intellectual actions of the characters in light of an ethical code.

Psychological Plane The reader is aware of the psychological forces influencing the characters' physical and intellectual actions in light of an ethical code.

Philosophical Plane The reader is aware of the universal truths expounded by the author through the physical, intellectual, and ethical behavior of the characters under the influence of psychological forces.

Eileen E. Sargent, Helen Huus, and Oliver Andresen, *How to Read a Book,* IRA Reading Aids Series (Newark, Del.: IRA, 1970), p. 29. Reprinted with permission of Sargent, Huus, Andresen, and the International Reading Association.

Name _____   Class _____

WHAT IS YOUR APPROACH TO STUDYING A FOREIGN LANGUAGE?

Effective study methods contribute to increased learning. After you have responded to the questions, circle the number of the questions indicating changes you need to make. Respond Yes *or* No *to the following questions:*

_____ 1. Are you genuinely committed to learning this foreign language?

_____ 2. Do you feel that the teacher cares about you and your progress?

_____ 3. Is your family supportive and willing to help you upon your request?

_____ 4. Do you listen intently in class and carefully imitate what you hear?

_____ 5. Do you practice every day outside of class?

_____ 6. Do you speak out loud when you are reading, studying, or reviewing?

_____ 7. Do you believe that you will become a fluent speaker of this language?

_____ 8. Do you use the context to get the meaning of unknown words?

_____ 9. Do you work on small units until you gradually get the whole lesson?

_____ 10. Do you make a list of problem words for more frequent practice?

_____ 11. Do you study in half-hour intervals so that your mind stays alert?

_____ 12. Do you and your teacher look at errors positively as your opportunity to learn?

_____ 13. Do you reread for additional practice?

_____ 14. When a classmate is reciting, do you recite mentally with that person so you get a "refresher shot"?

_____ 15. Do you read and listen for meaning so that you can guess intelligently when you don't know a particular word?

_____ 16. Do you keep up to date on assignments since language learning is cumulative? Tomorrow's lesson will be built on what you learned today.

_____ 17. Do you finish reading a sentence before you look up an unknown word within it?

_____ 18. Even if you are unprepared, do you still go to class so that you keep learning from classroom work? In class may be the only place you hear the language spoken with appropriate explanations.

_____ 19. Do you seek additional practice by conversing in a foreign language with classmates outside of class? Fluency is the result of frequent experiences of communication in that language.

Name _____   Class _____

SELF-EVALUATION SHEET FOR A SHOP PROJECT

This check sheet is intended to focus your attention on any "need areas" and point the way to improvement. Before you begin your project, answer Yes or No to each of the questions below. Do not enter the shop to work until you can respond affirmatively to all questions.

After you finish your project, circle those numbers representing procedures that you need to improve before working in the shop again. After working on your project, you know the problems caused by lack of preparation. You know if you really were prepared for what you intended to do.

_____ 1. Do you know what materials and equipment you need for your project?

_____ 2. Do you know the sequential steps of your procedure?

_____ 3. Can you visualize what you do in each step?

_____ 4. Do you understand the technical terms, the symbols, the directions given?

_____ 5. Have you "zeroed in" on amounts, measurements, equipment needed?

_____ 6. Are you aware of CAUTIONS and WARNINGS?

_____ 7. Have you analyzed the diagrams and drawings for the quick "how-to-do-it" insights they offer?

_____ 8. Have you eliminated asking your instructor questions when the answers are clearly stated in the directions for what you intend to do?

_____ 9. Are you ready to proceed independently without further clarification from the textbook or your teacher?

After the project is finished:

_____ 10. Are you gradually eliminating the errors, the loss of time, the redoing of procedures that result from lack of preparation?

_____ 11. Are you moving toward handling your project largely on your own?

Name _____   Class _____

SELF-EVALUATION SHEET FOR READING LABORATORY PROCEDURES

This check sheet is intended to focus your attention on any "need areas" and point the way to improvement. Before the experiment, mentally answer Yes *or* No *to each of the questions below.*

If you do not understand, ask questions before you begin the experiment. The moment you step into the laboratory, you are saying that you are ready to conduct the investigation.

After the experiment, rate yourself from 1 to 4 on each of the points below. Poor = 1; Fair = 2; Good = 3; Excellent = 4. Now you know if you really were prepared for conducting the experiment.

Points to Consider:

_____   1. Do you know the purpose—the why—of your experiment?

_____   2. Do you know what materials you need to conduct the investigation?

_____   3. Do you know the sequential steps of your procedure?

_____   4. Do you understand the technical terms, the symbols, the abbreviations?

_____   5. Have you "zeroed in" on amounts, timings, temperatures, measurements?

_____   6. Are you aware of the cautions and warnings?

_____   7. Have you analyzed the diagrams and drawings for the quick "how-to-do-it" insights they offer?

_____   8. Have you eliminated asking your instructor questions when the answers are clearly stated in the procedures themselves?

_____   9. Are you ready to proceed independently without further clarification from the textbook or your teacher?

After the experiment, answer *Yes* or *No* to the following questions:

_____   10. Are you gradually eliminating the errors, the loss of time, the redoing of experiments that result from lack of preparation?

_____   11. Are you moving toward handling procedures for laboratory work largely on your own?

_____ 12. Is reflective thinking built into the way you read and the way you operate in the laboratory? Do you make predictions—anticipate outcomes—seek the basic reason why a thing does so-and-so—draw conclusions—make applications to your own experiences and the world outside the laboratory?

Please circle the numbers of the procedures on which you will focus when you conduct your next experiment. Report your progress at the bottom of every laboratory report. Attach this sheet to your lab report.

Name _____   Class _____

TEN WAYS OF STUDY THAT WORK

A new school year—with all its possibilities and promise—lies ahead for all of us. The marks you make this year can pay you well—in helping you enter the college you want, in bringing you nearer to the lifework of your choice, perhaps in college scholarships.

At this moment the year's ahead—make the most of it!

Efficient ways of study are not a matter of guess. Psychologists have been working for years on how to study. Research on the best methods of study has been conducted at top universities—including Stanford, Ohio State, and Chicago. There, careful experiments with groups of students have thrown light on ways of study that are best. By using these ways, you should learn more easily, remember longer, and save hours of study time.

The suggestions that follow are based on the results of these experiments.

1. *Make and keep a study schedule*

    Set aside certain hours each day for homework. Keep the same schedule faithfully from day to day. The amount of time needed for study will vary with the individual student and the courses on his or her schedule.

2. *Study in a suitable place—the same place every day*

    Is concentration one of your study problems? Experts tell us that the right surroundings will help you greatly in concentration. Your study desk or table should be in a quiet place—as free from distractions as possible. You will concentrate better if you study in the same place every day.

3. *Collect all the materials you'll need before you begin*

    Your study desk or table should have certain standard equipment— paper, pen, an eraser, and a dictionary. For certain assignments you'll need a ruler, paste, a compass, or a pair of scissors. With all your materials at hand, you can study without interruption.

4. *Don't wait for inspiration to strike—it probably won't*

    We can learn a lesson about studying from observing an athlete. Can you imagine seeing an athlete who is training for a mile run sitting on the field waiting for inspiration to strike before he starts to practice? He trains strenuously day after day whether he wants to or not. Like the athlete we get

Prepared by Ellen Lamar Thomas, former reading consultant of the University of Chicago Laboratory School, for students attending sessions on how to study.

in training for our tests and examinations by doing the things we're expected to do over a long period of time.

5. *A well-kept notebook can help raise your grades*

Research shows that there's a definite relationship between the orderliness of a student's notebook and the grades he makes. Set aside a special section for each of the subjects on your schedule. When your teachers announce important dates for tests and examinations, you'll find how priceless orderly notes can be.

6. *Make a careful record of your assignments*

Why lose time phoning all over town to find someone who knows the assignment? Put it down in black and white—in detail—in a designated place in your notebook. Knowing just what you are expected to do and when you are expected to do it is the first long step toward completing important assignments successfully.

7. *Use "trade secrets" for successful study*

Flash cards are "magic helpers." On the front of a small card you write an important term in history, biology, English, etc., and on the back, a definition or an important fact about that term. Carry your flash cards with you. At odd times take them out and ask yourself the meaning of the term. If you don't know, turn to the other side and review the answer.

The "divided-page" is another trick of the study trade. Make a dividing line down the center of a sheet of notebook paper. Then write important questions on the left side and the answers on the right. Use the "self-recitation" method of study. Cover the right-hand side and try to give the answer. Then check and recheck until you're sure you know the material.

A simple but effective study device is a "cover card." As you are studying, look at your notebook or textbook and read what you are trying to memorize. Then use your "cover card" to conceal what you have just read—and try reciting or writing the facts from memory. Check until you are sure you have mastered these facts.

8. *Good notes are your insurance against forgetting*

Learn to take notes efficiently as your teachers stress important points in class and as you study your assignments. Good notes are a "must" for just-before-test reviewing. Without notes, you will often need to reread the whole assignment before a test. With them, you can call the main points to mind in just a fraction of that time. The time you spend in taking notes is not time lost but time saved.

Name _____   Class _____

9. *Perhaps you've asked, "How can I remember what I've studied?" One secret of remembering is overlearning*

    Psychologists tell us that the secret of learning for the future is overlearning. Overlearning is continuing your study after you have learned the material well enough to barely recall it. Experts suggest that after you can say, "I have learned the material," you should spend in extra study one-fourth of the original study time. In an experimental study, students who overlearned the material remembered four times as much after 28 days had passed.

10. *Frequent reviews will pay you well—in knowledge, grades, and credits*

    Without review the average student can forget 80 percent of what he has read—in just two weeks! Your first review should come very shortly after you study material for the first time. The early review acts as a check on forgetting and helps you remember far longer. Frequent reviews throughout the course can pay you well—in pretest peace of mind.

    All this is helpful only if you follow through!

Name _____   Class _____

GETTING TO KNOW EACH OTHER

1. If you could visit any country in the world, where would you go?

2. What one day in your life would you like to live over again?

3. When you are thirty years old, what do you want to be doing?

4. What do you worry about the most?

5. If you had your choice, where would you like to live? Why?

6. What is the ideal number of children in a family?

7. If you could make one change in the world, what would it be?

8. What is the best book you have ever read?

9. What should be the major purposes of our government?

10. If you could choose one quality for a teacher to have, what would it be?

APPENDIX **D**

Feedback Form

Your comments about this book will be very helpful to us in planning other books in the Guidebook for Teaching Series and in making revisions in *A Guidebook for Teaching Study Skills and Motivation*, Second Edition. Please tear out the form that appears on the following page and use it to let us know your reactions to *A Guidebook for Teaching Study Skills and Motivation*, Second Edition. The authors promise a personal reply. Mail the form to:

Ms. Bernice Jensen Bragstad and
Ms. Sharyn Mueller Stumpf
c/o Longwood Division
Allyn and Bacon, Inc.
7 Wells Avenue
Newton, MA 02159

School Address:

Ms. Bernice Jensen Bragstad and
Ms. Sharyn Mueller Stumpf
c/o Longwood Division
Allyn and Bacon, Inc.
7 Wells Avenue
Newton, MA 02159

Dear Bernice and Sharyn:

I wanted to tell you what I think of your book *A Guidebook for Teaching Study Skills and Motivation*, Second Edition. I like certain things about the book, including:

I do, however, feel that the book can be improved in the following ways:

Some other things that I wish the book had included are:

Something that happened in my class when I used an idea from your book is:

Sincerely,